MW01243906

Twelve Insights for Mindful Living

An Awareness Approach to Health and Happiness

Daniel A. Johnson

Mindful Wellness Publishing, LLC
Tucson, AZ, USA

Twelve Insights for Mindful Living:
An Awareness Approach to Health and Happiness

Some names have been changed to protect individual identities.
The opinions, practices, and exercises offered in this book are based
on the authors' decades of research, study, observations, experiences,
and presentations on the subject of mindful awareness and whole-body
wellness. The author maintains a balanced and moderation approach
to all aspects of work and personal life. The recommendations in this
book are not intended as a substitute for professional medical advice.
Readers should consult their physician about any symptoms
that may require diagnosis and medical attention.

First Edition

ISBN paperback: 979-8-9850994-0-9
ISBN e-book: 979-8-9850994-1-6

LCCN: 2021922703

The Twelve Insights are registered federal trademark 97017542
and State of Arizona registered trademark 9241212.

Cover graphic: Getty Images
Cover and interior design: Jess LaGreca, Mayfly Design
Author photograph: Thomas Veneklasen
Editor: Joanne C. Hughes
Project director: Charlotte Meares

Mindful Wellness Publishing, LLC
Tucson, AZ, USA
www.MindfulWellnessPublishing.com
mindfulwellness@gmail.com
dan@thetwelveinsights.com

To your health, joy, and love—
gifts that I've been given.

Praise for the
Twelve Insights for Mindful Living

"Dan Johnson has provided us with an exceptional roadmap that will allow us all to incorporate much-needed mindfulness practices into our daily hectic lives. Read this book. It has the potential to transform your life."
—Richard Carmona, MD, MPH, FACS, 17th Surgeon General of the United States, Distinguished Laureate Professor, University of Arizona, Chief of Health Innovation, Canyon Ranch

"Dan's writing draws from creditable references in philosophy, sports, art, and medicine (natural and allopathic) and provides a solid foundation to support the concept of mindfulness. A real strength of this book is his ability to write as though he's talking directly to the reader. I really love the practice, exercises, and inspiration at the conclusion of each insight chapter. They provide a wonderful reinforcement of the concepts presented."
—Louis A. Giallonardo, Senior Vice President, the Segal Group, ret.

"The *Twelve Insights for Mindful Living* energizes me to further strengthen my mind, body, and spirit and empowers me to live my life's ultimate purpose and strive to be significant beyond success."
—A. Hamid Andalib, founder/CEO, EE Incentives

"'Is this book for me?' YES! The *Twelve Insights* is not only good reading but also a motivational life lesson about bringing mindful awareness to our thinking, feeling, and expressing, and becoming aware that life's possibilities are limitless. Throughout the years, Dan has shown a passion for the topics that he discusses and brings that deep learning to his book."
—May Young, Senior Account Manager, UnitedHealthcare, Public Sector

"In his down-to-earth *Twelve Insights* as in his wellness presentations, Dan challenges us to think in new ways, gives us tools to reduce stress, motivates us to reach greater heights, and shows us that an optimistic viewpoint has the power to change a person's world. Committed to supporting and accelerating the success of others, Dan effectively teaches us strategies to overcome personal and professional adversity, become more resilient, and confidently lead healthier, happier lives full of vitality, passion, and purpose."
—Brooke Shearer, Benefits Manager, Karsten Manufacturing Co., Ping Golf

Twelve Insights for Mindful Living

The journey is through mindfulness.
The destination is love.

Contents

Awareness I: Being Present for Myself

Acknowledgments

Before I thank so many extraordinary people who have inspired me and helped to shape the Twelve Insights over the decades, I want to and must acknowledge the Highest Power in the universe: Love. Truly, this book is the result of being shown and given the amazing gift of unconditional love and grace. I've been blessed to witness to them and to be mindful of their presence in strangers, acquaintances, friends, and families. My greatest mentor and teacher is the love of my life, my wife, Melinda, whose grace and love embrace all beings; her love shines light on all of life.

I'm indebted to history's great philosophers, spiritual teachers, and the many incredible current contributors to the fields of psychology, health, happiness, and well-being who encourage us to mindfully feel and express love for others, and the treasure with which we've been entrusted, our precious Mother Earth. You'll hear from many of these people in this book.

I greatly value the love and support of the Wellness Council of Arizona, founders Mel Zuckerman, president emeritus, Wellness Council of Tucson (WELCOT), and Jim Click Jr., along with the many dedicated professionals who have served on the board of directors for more than thirty-five years. Their vision—fortified by the focused work of the Wellness Council staff—has improved the health and lives of thousands of people in scores of organizations. It's been my honor to advance the Council's mission for the past quarter-century. Mel and his devoted wife, Enid, have inspired me and, subsequently, this book in so many ways. In 1978, Mel had a life-changing health experience that became the impetus to create with Enid and Jerry Cohen the internationally recognized health innovation Canyon Ranch Health Resorts, which embody "the power of possibility," as Mel likes to put it, and became the "original trailblazer of integrative wellness" that I and many others practice today. Mel and Enid shepherded the growing Canyon Ranch concept internationally until their retirement in 2017. In 2000, the Zuckerman Family Foundation funded the University of Arizona Mel and Enid Zuckerman College of Public Health. Dedicated to health equity, the institution became an international leader in research and pioneering programs in public health practices and policy. The Canyon Ranch Center for Prevention and Health Promotion followed a few years later.

High kudos go to the many people who have shared their fears and their cares, their hopes and their dreams and who have eagerly supported others with reaching their goals. Sharing our stories—the substance of life—bonds us and brings us strength, courage, and wisdom. Many thanks to my keen-eyed editor, Joanne C. Hughes, as well as to Charlotte Meares for her efforts to manage, consult, research, and contribute to the composition and completion of this work, my gift to you. My gratitude goes to my beautiful daughter, Makenna, for whom being mindful and sharing love comes naturally. An inclusion specialist with one of the nation's highest-ranked school districts, she brings her experience with the fundamentals of mindfulness to give a loving touch to children with special needs each day. She touches the lives of so many.

There are many wonderful people whose names I've not mentioned, but I see you, play golf with you, revel in your accomplishments and goal achievements, you and everyone I have included are the mortar in the foundation of my creativity. I think of you and I'll always remember the positive imprint you've made on my life and, in turn, on this book. To those who challenged me to remain curious about and interested in the world, people, growing, thinking, and feeling—because that's what you do—thank you for the lessons and the love and wisdom you imparted. To my clients, who have taught me more than I've taught them, well done! And, to my readers, thank you for picking up this labor of love. I wish for you a mindfully aware life rich with health and happiness.

INTRODUCTION
From the Insight Out

I love you. How do you feel hearing those words? What if the first, last, and only sentence in this book was "Love yourself and others unconditionally, for everything you need to know to live a fulfilling life of happiness, health, and well-being are contained within these words"?

Yes, I know. If only it were that simple. But life's complicated. Love—an action, attitude, and experience that neuroscientists call a prototypical emotion—requires more of us than does hatred. So, what's love got to do with mindfulness, really slowing down to give someone or something our full attention? Turns out, a lot. We're social creatures with a basic need for healthy love and belonging.

We also have a deep inner life. Sometimes our inner and outer selves are at odds. Many of us have scars nobody sees. Some wounds are self-inflicted. Many go back to childhood, when we didn't know how to protect ourselves. As adults, we're not immune from insult and injury, and some wounds may still be raw. No few of us have received physical and emotional pummelings that took or continue to take a toll on our spirit, body, and mind. Perhaps we're spending time, money, and energy undoing the doings of our early caregivers and adults whom we trusted. We humans crave a sense of well-being. And we have the power to achieve it. Just as we can train our bodies to be fit, we can train the mind to maintain equanimity amid the internal and external chaos. And we can achieve a body, mind, spirit harmony that fosters overall well-being. That's the reason for this book.

We often and casually use the expression "judging a book by its cover." The idiom reminds us that we'll miss something deeper when we make rapid-fire, superficial judgments about people and things. The details may escape us, such as why we chose fractal hearts for this cover. Chapter 14 reveals the secret behind that choice and the layers of meaning important to all of us.

When I was ten, my abusive stepfather gave me two gifts. One was the opportunity to acquire mental and physical strength. The other was a kind of back-door path to success. I can't say that he gave them to me unintentionally or inadvertently, but his beliefs and actions catapulted me into a new, exciting environment where, for the first time, I received positive reinforcement from an adult. I began to see myself—that kid who had never had a book read to him, who didn't know his alphabet when he entered first grade, who started school with what we now call post-traumatic stress disorder and was later discovered to be dyslexic, who was incessantly and viciously made fun of by other kids for having to wear the same old clothes—as a real person who had been involuntarily launched into becoming a self-reliant, self-actualized, explorative, resilient individual because the alternatives were unacceptable.

Resilience doesn't happen overnight. It isn't a quality someone can give you. It's a "becoming" characteristic. A silver lining of growth and development through our personal traumas, as we'll discuss further on. "The past doesn't determine your future unless you carry it with you in the present," author Marianne Williamson reminds us.

My mother's sad and tragic life was an inspiration in strange ways. Painful yesterdays became my teacher—the fitness trainer of resilience. My deep love for her and our entangled struggle for survival were a large part of the impetus to launch each day joyfully and mindfully, one giant step toward lifelong well-being. My memory of her resilience—she died when I was sixty—of her small and huge failures and successes, still strengthen my spirit and fire my desire to help others as she had come to do.

"In every success story, there is the grace of good fortune," said Nobel laureate Daniel Kahneman, who devoted his career to understanding how we think, form beliefs, and subsequently act. He gave us the formula: "Success = Talent + Luck. Great success = A little more talent + a Lot of Luck."[1] My formula is "Success happens when opportunity meets with preparation."

Though I didn't recognize it when I was young, grace sat at my table even in the darkest times.

As children and adults we're faced with situations that we're powerless to do anything about. They can feed our sense of learned helplessness. Or they can test our mettle. Yet, it's not only when things go wrong that we need to draw on our reserves, experience, knowledge, determination, and courage to make wise choices. When things go right, it's easy to relax our intent, purposefulness, and awareness and mindlessly forget to assess the reasons why and replicate them.

Early on, "things" went right for me for all the wrong reasons. I made it through high school not because I studied and worked hard. I didn't. I never read. I memorized everything I needed to parrot back on exams and in assignments. My superhero was Tarzan. Athletic, loincloth-clad Johnny Weissmuller negotiated the jungle armed with only a knife and a quick-witted mind that provided life-saving decisions just in the nick of time. I recognized he had qualities a lot of the people in my small sphere of inclusion didn't: awareness and mindfulness. And I wanted them. One false move in the jungle and it's curtains.

Life's like that, I began to think. And I began to think about thinking. The mind's work fascinated me. I saw that it worked for and against us. We could think positively, act accordingly and, often, things changed. I also saw the reverse was true. I didn't see positive outcomes from negative thinking. I watched attentively as people set goals and achieved them. Losing thirty or forty pounds wasn't just a physical accomplishment. People changed in other ways. When I was a fitness trainer, my clients' motivation became my inspiration.

Giving others an opportunity to experience the transformational processes that I had the great good fortune to know made and still makes me happy. Not for a minute or a day or a week, but ongoing. I believe divine intervention saved my life so many times in so many ways. Not the least of these was putting in my path people who believed in me, people who taught me to believe in myself. Call that intervention a higher power, or God, or cosmic consciousness, or just will; my awareness of it was palpable.

Surely, I experienced small aha moments throughout my tumultuous growing years, but the biggie, at nineteen, hit me over the head. I had a sudden—yes—awareness that I had squandered my opportunity to learn. That awareness had become painfully evident: I had no substantive idea how the world worked and what made people tick. Yet, I yearned to. I yearned to hear "I love you." Over time, I began to tell more and more people that I love them.

There's an art and science to living fully, to one's highest potential—loving, giving, and growing. There are decades of scientific proof that—for most of us—living mindfully and positively affects not only our thoughts, but also our actions. Most likely you've heard the maxim, "We are what we think. All that we are arises with our thoughts, and with our thoughts we make the world." That's poetical and inspirational even as it isn't a faithful translation of Buddhist scripture. This passage below is, and it's even more powerful and full of promise:

> All experience is preceded by mind,
> Made by mind.
> Speak or act with a peaceful mind,
> And happiness follows,
> Like a never-departing shadow.[2]

Two beautiful insights come from this. One is that we have control over our happiness. The other is the positive spin on "shadow." Shadow is not a dark and foreboding side of us. The takeaway is that there is a path to a peaceful mind. That's been my quest ever since I recognized I needed to take back my power and be the master of my own thoughts. Mindfulness—in meditation and through my thoughts, beliefs, and actions—has been the orchard I've chosen to cultivate. It has borne much fruit that I now share with you.

Mindfulness in Thought, Belief, and Action

Deepak Chopra, a pioneer in integrative medicine and personal transformation, moves into his golf backswing mindfully aware, keeping his eyes on the ball. "Now is the only time that really exists in golf," he says.[3] "The swing is always in the present, and when you walk up the fairway to address the ball again, the present moment is once more at hand." To Chopra, the Scottish game mirrors life.

For golfers serious about their performance, mindfulness is par for the course. In May 2021, a month away from his fifty-first birthday, Phil Mickelson made history with his epic victory in the 103rd PGA Championship. When that win wasn't a sure thing, his brother and caddy coached him to put thought into his swing. Mickelson pushed aside old gnarly issues that had tripped up his game and focused on the idiosyncratic swing that put him at the top of the leaderboard. "I've tried to stay more in the present," he later told reporters. "I was just trying to quiet things down. . . . I believed for a long time that I could play at this level again. I didn't see why I couldn't."[4]

A telling headline reads: "Phil Defeats Father Time." He did because he knew he could. Mickelson's positive self-talk and belief in himself are strategies that can work for you, whether you're a golfer or a welder, a runner or an architect.

You've been there—in the zone—that ever-present now at the crossroads of our past and our future. Those moments are filled with gratitude because we're truly connected to the many normally overlooked experiences that enrich our lives. Ironically, the present moment has nothing to do with clock time. On the course and off, my mindset during peak moments is feeling in control. Feeling out of control produces "anxiety, uncertainty, confusion, panic, and loss of self-confidence,"[5] depending on how severe the sensation is. When we sail without a compass and let the winds chart our course, we relinquish our control to life's currents and giant waves.

The goal is to restore control naturally and to embark on an aware, mindful lifestyle to enhance joy and happiness. When we're happier, we're more peaceful and can meet fate's storms with greater resilience. We may never know how far the ripples of our happiness and peacefulness expand. All we can do is be the rock that skips across the water to start the ripples' movement.

We don't accomplish great things unless we're focused on them. All too often our minds are somewhere else. Life is on autopilot. We're zooming through a hectic day hardly aware of taking a breath, not even pausing long enough to ask our body how it's doing. On our daily drive across town, we don't notice the park's new benches and flower beds bursting with crayon-bright blooms. The impact of being aware of our well-being escapes us because we're not in the moment.

That's precisely where we need to be, say experts at Harvard School of Medicine, if we want to reduce stress and increase overall happiness. Traditional Western medicine has come down fully on the side of the mental and physical health benefits of mindfulness practice brought to its attention by professor emeritus Jon Kabat-Zinn, former director at the Mindfulness-Based Stress Reduction Clinic at the University of Massachusetts Medical School.

Mindfulness habits enable us to shift our behavioral and perceptual gears and adopt positive attitudes that contribute to a satisfied life.[6] When we're in the moment, savoring life's pleasures—tiny or huge, our brains turn on the positive-emotion switch. The more we recognize those instances when we feel good, the more we come to expect them—an outlook we describe as optimism. Optimists set and achieve many of their goals. Positive emotions strengthen our reserves and act as a buffer between our vulnerabilities and hard times. We're more resilient both physically and mentally. Scientific studies demonstrate that resiliency leads to longer, healthier lives and an enhanced sense of overall well-being.

Is This Book for Me?

The *Twelve Insights for Mindful Living: An Awareness Approach to Health and Happiness* arises from my lifetime of learning, listening, training, and teaching. Each insight begins with the "He(art) and Science" behind the intuitive, intangible, and tangible benefits of living mindfully aware as well as the research to back them up. For many of us, the proof is in the pudding.

The practices and exercises help you integrate each insight into your daily life. My intention is to give you tools to achieve both necessary (life-saving) and desirable (life-enhancing) goals. Perhaps you need to be supported in making a lifestyle choice, such as "I need to lose weight and restore my health so I can be with my kids as they grow up." Or "I want to get fit for my climb of Mt. Kilimanjaro." Or "I want to leave stress at the office and not bring it home to my family." Better yet is to phrase goals positively: "I want to stay calm when my boss gets out of control." Maybe your goal is to release pessimistic thoughts and feel more joy. Let go of anger and rage. Forgive a transgressor. Forgive yourself. Overcome addictive behaviors such as overeating or substance abuse. Reduce chronic pain. Lower blood pressure. Recover from heart disease. Become a cancer survivor. Train for an Ironman. Deliver a new life.

What do you want to bring into *your* life? What habits are you ready to toss in the self-defeating trash bin? As you embark on the path to goal achievement, you'll recognize that happiness isn't a destination—"I will feel happy *when* I achieve this goal"—but an ongoing, positive mindset—"I feel happy *now* as I work toward my goal." We don't need to wait until things get easy to be happy.

No matter the goal, learning to be in the moment at work, at home, and at play nurtures body, mind, and spirit. Forget about multitasking for a while. Experiment with being single-focused using the Twelve Insights tool kit. Cultivate mindfulness while meditating. If meditation isn't your cup of matcha, then develop the ability to practice mindfulness while walking, gardening, making love, buttering toast, wandering mentally past the moon and stars into deep space, or sitting in the bleachers during little-league practice.

Religious practitioners may prefer deep engagement into mindfulness through prayer. Others are inclined toward mindfulness through contemplation or Simran—a Sanskrit word meaning the act of remembrance, reminiscence, and recollection that lead to the realization of the highest aspect of one's self and discovery of the purpose in one's life to answer the question, "Who am I?" Secularists have found non-spiritual prayer a profound pathway to mindful awareness. As you see, there need be no deity associated with meditation or mindfulness practice. There is simply you, orchestrating choices to connect to something larger than the self and disconnect from something that is counter to your well-being.

Whether you're among the 84.4 percent of the world's population who puts faith in one of the more than four thousand religions, or you count yourself among the 15.6 percent who ascribe to no particular faith or who consider yourself atheist,[7] this book *is* for you—a miracle of creation.

Colors of Contentment

This is not a "fix you" book. You're not broken—even though sometimes you may feel sure that's the case. But there may be parts of your life that need a tune-up or, perhaps, a complete overhaul. The actionable insights collected here are a portable game-changer. The awareness approach smoothly integrates mindfulness into the things you do every day, wherever you go.

As you flip through the *Twelve Insights for Mindful Living*, you'll notice something else that sets this book apart from other mindfulness books on the shelf. We mindfully chose not to include stock images of broad smiles flashing perfect teeth; climbers scaling vertical rock faces; trim, athletic bodies racing to finish lines; and the requisite, politically correct mix of ages and ethnic groups collaborating over community development plans.

Instead, we've given considerable thought to how to craft this book to offer you that thirteenth loaf. Vogelkop gardener's male bowerbird gave us an idea. These feathered friends adorn their elaborate bower architecture with whatever pleases them aesthetically—and that's colorful. Each to his own. University of California, Los Angeles, physiologist and author Jared Diamond contends that bowerbirds' selective picking and choosing until they get an arrangement that pleases them seems very humanlike. Really, it's a "culturally transmitted creative process."[8] We agree, although we humans don't create art in anticipation of sex (well, maybe some of us do). And the philosophical question, "What is art?" is for another time and place.

"It is difficult to conceive of a pigeon Picasso or a baboon Botticelli," says molecular biologist Nathan Lents who writes about human evolution. That's because few animals have achieved "the faintest hints of the beginning of culture. Art reflects culture, transmits culture, shapes culture, and comments on culture."[9] And prehistoric cave walls attest to this: they became a canvas for human thought and expression. As Lents points out, humans' early art became creative visual representations of memories: where to find plentiful game or the location of a year-round waterhole. We may never know what else early art achieved, but we do know that over the ages the act of creating and viewing affects us emotionally and behaviorally. Lents also proposes that "artistic ability was likely to confer some advantage on those that had it" and, eventually, through natural selection, wound up in our DNA. We've all heard, "She's an artist; it runs in the family." Our human family, that is, which goes back a long way. Art has been with us, perhaps, every step of the way. It permeates our lives. The capacity for it is embedded in our genes, even if we can barely draw stick figures and distinguish between purple and magenta.[10]

For these reasons, we have included stress-reducing coloring pages that may even bring out the cave painter in you. You don't have to be artistic to reap the benefits of coloring. Creativity and mindfulness share myriad characteristics. For many people, mindfulness coloring induces a beneficial calm, aware state very much like meditation or focusing on the breath. Working creatively brings us fully into the present moment to balance the sensory overload that wears us down.

The He(art) and Science Approach

"Mindfully engaging in art is linked to improved self-confidence, feelings of safety and resilience," and aids in trauma recovery, according to researchers Kalmanowitz and Ho.[11] Rather than focus on the end result, be aware of the process of applying colored pencils, crayons, or artist markers to these special pages. They can be great mood enhancers.

The United Nations Educational, Scientific, and Cultural Organization (UNESCO), in collaboration with the Mahatma Gandhi Institute of Education for Peace and Sustainable Development (MGIEP), created an online series of art activities for mindfulness and well-being based on positive psychology pioneer Mihaly Csikszentmihalyi's famous "flow" state of perfect engagement and attention.[12]

Many of the techniques to reduce stress are adaptations of ancient practices that scientific research is proving to be beneficial to our health and well-being. You'll find no pseudoscience or chicanery here.

Think of the Twelve Insights like one of those multi-tools that put the realm of all possibilities in your mental pocket. There's something for any situation. And we've included the full list of Twelve Insights as a quick reference in the back of this book. You can also download a copy from our website to stash in your wallet or briefcase when you're on the go.

The Twelve Insights' tool kit looks basic, but it's actually bottomless. In fact, it's as deep as you want to go to use the practical applications of mindfulness and awareness to achieve dynamic changes in your life. You say you've been there and haven't been able to do that? Perhaps the reason is because you've not set yourself up for success. Goals shouldn't crush us. Understanding the what and why of goal achievement can be empowering. Getting specific about a goal is a start. The Twelve Insights will take you to the next step.

The Downside of Success and Upside of Failure

We've used the term goals since we were youngsters and our teachers stuck little gold or silver stars on our report cards as recognition for doing our best. Yet, do we really understand the nature of what it means to do our best? And what happens when doing our best isn't enough to achieve our goal? We'll explore the yin and yang of success and new ways to think about failure to achieve a goal.

After all, goals are mental constructs that exist only as we create them. It may seem like running a marathon is a reality, but the goal that got us there was a cognitive representation, an idea concocted in the mind.

"Goals are a form of self-regulation adopted by humans to achieve specific aims. By focusing people's attention, goals facilitate responses that are compatible with people's objectives."[13] Oddly, goal-directed behavior in the now requires us to create a mental image of doing or not doing something in the future, maybe starting this moment or in a moment to come.

Goals would remain only concepts were it not for commitment, the degree to which we are willing and eager to follow through. Aristotle understood goal-directed behavior's impact on imagined futures. While our commitment and the degree to which we commit is a conscious decision, "once in place, goals may be activated through an automatic process, influencing behavior outside an individual's conscious awareness."[14]

Little attention was given to goals in the psychological literature until the study of behavior became fashionable in the 1920s. American psychologist Edward Chance Tolman saw that behavior "reeks with purpose" as we choose to move toward or away from situations or objects of our goals, just as we would choose to attain success and avoid failure, whatever constitutes our definitions of and standards for each. We knew when we achieved success as measured by society's conventional standards—"achievements" like getting our first car, landing that first job, committing to a partner, and buying a home. We gauge our successes and failures by interpreting how well or how soon we arrive at societal milestones.

Milestones are like road signs that show us where we are in relationship to where we were. Positive milestones mark turning-point moments, or new chapters, in our careers or personal lives. If we approach each tangible milestone with a growth mindset, we move forward. As conventional milestones crumble—we may feel caught between an awareness rock and a social hard place. When that happens, we often refocus on those core or invisible life values, milestones that define our sense of self, our relationships, and our place in the world. From that three-dimensional perspective, we become aware that we are inseparable from our thoughts and our thoughts are inseparable from how we live our lives in harmonious agreement or discord with our true nature, our interpersonal relationships, and our global family. In 1990, Voyager I space probe took a portrait of us at home on our Pale Blue Dot. This milestone for humanity occurred as a fraction of a yoctosecond in our perception of time's arrow. Yet, every moment is a chance to begin again.

Around the world, across cultures, the strain and stress of health, economic, environmental, and social justice issues exhaust and challenge us to build stronger, more resilient selves and more tolerant and intentional global communities with which we're inextricably entwined.

More Is Better

If you've tried this program and that trendy practice to achieve your goals only to be derailed, take heart. The insights included here aren't a one-shot vaccination against mindlessness that lets you slide into tomorrow with old habits that failed you yesterday. They also aren't like 800-calorie-a-day diets that are unhealthy and can't be maintained long-term. The Twelve Insights are healthy, sustaining mindsets and actions that cost only habits you're ready to relegate to the past.

You don't have to wait for the benefits to set in. The *Twelve Insights for Mindful Living* offers strategies for developing fresh perspectives on the way you perceive and react to stressful situations in the present. You'll learn how to make safe and wise choices easily and quickly without judging or laboring over them. Living in the past is like choosing to see through a glass darkly. Time and our faulty memories distort what we perceive in our rearview mirror. Misconceptions about past thoughts, feelings, and behaviors can result in our languishing in destructive habits. Awareness helps us see more clearly, remove false beliefs, and choose to release the hold a habit has on us.

Living mindfully doesn't mean you're shielded from road rage or insults from the next person in the grocery store line. But you'll learn how to respond to harmony hiccups in healthier ways. You'll feel—perhaps for the first time—the joy of discovering silver linings in clouds and the hope of crocus buds pushing up through the snow. Small wonder that these resilient little symbols of hope are associated with positivity, joy, and happiness—an excellent metaphor for us as we set our sights high but cut ourselves some slack as we emerge from the winter of our discontent.

How Do I Use the *Twelve Insights* Book?

Where do you start? First, decide if you want anything in your life to be different. Nothing happens to change your circumstances or how you respond to them until you're motivated to open a door and venture—or adventure—into what's on the other side. Sure, that's often scary. Many firsts in life are.

Motivating human change is my passion. I've worn many hats: from sponsored athlete to fitness trainer, from a member of the Arizona Governor's Council on Physical Fitness to executive director of the Wellness Council of Arizona, from originator of the STRIVE motivational programs that focus on inspiration, human dynamics, and individual potential to a health and wellness coach. I help guide others through change and try to practice what I preach—functioning best when I'm mindfully aware.

I didn't just one day decide to live a mindful life and build a successful organization sharing the strategies you're about to learn. Like many good things, getting from "there" to "here" was an evolutionary process. Along the way, I've had many teachers. Employees from more than two hundred local, regional, and national organizations who attended my workshops and seminars candidly and openly shared their challenges—from small to seemingly insurmountable. Their feedback, questions, and commitment to leading healthier, happier lives helped shape the book you hold in your hands. To the many who achieved hard-won goals, congratulations! I applaud you. To those of you who have returned to the starting line, ready to begin again, I give my support and my commitment to honor your goals.

Albert Einstein was clear: "information is not knowledge." Even the abundance of material between these covers cannot do for you that which you must do for yourself. "Knowledge comes, but wisdom lingers," wrote Calvin Coolidge. "It may not be difficult to store up in the mind a vast quantity of facts but the ability to form judgments requires the severe discipline of hard work and the tempering heat of experience and maturity."

I've spent decades deepening my understanding and practice of mindfulness. This book might not be written had I not long ago delved into ancient wisdom and been inspired by leading mindfulness teachers—spiritual and secular. I share with you my own and others' "Aha!" moments and serendipitous breakthroughs to overcome obstacles. Their real-world stories, struggles, successes, and failures inspire me, and I hope that they inspire in you a sense of discovery—your own power—insights that you can apply to your life now. Not yesterday. Not tomorrow. This moment.

Just "Be Here Now"

In the early sixties, Richard Alpert did what many successful Harvard professors did: experiment with hallucinogens to find that state of higher consciousness. Ousted by Harvard, heartsick and emotionally dysfunctional, he wandered to India and onto the path of enlightenment and transformation. The student was ready and his teacher appeared. Guru

Neem Karoli Baba renamed the sojourner Baba Ram, "servant of God," ultimately, Ram Dass, and kept him focused when he struggled with the reminder: "Be here now." In 1971, Ram Dass published the breakthrough book by that title and launched a mindfulness revolution in the West.[15]

You don't have to go to India or anywhere else or buy something—not even this book—to get to a "here" and be in it now. Just stay right where you are. Keep it simple, Ram Dass said. "We don't need to wait until we are enlightened before we act in the world, and we don't need to withdraw from the world to become enlightened." What is enlightenment? It's more than improving oneself by acquiring knowledge and wisdom. Enlightenment comes through awareness and insights.

Did you notice that to be here now and embark on the journey to mindful awareness, you are the one to take the action? Mindful awareness isn't like an honorary degree that's conferred on you. You actively engage in achieving the progress you desire. You may not think so now, but you're in charge of all that you focus on. Get into the flow, into the Twelve Insights' mindfulness techniques specifically designed to work with and through your unique personality and, perhaps, the self-limiting beliefs that have held you back in the past.

Sounds easy? Well, it is and it isn't. We can run many miles on a small tank of high-octane attention before it runs out. Then there's a snafu. We're on our way to a luncheon meeting, but we're sandwiched between semis on the freeway. The boom car in the next lane is pounding out 150 decibels of Kicker pumped-up bass that reverberates through our body. While we're spinning this afternoon's PowerPoint presentation through a fast rehearsal before the big board reveal, our mind's replaying the fear of dad's heart attack last night and the sound of the gurney wheels as he's rushed into the emergency room. Our concerns and patience are being hammered by the car stereo next to us. It takes mindfulness to get through moments like these without precipitating an accident or road rage.

According to the *Harvard Business Review*, we're wired toward stress that isn't productive. "Don't fool yourself into thinking distractions aren't harmful to your focus—they have high cognitive costs."[16] We need to pivot from distractions that could endanger us and focus on immediate actions that lessen or remove the physical or emotional danger. "Stress can be good or bad."[17] Which effect it will have on us depends on the attention we give situations that are and aren't under our control. Attention is a limited resource. Furthermore, our minds take a buckshot approach to attention, and that wastes precious time and energy that may be critical in certain situations. We need to pay attention to our attention—be aware of our awareness. We'll learn more about scattershot thoughts and how distractions pull us into a default mode in Insight 10. And, we'll provide a mental app for that.

Don't Curse the Sand Trap

"Always say 'yes' to the present moment. Surrender to what is." When you do, Eckhart Tolle tells us, life starts working for you.[18] Among the monkey wrenches in our wheel of achieving our goals is negative self-talk. Words matter. Seemingly subtle nuances between words can change the brain's chemistry.[19] Big results are possible with small efforts to walk our talk. Being mindful of our self-talk means we don't curse the sand trap. The more we practice what to do when what we did lands us where we don't want to be, the faster our brain can use awareness to guide us in new situations. When we shift our attention and focus, without judgment, we can accomplish more in less time. The actions can become automatic, natural, fluid. We can feel vitality rather than exhaustion. Swap depression for contentment. Let doomsday emotions take flight and live optimistically. Release the tension and stress that sabotage well-being.

The iconic host of "The Joy of Painting," which aired on Public Broadcasting Service (PBS) from 1983 to 1994, Bob Ross appeared to take well-being to another level. Known as much for his wide philosophical brush strokes as for his alla prima technique on canvas, Ross focused viewer attention on "happy little clouds." Now and then he'd read a fan letter before the camera. "Bob, everything in your world seems to be happy." Bob looked his invisible viewers in the eye and silkily responded, "That's why I paint. I can create the kind of world that I want, and I can make this world as happy as I want it. Shoot, if you want bad stuff, watch the news." He often stroked the airtime with a Ross maxim. Here's my favorite: "We don't make mistakes. We have happy accidents."

My happy accident, painted when I was ten onto the nearly blank canvas of my mind, changed my future. A sage adult, quite unlike the loveable hippie Ross with the soporific voice, coached me about life and success. I didn't know it then, but when I gave myself a new label, I gave myself a new life.

I expanded my limited perception of myself from that of a one-kid business to that of a budding entrepreneur. The awareness practices stuck. In my twenties, I dropped more self-imposed limitations and worked on fitness, my own and the increasing numbers of people who wanted me to be their personal trainer. My joy was introducing people to the benefits of being strong and healthy. They discovered the byproduct of getting in shape was feeling less stressed, more relaxed, more capable of handling whatever life dished out. At the same time, I sold health club memberships. The related skills and mindsets became stepping stones to bigger and better things. I began to work with cardiac patients, teaching them how physical and emotional fitness could help them lead healthier, fuller lives. Coaching individual athletes how to attain peak performance flowed into launching successful fitness centers. When business leaders recognized the correlation between workplace productivity and employee health and happiness—and reduced healthcare costs—they invited me to teach wellness techniques on blue- and white-collar levels. My work bore out the research. Studies show that executives and business leaders who practice mindfulness create a downstream effect on those around them. Over time, I winnowed the practices I used down to their essence—the Twelve Insights.

A Baker's Dozen

Unlike donuts, cupcakes, or loaves of bread, the Twelve Insights don't come in a baker's dozen. The seemingly quaint practice of English bakers giving a little extra so they weren't flogged or fined for selling a short weight began in the Middle Ages. There's no short weight between these covers. The Twelve Insights measure up, and the more you use them, the more they catalyze your own positive responses from less-than-favorable situations to create the life you want. Even so, we've added something special, which you'll see below, and that may feel like a baker's dozen after all.

There is no magic number of insights. Over many years, I've syncretized, distilled, and compiled inspirations both sacred and secular. I've listened, observed, and researched. The resulting insights here offer optimal ways of thinking, being, and doing that have helped me and my clients clear perceived physical or emotional hurdles. Many cultures resonate with the sacred number twelve. Twelve hours on a clock, months in a year, pairs of ribs in the body, apostles of Jesus, knights at King Arthur's round table, Olympians in Greek mythology, signs of the zodiac, days of Christmas, tribes of Israel, imams in Shi'a Islam, and steps of Alcoholics Anonymous (AA).

Of course, we could live in peace, health, harmony, and happiness with just one insight: Love. Love others. Love self. Love something higher than self. Love our earth mother. Love the river of diversity that runs through it. The Twelve Insights assume and subsume these and other values.

The more I witnessed workplace stress and anxiety that carried over into workers' personal lives, the more urgent was my call to share awareness and mindfulness techniques for living happier and healthier. And that's what you'll find in the following chapters. You may recognize situations that are similar to yours. Perhaps you've faced on-the-job obstacles that seem to get in the way of achieving your desired level of employment or professional success. Maybe you've felt that bad luck follows you around like a shadow on a sunny day. Or worse. Maybe you're exhausted from trying to be someone else's version of you, someone willing to live under rain clouds rather than reveal your shadow to others—and to yourself. Practicing awareness, we can meet, understand, accept, and love the shadow, which psychiatrist Carl Jung credited with great creative power. We can be best friends forever. At the least, we can practice kindness toward self.

Chapter 1, "Focus on the Now," explains the benefits of living fully in the present. We are world-building by setting the foundation with each of today's ephemeral moments. Each now is tomorrow's legacy. What do we want our future to look like? Think of the future as each successive rung on a ladder of infinite rungs that disappears into the clouds. We raise our foot onto the next higher rung. We perceive fluid motion. That action is one "now" moment in a sequence of many, like a film in slow motion. One frame at a time, each aware now step inches us closer to the future we envision—the goals we set.

In chapter 2, "Grasp the Highest Star," we'll delve into the differences and similarities between mindfulness—including the subtleties that distinguish Buddhist mindfulness meditation from Western flavors of mindfulness—and awareness. We'll explore the reasons why and how mindfulness can trigger positive behavioral changes and bring you closer to your goals. We'll discover that it's easier than we thought to turn insights into positive habits that contribute to our well-being. When we become aware of experiences and emotions that interfere with our well-being, we can reach into our mindfulness tool kit and pull out healthy distractions.

The Three Levels of Awareness

Just as we accept three interconnected aspects of the self—body, mind, and spirit—I've equally divided the Twelve Insights into three levels of awareness.

Awareness One: Being Present for Myself, traverses inner territory. Socrates said, "Know thyself." But what constitutes the "self"? Where does self-identity come from? Why is self-knowledge important? How can we change who we are? Why would we want to? The first four insights begin in chapters 3 through 6:

- ❧ "Accept the miracle of you"
- ❧ "Imagine the 'I'm possible'"
- ❧ "Check in with myself"
- ❧ "Leverage the power of optimism"

Awareness Two: Being Present for Others, maps our socioemotional wandering beyond our home turf. Venturing into territory unknown, we discover "non-selves." Our journey can feel like we've entered a traffic roundabout where we influence and are influenced by the other vehicles going our direction. We can return to where we started or explore side streets. Here are the insights of side streets in chapters 7 through 10:

- ∾ "Walk my talk"
- ∾ "Accept responsibility"
- ∾ "Offer and accept a hand"
- ∾ "Forgive and release"

Awareness Three: Being Present for the World, examines the continuity or discontinuity of self in connection to our environment. In human development, continuity refers to gradual change or maintaining the status quo. Discontinuity implies more abrupt changes—a consequence of our choice or of occurrences beyond our control. Chapters 11 through 14 conclude the Twelve Insights:

- ∾ "See with 3D vision"
- ∾ "Breathe life"
- ∾ "Ground yourself in nature"
- ∾ "Live in love."

Over the decades, I've heard the "Yes, buts," the reasons why we can't overcome inertia until this happens or that ship comes in. What I found is that when we decide to, we can turn hurdles into hoorays, obstacles into opportunities. We can change a "tomorrow come never" attitude to "now is the time."

I encourage you to discover the relevance of each insight for yourself. If the insight fits, follow through with the tool kit's awareness practices and exercises. Working through these mindfully, fully present in the moment, anchors your commitment to the goals that you've set and confirms your progress. Step up your game and defeat all self-imposed limitations. Trade par for a birdie or better.

Practicing awareness and mindful meditation isn't a one size fits all. Nor is it appropriate or healthy to take the practice—or any endeavor—to extremes. Like the Greek poet Hesiod, c. 700 BCE, we endorse healthy moderation in all things. If you've already had an insight that your health, well-being, happiness, and success depend on moderation, you're right. And that middle ground is fertile soil for developing your most mindful self.

ONE

Focus on the Now

Happiness is a sign that things are going well. Conversely, things usually go well when we're happy. Oftentimes, we're conscious of feeling happy when we've stepped over a threshold—marked a "first" in our lives. That over-the-moon first kiss. Buying our first house. Birthing our first child. Standing tall after the boss's glowing introduction of us to the new client. In each of our lifetimes, there are only so many firsts. Intuitively, we know that those good feelings don't last for long. So after the adrenalin rush wears off, what is happiness, and how does it affect our well-being? That depends on our perspective, culture, upbringing, genetics, and events beyond our control.

Neuroscientists and psychologists tell us that people who have more intimate relationships are happier. Or do we have that backwards? Do happy people have more intimate relationships? Decades of research show us that happy people sleep better, are less likely to get sick, are likeable, generous, and tend to squeeze every juicy bit of pleasure and meaning from the things they do at work or play. That means some people derive joy not just from first-time or fluke events, but also from their competencies that fuel positive outcomes.

One Size Doesn't Fit All

Social psychologist Sonja Lyubomirsky and her lab's colleagues tackled an enigma: why is it that what should make us happy doesn't and what shouldn't make us happy does?[1] Immediately, we see one problem: who's to judge what should and shouldn't be right for me or for you? Another problem? Many of us in highly developed countries are obsessed with "finding" happiness and being happy. "Don't worry. Be happy."

Carol Graham, senior fellow at the Brookings Institution, senior scientist at Gallup, and author of numerous books and articles on happiness and the "paradox of happy peasants and miserable millionaires,"[2] found that despite socioeconomic and cultural differences, there's little difference between what makes people happy from one country to another.

What insights are there to discover in the circular language of happiness, well-being, health, and joy? After all, life is messy and complicated. Not everyone approaches nirvana on the golf course as do Deepak Chopra and Phil Mickelson.

Surveys to determine the importance of being happy reveal startling results. People who rated happiness as their highest priority reported that they felt positive emotions 50 percent less often than those who valued many other aspects of life. Additionally, they experienced 75 percent more depressive symptoms and approximately 15 percent less emotional well-being.[3]

Chasing Rainbows When the Gold Is at Your Feet

Consistently, researchers find that the more we pursue happiness, the more it eludes us. Ever notice how the faintest stars appear when we look at them indirectly? Astronomers call that "averted vision." Basically, it explains why when we're looking off to the side, faint objects become visible. Happiness is like averted vision. Does that mean we shouldn't pursue it? Of course not. Remember that our founding fathers said we had a "right" to pursue happiness. They were right not to define it.

Who doesn't want to live happily ever after? There are three psychologically huge little words we carry around like baggage chained to us that drag down or prevent our ability to find joy in the moment: "if," "when," and "unless." "If I get that job . . ." "When the baby comes . . ." "Unless

Kris loves me . . ." It seems forever ago that the phrase "happily ever after" was frequently associated with marital bliss. You say, "I do," and the rest is history. But the composition of the American and worldwide family structure has changed dramatically, and looking around us confirms research conducted by the Pew Research Center. While family is precious to many of us, and we love being around family members, we don't live fairy-tale lives—solo, with partners, within the family, at our jobs, or within our local or global community. We are the only ones responsible for our happiness.

On *Sesame Street,* Kermit the Frog sings "It's not easy being green." He laments blending in with so many other ordinary things that people pass him over. "'Cause you're not standing out like flashy sparkles in the water or stars in the sky."

We want to be special. We want to take a deep breath until our lungs are bursting with recognition that we're not just *one of everything,* we're *one of a kind.* We *are* flashy sparkles on the water, and we're *made* from the stars in the sky. We want to live full and happy lives, but happiness isn't easy when it seems like everything conspires to throw water on our inner fire. Perhaps it's time to look at happiness using averted vision. We see it and feel it when we're focused on well-being, health, balance, and service to others.

Happiness is like cherry blossoms. The tree blooms when we've planted it in a sunny place in well-drained soil, watered it sufficiently, and removed infected leaves and branches before they became systemic problems.

Throughout this book, as we become the strong tree, we'll prune out obstacles and gain insights into our long-held conceptions and misconceptions about happiness. Because society and the social media play key roles in shaping our definition of a happy life, we'll touch on their influence. We'll look at how we become trapped in a cycle of unfulfilled expectations that inevitably collapses our ideals and crushes our dreams, spirals us into unhappiness, depression, or other emotional states mutually exclusive to feeling overall well-being. Between our addiction to the past and obsession with the future, there is being fully present in the now. There is our treasure.

True happiness is to enjoy the present, without anxious dependence upon the future, not to amuse ourselves with either hopes or fears but to rest satisfied with what we have, which is sufficient, for he that is so wants nothing. The greatest blessings of mankind are within us and within our reach. A wise man is content with his lot, whatever it may be, without wishing for what he has not.

This prescription for happiness didn't emerge from trending research on mindfulness's focus of living in the now. Roman statesman Lucius Annaeus Seneca, born in 5 BC, gave it to us. Roughly a hundred years later, Marcus Aurelius, affectionately called Seneca the philosopher king who saw himself a mere student, insightfully wrote to us across the ages: "The happiness of your life depends upon the quality of your thought. Therefore, guard accordingly and take care that you entertain no notions unsuitable to virtue and reasonable nature." In his *Meditations*,[4] Marcus Aurelius addresses the quiet and yet hard questions we still ask ourselves: Why are we here? How should we live our lives? How can we protect ourselves against the stresses and pressures of daily life? How should we deal with pain and misfortune? How can we live knowing one day we will not? They beg response, and the *Twelve Insights for Mindful Living* brings crisp understanding to these and other timeless questions about how to live, love, laugh, and be happy.

To everything there is a season. "A time to break down and a time to build, a time to weep and a time to laugh, a time to mourn and a time to dance, a time to cast away stones, and a time to gather stones together, a time to embrace and a time to refrain from embracing. . . ."[5] On the other hand, not all goals need timelines and target dates. We can set a direction and move toward it, reveling in the journey, open to whatever we discover along the way.

More than twenty-three hundred years ago, Aristotle reasoned that we can cultivate *eudaimonia*—happiness and flourishing—in every season. "As it is not one swallow or one fine day that makes a spring, so it is not one day or a short time that makes a man blessed and happy."[6] We don't make one decision to sow our fields with seeds of rational thinking and right actions only to make another decision to abandon them to circumstances. Our ultimate purpose is to tend them daily so our crop will flourish.

You'll Know It When You Feel It

Jerome Kagan, Harvard University developmental psychologist, urges us to be aware of the difference between feeling momentary happiness triggered by some occurrence and evaluating our satisfaction with life overall, through it all. For Kagan, the question is not "How often did you smile yesterday?" but "How does your life compare to the best possible life you can imagine?"

Yes, stuff happens. A lot of it is beyond our control. Nature's fury. Market crashes. Flights canceled. Global economic downturns. Company closures. Interstate pileups. Pandemics. Remember, it's not the story that defines us, but our perspective ("I was in a pileup; my car was totaled; but I walked away and am home with my kids!") and how we choose to respond that colors our lives.

Twenty-first-century behavioralists and neuroscientists are arriving at many of the same insights as did ancient philosophers who had a pretty good understanding of human nature. And many thoughts and theories have either stood the test of time or have come back around again. For example, when we're content with the life we have and know that we're on the right path, we can effortlessly flood our inner self with quiet serenity and peace, conspicuous by the absence of worry, anger, guilt, and a disconnect from self and others. It's not necessary to parade "I'm happy," grinning like a Cheshire cat (although most of us know at least one person who smiles all the time). If smiling at everyone's not authentic to you, don't do it. Just feel it. Every ounce of energy given to and expected from this book is a step toward living a full and purposeful life, in the flow of body-mind-spirit well-being.

When life is out of sync, however, we feel a disconnect between what we want from it and what it brings to us. We can't always put our finger on it. It just feels like there's nothing to be happy about; nothing to be grateful for. Everything's a mess. Ties to family and friends feel severed. Connection to our faith community and workplace feel strained. Self-esteem and self-acceptance seem to have flown out the window. The sense intensifies that life's about aimless wanderings. It feels like we're in survival mode. Our muscles are tense, ready for fight, flight, or freeze. Our bodies are overreacting to phantom fears. Our brain is jigsaw puzzling past and current events, forcing pieces into places that don't fit into a picture that's misassembled.

But our brain is trustworthy and wouldn't deceive us. Right? Sorry. Our mind is a consummate liar. Much of the time, it's like a gossipy neighbor who snoops on everyone, making up juicy tidbits of misinformation when there's none to scramble, and spreading falsehoods about others behind their backs. Where does our brain get the information it brews for our morning cuppa? Everywhere. Where attention goes, the mind follows. Don't expect certified organic, fair trade there. Memories are unreliable. Social media relentlessly churn between truths and alternative facts. Tomorrow isn't here yet. So, what's left but to use the fine sieve of awareness to sift facts from fiction in the present? Detect an irony here? Aren't we using the mind to tame the mind?

We could say that. The difference is that we've made the choice to be keenly focused, aware, watching, and listening for truths, large and small. We've corralled that herd of wild mustangs galloping through our one hundred billion neurons. We also discovered an army of pesty automatic negative thoughts, or ANTs. In Insight 4, we'll spend time nurturing optimism, our positive thoughts—training those beautiful mustangs—and developing strategies for safely disposing of those ANTs. That progress alone is cause for joy. And there's stuff all around outside us that can connect with what's inside if we truly open our awareness eyes. We don't have to look to see.

Sometimes we're conscious of bliss. From the Middle English word *blisse*, bliss—perfect happiness—may arise as an awareness in fleeting moments triggered by a known or unknown event. Sometimes bliss can feel like an altered state of body-mind euphoria, a natural high. Mothers know that feeling when they hold their minutes-old babies. At other times, bliss arises as a wave of all-pervasive pleasure, as the sensation of stepping out after a storm to stand in awe of a vibrant double rainbow, visible end to end. We may know it as the feeling of expansiveness in our chest when we've buffed that last coat of beeswax onto the cradle made for our first grandchild.

When you recognize a blissful moment or episode, it's because you've become keenly aware of the sensations in your body and the thoughts "fluttering around in your mind," as author Joseph Campbell put it. Through the Twelve Insights, we'll work with that "fluttering," practice focusing on one thing at a time, letting the distractions slip away, and embracing the sensations of our aware self.

Relationships Matter

Self-awareness seems self-explanatory. It's my relationship to myself, yes. But being self-aware is not the same as being selfish. Oneself becomes the focus of attention as the building block of creating a self-concept. Research has shown that even infants have a rudimentary sense of self-awareness, that they are a separate being from others. Life's experiences change us. Self-awareness is the mirror that reflects back to us our thoughts, beliefs, desires, dreams, and actions. And more. What we see is shaped by our perception at any one moment. Our self-awareness evolves. Informed by our past, our understanding deepens.

Often, after a lecture or workshop, someone comes up and tells me that they feel like they'll never break through old complex emotions, memories, and pain. I tell them that they may feel stuck with a reflection of themselves that's no longer true. In fact, that reflection isn't who they are. That perception has to change before they can get where they want to go. When we're out of sync and out of control, it does feel like everyone's making choices for us. We find ourselves doing things that others want or expect us to do. Or we've fallen into patterns of not doing the things we love. We've let the small things that matter to us fall off our happiness to-do list because we perceive there are big things that have a higher priority. Sometimes big things won't wait.

We're dancing with terms such as awareness, but what is it? K. Abdul Gafoor defines awareness in a paper presented to the November 2012 seminar *Emerging Trends in Education* at the University of Calicut, Kerala, India. He calls it "The state of being conscious of something, the ability to directly know and perceive, feel, or be cognizant of events, objects, or sensory patterns."[7] The objects of our awareness can be self, social, political, or environmental. Gafoor makes an interesting point: an individual can be aware of the "sense data" and yet not understand it. Awareness itself doesn't contain knowledge. The implication is that we have to interpret that data and make sense out of it, or it remains experiential and not capable of producing growth. More specifically, the awareness needs to be processed mindfully. We'll come back to this concept later.

Is awareness the same as consciousness? "Perhaps no aspect of mind is more familiar or more puzzling than consciousness and our conscious experience of self and the world."[8] As Neolithic burial practices demonstrate to archeologists, what the essence of consciousness is has been a mystery since the dawn of man. Surprisingly, there is no ancient Greek equivalent word to consciousness. In 1640, René Descartes combined his concept of *pensée*, or thought, with his understanding of "all that of which we are conscious as operating in us." The American Psychological Association (APA) tells us that "it is possible to be aware of something without being explicitly conscious of it." The APA's recognition underscores my efforts to teach participants how to turn on the mindfulness switch and be fully conscious of their minds' wanderings.

As you've seen, the Twelve Insights are grouped into three categories or types of awareness. The first is self-awareness, which we've been discussing above. The second is our awareness of others. This relationship, also called social awareness, identifies the ways in which we engage with and respond to others—including family—in one-on-one or small-group situations. This dynamic presupposes our ability to be keen observers of others' thoughts, words, emotions, and actions and translates them into responses that transmit our understanding. The third type of awareness takes in the broader scope and expands our feedback loop as our relationship to the world. Because our world includes larger groups with their own ethics, values, rules, and dynamics, it's also called organizational awareness. Organizations operate on their own levels of hierarchy, policies, processes, and protocols. Protocols are like a spoken language. The problem is that their messages aren't always clear. Sometimes there's ambiguity about where we belong in a hierarchy and how we're to interact across the various organizational leadership levels.

The Road to Mindfulness

Take a right turn onto awareness and you'll arrive at mindfulness. The University of California, Berkeley's, *Greater Good Magazine* defines mindfulness as "maintaining a moment-by-moment awareness of our thoughts, feelings, body sensations, and surrounding environment through a gentle, nurturing lens." Sounds good, but there's more. "Mindfulness also involves acceptance, meaning that we pay attention to our thoughts and feelings without judging them."

In my presentations, I stress the nonjudgmental component because it's too easy for participants to slip into self-condemnation for some occurrence in their past or into their past's effect on the future. Now is where I want their awareness to be. Acceptance means receiving your awareness with an open heart, compassionately. Compassion goes hand-in-hand with mindfulness. Compassion is often what's missing, according to Stanford University professor of neurosurgery Jim Doty.[9] Ultimately, the goal of practicing compassionate mindfulness, says Doty, "is to develop less ego, not to use this practice to support one's ego."

Doty warns us about the use of this powerful practice for the wrong reasons. Science has demonstrated that the better we get at practicing awareness, the more fear recedes. And the more that fear recedes, the more emboldened and confident we become. In moderation, that's not a problem. Without the overlay of compassion, however, increased awareness alone can lead some people to become manipulative. Compassionately practicing mindful awareness regulates the fountain of unconstructive thoughts, habits, and actions that interfere with development of healthy relationships with ourselves and others.

We'll discuss taking any thought, idea, or action to extremes again later. Here, the emphasis is on balance that enables us to make clear and informed, positive choices based on unclouded perceptions. We're not misled by expectations that aren't grounded in reality. We don't decompose emotionally or think the sky is falling when things don't go our way.

We can accept that we'll be buffeted by storms and high seas over which we have no control. As the captain of our own ship, we can control how we respond. We have an inner helmsman at the wheel. Our intuitive navigator is charting a course through the treacherous personal and professional reefs with emotional intelligence, or EI for short. When our EI kicks in, we mobilize our emotions to work for us rather than against us. We manage stress in positive and constructive ways and communicate thoughts, ideas, and instructions effectively and empathically. We rise to meet fear and challenges. In action, EI means that even though we aim for safe harbor, we empowered our crew to put on their own EI life jackets, and we've checked the lifeboats. Now, mindfully and in the present moment, we're prepared to tackle each swell as it comes.

Did you notice how many interrelated psychological and physiological functions are going on simultaneously here? You'll see many of the Twelve Insights in practice as we navigate through them. In stressful situations, we're not thinking about happiness. There's no time or place for self-indulgent worry. Freezing isn't an option. Focus isn't on me. It's on us. Our perception triggers automatic neurological and cellular responses. A rush of hormones sends one message. Our awareness rescinds it. Within a flash, we've sorted through the mixed messages and made informed rather than emotional choices.

Touched by a Hummingbird

Susan Sontag's nudge to "do stuff" is short, sweet, and spot on. "Do stuff. Be clenched, curious. Not waiting for inspiration's shove or society's kiss on your forehead. Pay attention. It's all about paying attention. Attention is vitality. It connects you with others. It makes you eager. Stay eager."

I can relate to eagerness, too. In Arizona, winter often feels like spring in other parts of the country. One year, I dutifully did the "dormant season" pruning and patiently awaited nature's awakening. On a perfect April afternoon, I was eager to get into the back courtyard, dig holes, smell the richness of the potting soil, and plant green things. Working with plants and constructing rockwork features had become one of my many opportunities to seize the mindful moment and reduce stress through working meditation.

Emblazoned on the front of my t-shirt was a large, radiant sunburst that looked like a golden sunflower. Immediately, our courtyard cadre of hummingbirds checked me out. Disappointed by the deception, they took off. All except one black-chinned fellow, that is. In slow motion, I stood straight and tall, becoming the sunflower on my chest. Little black chin accepted my offer to connect. We touched. The vibration of his wing hum amplified through me as he searched the sunflower for the tiny florets he had learned to expect. Even past his discovery that nectar was an illusion, he lingered, hovering. I longed to have something for him. But, perhaps, I had. For those awesome, intimate moments, the gift of our mutual awareness was reciprocal.

Among students of mindfulness, Jon Kabat-Zinn's raisin exercise is legendary. So is the molecular biologist's pioneering work to bring mindfulness meditation to medicine and society. "I bent over backwards to structure it and find ways to speak about it that avoided as much as possible the risk of it being seen as Buddhist, new age, Eastern mysticism or just plain flakey," Kabat-Zinn explained in a 2017 interview for the *Guardian* about secularizing mindfulness four decades earlier, mission-bound to change the world's consciousness.[10] When he and colleagues launched the University of Massachusetts Stress Reduction Clinic in 1979, his goal was to teach people to mitigate intense physical and emotional pain with mindfulness meditation—"the awareness that arises from paying attention, on purpose, in the present moment and non-judgmentally." The UK has gone all out with spreading the benefits of Kabat-Zinn's mindful meditation to schools, prisons, and even to political offices. Fully in the social equality camp, Kabat-Zinn warns that when the human mind operates mindlessly, it "winds up becoming a prisoner of its myopic perspectives that puts 'me' above everything else."[11]

Kabat-Zinn's raisin relaxation icebreaker exercise takes participants' minds off "me" and focuses attention on the senses of sight, smell, touch, and taste. The guru of stress reduction isn't blindsided by rare incidents in which mindfulness meditation practitioners experienced less-than-positive effects. "If in the past fifty years I had found something more meaningful, more healing, more transformative and with more potential social impact, I would be doing that," he concedes.[12] So far, the millennia-old practice gone secular is still a powerful tool in our tool kit. This moment, the endorsement of millions of mindfulness meditation practitioners worldwide is rock solid. Before exposure to combat situations, soldiers learn meditation techniques as a coping tool to prevent Post-Traumatic Stress Disorder (PTSD). In a 2002 collaboration with Welsh psychologist Mark Williams and colleagues at Cambridge and elsewhere, Kabat-Zinn combined his program's techniques with those of cognitive behavioral therapy (CBT) to create mindfulness-based cognitive therapy (MBCT) that's been shown to be at least as effective as antidepressants. Kabat-Zinn acknowledges that we've barely "scratched the surface of what human intelligence is all about."

What we're capable of is up for grabs. For now, it's enough to seize the moment and connect with a hummingbird.

Everything That Happens, Happens as It Should

"And if you observe carefully, you will find this to be so," completes the quote by Marcus Aurelius, a Roman emperor who ruled by reason. Maybe you've wanted to put distance between you and the person who said this to you when what you wanted was empathy, not philosophy. In the wake of horrific events—nature's or manmade—how do we relate to the statement that everything is happening as it should? Or for a reason? The idea makes us shudder. It seems fatalistic. Are we in control of our lives or are we at the mercy of the winds of fate? Let's find out.

I remember that my mother and my biological father screamed and shouted at each other a lot. When I was five, my mother threw him out. Their divorce was acrimonious. My father, a military policeman, had come home with his gun still in his holster. Livid, he held his pistol to my head, shouting to my mother that if he couldn't have his son, neither could she. Their standoff lasted four excruciating hours. Miraculously, and somehow, it was settled. We three kids stayed with Mom. To make ends that never met, she worked as a barback, a person who makes the bartender's work look easy. Alcohol consumed her.

Throughout my growing years, I only heard her say "I love you" a few times, during moments she wouldn't remember but I'd never forget. Given my youth, I couldn't know the extent of her struggle or the abyss of her depression. I ached when I saw her suffer. One night, she was driving home from the bar where she worked. Not in control of herself much less of a powerful machine on wheels, she plowed into a parked car. Her face hit the steering wheel so hard that the impact knocked out four upper front teeth. Instead of heading to the emergency room, she pressed a handkerchief over her mouth and managed to drive home. When I saw her, she was a bloody mess, physically and emotionally. Those words—I love you—came from a broken place and evaporated with the alcohol. But I held onto them and never let them go. They became solid gold over the decades that I watched her transformation through AA—its own story in chapter 14.

Nights, I curled up in an alcove of our rundown little house across from a trailer park. One day, when I was six, neighbors asked Mom if they could take my older sister, Paula, and me to church so we could join in a special group function afterwards. That next Sunday, they picked us up. When everything was over, the neighbors and the group leader each thought the other had arranged to take me home. Their wires had crossed. I faced an empty parking lot. Suddenly, I was aware of total aloneness. I believed I was lost forever. Crying, I started walking down the road in the direction we had arrived.

A grandmotherly woman pulled up beside me. "Are you alright? I'll take you home," she said. She asked for my address, but I didn't know it. "Never mind," she said. "Get in." I described my house, the street and the turns, and the way I remembered coming in earlier that morning. When we arrived, my house was empty. The grandmotherly woman handed me over to a neighbor. That evening and for all her years, my mother made no mention of what happened, as though it was of no consequence that her young son had been abandoned. Ignoring reality and losing her temper were as much an addiction as was alcohol. I loved her anyway.

I was learning the hard way to use a technique that changed my life, even though it would be years before I knew what to call it: mindfulness. I just knew I had to pay attention to what was going on in my head and to the world around me.

My mother remarried. I remember her saying that the money always ran out before the month did. I was ten when my stepfather took me aside. "Look," he said, "your mom's going to have a baby, and I'll have six mouths to feed. I'll provide a roof over your head, food on the table, a few school clothes, and one pair of shoes for the year. Anything else is your responsibility." That "responsibility" meant work—every day after school until supper and eight to five on Saturday. My stepfather required that I take Sundays off.

He bought me a not very gently used girl's bike. We welded a bar on it so it would look more like it was intended for boys. My stepfather made it clear: the bike was for one thing—transportation to a job. I quickly under-stood the term "pounding the pavement" as I followed his instructions to go business to business until someone hired me to do something, anything. No one did. That is, until I got to the barber on Broadway Boulevard. That was the kick in the one of two pair of pants my stepfather allotted to me per year that I needed to become an entrepreneur. The bonus was that I also recognized the significance of adding value to someone else's business. What could I do for the barber? How about shine shoes? On the condi-tion that I did a good job and didn't get polish on his clients' socks, my wooden shoeshine box and I would be welcome. Suddenly, I was not only employed, but I was also part of a team. He cut hair while I shined toes and heels. I charged two bits. I was pretty happy picking up a few dollars each afternoon. The barber's customers were happy to be slicked up head to foot.

In fact, I learned that if I swirled and rubbed the polish in deep and worked fast with my buffing towel, clients could feel the soothing warmth through their shoes and relax as if they were getting a foot massage. I'd give the buffing towel a few crisp snaps that made me look like a pro. I had no doubt my little TLC made people feel good because their tips were always bigger than the amount I charged. It was great to earn in-come. Still, something wasn't right.

"Tell me about your business," said one of the barber's two best clients, both encyclopedia salesmen who watched my polish and buff routine.

"I hate being a shoeshine boy," I admitted. "The kids make fun of me. Worse, one older kid always waits in ambush as I cut through the park. And if I can't ride fast enough, he knocks me off my bike and beats me up."

"Then stop being a shoeshine boy," he advised the all-ears ten-year-old.

I told him I couldn't stop. I needed to earn money.

"Then shine shoes. But change your business model and give yourself a more professional title, one people will respect and that will bring you more business. You'll certainly find plenty of leather-shoe-wearing poten-tial customers in the offices and retail stores around here if you go door to door. Oh, by the way, quit taking the shortcut through the park!"

On the advice of my new "executive coach," I painted *Shoeshine Preservation Expert and Consultant* on the side of my shoeshine box. I expanded my territory to office buildings and retail stores. The more shoes I shined, the more referrals I got. I passed my courses in street economics, human dynamics, and free enterprise and benefitted from the law of supply and demand. I outsourced my overflow business to friends and kept a percent of their profit.

But the biggest lesson was the priceless one. I had never had an adult take interest in me before, much less mentor me. It gave me wings.

Next, I peddled Fuller Brush. At seventeen, I scrubbed whatever needed scrubbing at European Health Spas. In my spare time, I worked out. The more fit I got, the more spa clients wanted my help to get their bodies in shape. Fitness consulting fit me. It also left me time to earn commissions on spa membership sales. The experience yielded a valuable insight: nobody likes to be sold anything, but everybody likes to buy something. Fitness became my passion. I studied how the body works, what fuels it, what fuels our minds, how our minds help determine what we can achieve with our bodies. Through the years, I co-owned and operated more than twenty fitness centers and athletic clubs.

I'm a firm believer that more often than sometimes, things happen serendipitously that can change our lives. That's how it felt when I was invited to give my first talk on personal and professional development based on mindfulness for health and well-being to one hundred fifty club members. I've been blessed and now conduct trainings and presentations at many dozens of organizations that employ thousands of people. Along the way, I had a Marcus Aurelius moment: an insight about why things happen as they should. I'll share that in Insight 5.

The Illusive Mind

Underpinning each of the insights is present-moment awareness integrated with becoming mindful. Mindful of what? Mindful that while we're meditating—using whichever practice works for us—we're in the present moment. That's where the work is. Not plodding in the past or flirting with the future. Mindful that we haven't wandered off and gotten lost in a jungle of thoughts or entangled in vines of dried-out beliefs. Just as we should do if we find ourselves lost in a forest, we need to stop wandering, take a deep breath to calm ourselves, recognize that "there are many good sides to getting lost,"[13] retrace our steps to a familiar place, and return to the here and now. Throughout the *Twelve Insights for Mindful Living*, we'll practice stepping into the present and onto the path to harmony, health, and happiness.

> Can we bring more peak moments into our lives?
> Can we make precious moments last longer?
> Is living a fulfilling, joyful life possible in today's world?
> I'll give each of those questions an unqualified "yes."

Decades of studies demonstrate mindful awareness is not only effective in neutralizing fear, anxiety, worry, anger, and such that undermine our well-being, but the practice also helps us "avoid, suppress, or over-engage" with our distressing thoughts and emotions.[14] When Jon Kabat-Zinn applied the Buddhist practice of mindfulness meditation—at least 2550 years old and secularized for clinical settings—to his ten-week stress reduction and relaxation program, chronic pain patients who hadn't responded to traditional Western medical treatments reported not only significant reduction in pain, but also shifts toward positive moods.[15] As they practiced acceptance, patients experienced events in the moment (as well as those retrieved from memory) without becoming excessively or obsessively preoccupied with them.

Electroencephalogram (EEG) studies on meditation from the 1950s and '60s found that the alpha and theta brainwaves patterns of meditation practitioners are associated with those of rest and sleep states.[16] Recent corroborations indicate that because mindfulness meditation also reduces distractions from vague thoughts and because attention is a trainable skill, it increases the brain's neuroplasticity,[17] its capacity to continue developing and changing throughout life.

That's a lot of science behind the claims. We live in a complex universe. We ask the why of something and receive interrelated answers because all things are connected. While we love solving puzzles, our brains are hardwired to crave simple, elegant solutions, such as a tidy theory of everything.

Millions of years ago, hominids, including our *Homo* ancestors, walked away from what they knew and wandered into no-man's-land in search of something better, warmer, wetter, safer. Perhaps a place of more plentiful game and wild foods. Push and pull factors spurred them onward, despite the danger. They didn't know their destination. They only knew their purpose. Find a place more hospitable. They followed their instincts, the weather, water courses, adapting to nature's challenges along the way, intersecting and interbreeding with other early adventurers, innovating to meet necessity and, perhaps, comfort.

Before the intricate maps of our forebearers, our distant ancestors dispersed over land and by sea ever aware of their relationship to the canopy of stars, sun, moon, and constellations. Mindful of the movement of shadows across the plains, the ripples in watercourses, the buildup of massive storm fronts, they logged the information tracked by their senses and retrieved it as needed. Attention to detail and adaptability made us who we are.

Ceaselessly, and more than lightning fast, nerves bombard our brain—our living computer—with millions of bits and bytes of electrical and chemical impulses through an extraordinary conduit, the spinal cord. Twelve pairs of cranial nerves connect the eyes, ears, and other sensory organs to this control center. Perhaps we've become afraid to trust our senses, which served us fairly well since the dawn of . . . well, you know. We've retrained our senses to be aware of the subtle ping of our smartphone's text message notification and the distant flash of red lights in our car's rearview mirror rather than to react with fight or flight at the snarl of a too-near saber-tooth tiger. And we're still reinventing ourselves and our world through the filter of our skewed perceptions.

Physicist Lee Smolin, in a 2013 *Science Friday* interview by host Ira Flatow, discussed our destiny and our control over it in his book *Time Reborn: From the Crisis in Physics to the Future of the Universe*. Einstein believed time is an illusion; Smolin thinks otherwise. "It's certainly true that everything we experience and think and feel is experienced in a moment of time, which we experience as a flow of moments." The kernel is that, for many of us,

what we think about, what we really value or really aspire to [is] outside of time. We have no choice about going forward in time. We have no choice about where we are in time. We have no choice about the fact that almost everything that goes on in our lives is irreversible and can't be restored or reversed. Where you are in space just represents your perspective, and you can choose, to some extent, your perspective.[18]

Our tool to attain for ourselves greater perspective is mindfulness. We can use it to virtually freeze-frame our awareness of an occurrence, thought, emotion, or sensation in that impossible-to-harness now before our perception of reality catches up and relegates that experience to what we call the past. We can also use mindfulness to heighten our awareness of and bring attention to the changes or flow from this now to that now. We can visualize the invisible processes as our bodies produce visible changes—the microscopic rhythms and pulse of the protoplasmic stream, the primordial heartbeat that's detectable from the lowly slime mold to the ebb and flow of our lifeblood.

Can we bring more peak moments into our lives? Can we make those precious moments last longer? Can we bring more awareness to our job, to our day-to-day activities, not just the special ones? Is living a fulfilling, joyful life possible in today's world?

I'll give each of those questions an unqualified "yes."

The late Joseph Campbell, professor of literature, mythologist, and pioneer in the study of bliss, whom I admired greatly, reflected on our challenge and our greatest flaw: "the sin of inadvertence [mindlessness], of not being alert, not quite awake."[19]

We can't hear the music if we don't listen. Let's remove our earbuds and tango with life on a whim. Amazing things happen when we least expect them.

TWO
Grasp the Highest Star

"**G**rasp the highest star" is an invitation. Not to a destination. It's an invitation to stretch yourself and embark on an unimaginably rewarding journey toward the you you've dreamed about. The you who's ready to leave behind old, self-defeating habits and develop positive habits characteristic of a satisfying life and critical to reaching your fullest potential. Fullest potential doesn't mean that one day you'll be recognized as the world's greatest surgeon, salesperson, scientist, or skier. Nor does it mean you'll be the richest or the smartest person quantitatively, or that you'll be number one in your chosen field. Number one spots are fleeting positions quickly overtaken by someone whose goal is to top your victory.

Sadhguru, Indian yogi, author, and lecturer, expresses the challenge: we know what a "full-fledged" apple tree is, but we don't know what constitutes a full-fledged human being.[1] Just as there are many kinds of apple trees that bear fruit of considerable variety—or not at all—we appear to each other as infinitely unique. Yet, from the perspective of our genome, "we are all essentially identical twins."[2] In fact, you and I are genetically 99.9 percent alike, as we'll explore in Insight 1.

For those whose daily inner work is "in-joying" a full-fledged life, body and mind are under control. There is no need to blame anyone for restricting them from living a successful life—and everyone's definition of successful is as unique as we are. We can think of living a full-fledged life, an authentic life to its fullest potential, like walking a beautiful path carpeted with the red, gold, and amber leaves. We're immersed in cosmic excellence and totally aware of our natural experience of happiness and joy. The word "excellence" originates from the Latin *excellentia*, the quality of being extremely good. Human excellence, then, is a state of being often associated with virtue and ethics.

Aristotle recognized "excellence is not an act, but a habit." Habits, of course, are those things we do repeatedly. When they're healthy and positive, they're stepping stones along the path to living our fullest potential. When we associate value with our habits, we're willing to expend the effort to achieve a level of excellence. And when we recognize our excellence—not perfection—that brings us ongoing joy. Habits associated with excellence are directly a consequence of awareness. The Twelve Insights help you identify your excellence and strengths and build on them.

Sure, winning a race or getting a raise brings us joy, but that wears off. We feel fulfillment in our cumulative practice of choosing healthy habits that create an ongoing sense of satisfaction. Yes, there will still be moments when we think we've fallen into an abyss. But living mindfully aware has taught us not to believe our thoughts. There is no abyss. It's an illusion. We'll talk more about believing your thoughts in Insights 4 and 9.

Ask yourself this: through whose eyes am I envisioning my fullest potential? Family's? Friends'? Colleagues'? What individual or test is capable of predicting my future and my best self? Others see you as if through optical filters that selectively transmit light of different wavelengths. People bring their perspective not only to every aspect of their own lives, but also to their relationship with you and their surroundings.

This myopia reminds me of the Indian parable about the five blind men and the Rajah's elephant. Each man, never having seen an elephant, had formed his own preconceptions about what an elephant was and how it must look. When they were taken to examine the Rajah's great and wonderful beast, one touched only its tail. Another ran his fingers along the elephant's trunk. Yet another felt the spear-like tusk, and so on. Their individual experiences reinforced their singular viewpoints. The wise Rajah reprimanded them for forming conclusions based on their limited information. "Each of you has touched only one part of the elephant," he said gently. "If you put the parts together, you will know the truth."

Others' perspective of you may be only partially true or not at all. Who can see into your mind and heart better than you? Do you look in the rearview mirror, dissatisfied with where you've been because you think you should have accomplished more? If so, are you one of the five blind men trying to describe the elephant by touching only its tail or its trunk? Awareness and mindfulness are the glasses through which we get a clearer view of those things that bring satisfaction to our lives and those that increase stress and anxiety. For many of us, doing what we love and loving what we do is a great place to be.

"Working hard for something we love is called passion," says Simon Sinek, international motivational author and speaker. "Working hard for something we don't care about is called stress."

Robert Steven Kaplan, professor at the Harvard Business School, studies stress and the dissatisfaction people experience when their relationship to their work feels unfulfilling. There are two deceptively different questions we can ask ourselves, Kaplan says. "Am I reaching my potential?" and "How do I rise to the top?"[3] Each requires us to look into our heart of hearts and come to our own definition of success. Not someone else's. Only then can we walk the path toward whatever it is that fulfills us rather than drift into a career for which we're not emotionally suited. Loving what we do gives us the emotional intelligence to weather storms. But achieving success goes beyond being passionate about a thing and committing to it. We also have to be willing to obtain the critical skills required for the goal's achievement.

Often before we can go forward, we need to take a step back. Many times we sidestep responsibility and accountability and blame others for where we are or why we're feeling unfulfilled. Frequently, we feel like victims of circumstance, the boss, co-workers, bad luck. Kaplan reveals a harsh truth: our career wounds are self-inflicted. "Taking control begins with understanding yourself. Those who identify their dreams develop the skills to realize them and demonstrate courage will find fulfillment— even if they hit bumps along the way."

"To win, you need to fail, and fail hard," said successful actress, comedian, producer, and writer Aisha Tyler during an interview for *Forbes* about her book *Self-Inflicted Wounds, Heartwarming Tales of Epic Humiliation*.[4] Books, workshops, seminars, and the educational system pass along a lot of information, facts that we sift through for relevance. For good reason, the maxim that experience is our best teacher remains true. Our missteps and so-called failures shape our understanding of ourselves and how we interact with events and people far more than success. In Insight 9, we'll plunge more deeply into the sea of regret and failure and explore coming up for life-saving air when our lungs feel like they're bursting.

We can learn to survive a tsunami of workplace, home, health, spiritual, financial, and personal issues that feel crushing. Awareness permits us to adjust our perspective, examine our thoughts, discard our limiting beliefs, and emerge confident that we're making informed choices about our future.

Choice Not Chance

If a wizard offered you the chance to be either the smartest person in the world or the most aware, which would you choose?[5] Not surprisingly, more people answered Deepak Chopra's revealing question with "smarter." But which is the wiser choice?

Awareness. Here's why. Smartness and wisdom don't always reside together. "A smart person will give you smart answers, but a wise person will ask you smart questions."[6] Wisdom is the fertile ground from which good choices spring. There's a direct correlation between wisdom and awareness. We're like a gold nugget nestled in a sandy creek bottom, aware of but undaunted by the rumble and jumble of pebbles jostling above us when the flow becomes swift. While we're conscious of the tumult of our surroundings, we're not reactionary. Even when the rush dislodges us and washes us downstream, we remain calm, in control. Experience has taught us that we'll come to rest in a new place where it's safe to settle once again.

Like water, the mind's current is a powerful force that can dash our thoughts and feelings against the rocks. The mind "can enslave us or empower us. It can plunge us into the depths of misery or take us to the heights of ecstasy," acknowledges author and speaker David Cuschieri.[7] Our task is to use our power wisely and, through awareness, clearheadedly make our best choices.

We use awareness, mindfulness, and living consciously as though they're interconnected because they are. They form a circle—or cycle—of actions and non-actions that define how we approach life. Our quest is to be aware not only of what's going on in the outer, but also to what's going on in the inner. That means discovering and understanding our triggers, maintaining control, and responding rather than reacting. To live consciously is to live in the present, fully aware and better equipped to make mindful decisions. Awareness shines a light on the way out when we're feeling trapped in a phantom reality that no longer serves us—if it ever did. When we're in the midst of pain and tough times, it's hard to believe that we're not really trapped or stuck unless we choose to be. We make up all sorts of excuses to stay where we are. Someone whose opinion about us matters calls us egocentric, or leaves us for someone else, or tells us we'll never change. Maybe our parents punished us for being "selfish." Perhaps we've developed a pattern of self-criticism that's destructive and debilitating. Whatever we perceive is holding us back from reaching our wished-for stars, that's where we focus our awareness, survey our experience, tap our wisdom, and choose to step forward mindfully.

As we go through the insights, you'll see me remind you often of a powerful lesson Deepak Chopra teaches: "Don't believe the lies your mind tells you. There are no tricks or shortcuts to living an aware, mindful life." There are no magic elixirs. There is only the work that each of us must do unique to who we are and where we are. We can succeed, fail, or somewhere in between. It's all a matter of perspective. Failure to one person is a successful lesson or opportunity for another. We're not cookie-cutter beings. The dynamics of our upbringing and genetic inheritance make us unique. Researchers have attempted to quantify and qualify the effects on us of nature vs. nurture, but, it's complicated. The universe is complicated. Body, mind, and spirit growth are complex processes. Yet, as you'll discover, you can change habits that have sunk your ship in the past. Awareness helps you establish the rules, set the pace, and keep the scoreboard. Join me on a little thought experiment.

Go In to Go Out

Let's begin your journey at the front door of the self. Feel welcomed. Close the door behind you; close it to judgment about everything you have ever been and done. Close it to self-recrimination, shame, and regret. Sit at the table of self-awareness. Feel the awesomeness of this new place. It has no walls, no ceiling, no floor. Like the vastness of space, your new home is limitless. There's no bottom to the depth you can search. Look up. Across from you is your spiritually malnourished, confused, unhappy, battered, wounded self. What is that self hungry for? Positive self-worth? Meaningful actions? Purposeful existence? Healthy relationships? Invite your other self to share your seat to see life from your new perspective.

Embrace. Become one. Order the daily special: presence in the now. Drink up amazement; it's not on the rocks. Nourish body, mind, and spirit. Sense the fullness of gratitude, love, kindness, compassion, and empathy. Hold that feeling as if it were an open passageway to the future. Step into each new now moment aware of your uniqueness, goodness, power, and healthy self-love. Know that nothing is stopping you from achieving your highest self. You are body-mind-spirit.

Living a fulfilled life is the joyful journey of accumulated moments in which our vision matches our circumstances, and we bypass the sideroads of limited thinking. Nothing limits us, except fear.

Forget Fight, Flight, or Freeze

Evolution has hardwired us to automatically respond to situations that threaten our survival. Aware of or aroused by danger, our active defense response, described in 1915 by physiologist Walter Bradford Cannon, is fight, flight, or freeze. Almost a century later, Maggie Schauer and Thomas Elbert redefined the response as the "defense cascade."[8] Whether our mind perceives a snarling wild animal rushing toward us or an oncoming train, our bodies release the hormone adrenaline and the stress hormone, cortisol. To prepare us for whatever is to come, our hearts race; blood vessels dilate; respiration increases; glycogen converts to glucose, fueling muscles and brain cells; pupils dilate; our minds quicken. In a state of heightened awareness, we focus on the threat, potential escape routes, or the options to freeze or fight.

The defense cascade model includes a phase called "quiescent immobility." It refers to the period after a threat or danger has passed and a state of quiescence sets in that promotes rest and healing. In that state, animals generally return to normal functioning. Humans, however, may not reach quiescent immobility as naturally, or at all. They're caught in a lingering state of arousal and fear.

Sometimes, there's no impending doom. The perceived threat tricked our bodies into reacting when there's nothing to fight or flee from. Research has shown that those of us who have experienced trauma are more likely to overreact to stress and anxiety and develop an exaggerated response. We'll explore coping strategies to mitigate these responses in Insight 5, "Walk my talk."

If we're lucky, the saber-toothed boss isn't eyeing our position as an hors d'oeuvre to be devoured by plant-wide reorganization. Still, stuff happens. When it does, we need to be aware of what's most important to us so that we can mitigate the stress and make decisions mindfully. Have you been chasing the "wrong" goals? Was the job loss a blessing in disguise? Did it open an opportunity for jumping onto a leadership training track within your current company? Was it a prompt to start the business you've dreamed about? Was it the incentive to get in the RV and see the country for a month or more? Or was it the impetus to start marathon training? Have you taken quiet moments to listen to your heart's desires? Are you aware of what lights your fire?

"Follow Your Bliss"

In 1987, Joseph Campbell made those words a household mantra. Later in this book, we're going to launch into another thought experiment to discover your bliss. Decades before I started working with groups, Joseph Campbell took his university students through their experiential paces to focus on being mindful of their happiest moments, "not simply excited, not just thrilled, but deeply happy."[9] We all know how painful it is to feel pinned between a rock and a hard place. But that other feeling, that quiet warmth and sense that all is right with our world in that special moment is where we want to be more often.

All of us have the capacity to be awakened to this other place that we can reach at will and feel bliss. There's no roadmap to get to my happy place and yours. Getting there takes a technique "that each one has to work out for himself somehow," Campbell admits. "No one can tell you what it's going to be. You've got to learn to recognize it. If you do follow your bliss, you put yourself on a kind of track that has been there all along, waiting for you."

Life's Not Always like a Box of Chocolates

Like many mothers, Forrest Gump's mom was right: when it comes to life, we never know what we're gonna get. What if we don't like Brazil nuts? Or nougat? When we picked this chocolate over that, we made a choice. Do we always have to live with our choices? Unlike chocolates, life seldom lets us bite into an experience, decide we don't like it, and put it back in the box.

A lot of counselors and coaches say you should stick with your decision, no matter what. That's not always a good idea. If I start snowshoeing across a frozen lake and suddenly hear the ice crack and pop, there isn't a shadow of a doubt in my mind that I'm going to reverse my decision. I'm going to slowly, carefully, inch my way backwards to the shoreline, distributing my weight as equally as possible on my snowshoes. Some people seem to walk out on thin ice more than others. Aware, I'm listening and paying attention to the murmurs of the ice and, based on that new information, I choose to change my course of action.

When counselors and coaches talk about the subconscious decision-making process that sabotages our happiness and well-being, they're referring to psychological reversal. Sometimes, without being mindful of our needs and the consequences of our actions, we lapse into self-destructive habits that cascade into choices we regret or that make us miserable. Just as things were looking up, we plunge into icy water or feel we've picked the wrong chocolate. In Insight 3, we'll explore healthy thought processes that increase our odds of experiencing positive outcomes.

Since I was that ten-year-old entrepreneur with a shoeshine box, I've led a vision-based life. No, that doesn't mean everything worked out perfectly or that I'm clairvoyant or see the future. The past is the history book full of lessons for today and tomorrow. It does mean that every morning I mindfully put on my special 3D glasses that enable me to *discover* my truths, beliefs, and gifts, *develop* a plan of action, and *disperse* my joy and sense of purpose as I make my own reality. With that clear perspective, I assure that my actions are vision-driven. We'll do this in Insight 9 and hitch our vision to our wisdom. Like Mary Morrissey, dream-building coach and empowerment specialist says, "I love my life. It's not perfect, but I love it." Life won't ever be perfect. But we can love the life we have when we recognize our power to consciously create it.

Just as our physical vision is stereoscopic, which gives us a sense of visual depth, mindful awareness is a psychological perspective, which sharpens our appraisal of reality. We can more clearly discern where we are (what's happening around us?), how we are (what are we feeling? are we in danger?), and what are our best choices among the options (fight, flight, or freeze, or none of these?). Goal achievement becomes our focal point, and our clarity of vision defines the steps toward it.

In 1977, eleven years before Nike launched its world-famous "Just do it" slogan, what is now an international corporate giant ran with "There is no finish line." Its original motto was realistic and optimistic: we set one goal, achieve it, and set another. One finish line is the starting line of a new adventure. In a sense, the finish line keeps moving forward a length or more ahead of us. That parallels learning and growth as lifelong pursuits to keep body and mind in shape. As I've said, we have to do the hard work. That's as it should be until our lifeforce can no longer manifest our dreams in time and space.

Each time I present the Twelve Insights to groups, especially during extensive and demanding seminars—demanding in the sense that we pull no punches, ask tough questions of ourselves, and respond openly with honest, deep answers—I wonder who's the student. I learn from participants' courageous life choices, wise decisions that demonstrate they've put mindfulness techniques into practice. The most extraordinary people have proven to me that mindfulness bolsters resiliency. I've lectured to and led trainings for executives, judges, healthcare professionals, educators, students, blue-collar employees, and leaders, and I've witnessed the tenacity of the awake and aware human spirit and marveled at participants' near superhuman determination to win when winning seemed a distant dream.

I add my mother to these successful people. Over many decades, I witnessed her personal transformation as she made a commitment to herself through Alcoholics Anonymous. Not every AA member makes such long strides. For Mom, her first step was not blaming anyone else for selecting a chocolate that was so distasteful. She knew she couldn't put it back in the box. Mom started where she was and, once she made her decision, she was all in.

Ram Das gave us this advice: "Wherever you are, be all there." Start with whatever chocolate you picked. Forget about the nut and focus on the chocolate. Find the thing you love about the thing you have.

The Two Faces of Janus

Maybe you remember Janus from high school Roman mythology—he had no Greek counterpart. As the god of gods and a benevolent creator, he became associated with the beginning of everything. Janus was depicted with two faces that look in opposite directions, symbolizing transitions from what was (the past) to what's ahead (the future). The richness of this duality paradox is that between the "then" and the "yet to be" there is the "now," and this dual nature meets at the mind level. Janus represents the middle ground of the duality paradoxes: life and death, beginning and end, change from one condition to another, one vision to another. In his hand, Janus holds a key to open metaphorical and literal doors and gates.

The lesson of Janus is further explored in Insight 3. There, we'll look at how a single moment can present us with seemingly opposing—even mutually exclusive—yet equally desirable choices. When one door to a chapter of our lives closes, we may only need to turn around and be aware that another opens.

Awareness—the Portal to Mindfulness

As I've worked with individuals and groups, I've found that it helps conceptually for workshop participants to think of awareness as the portal to mindfulness. While both refer to states of mind, awareness arises when we activate our senses and focus attention on the present moment and orient or ground our physical and emotional selves—our thoughts, feelings, and behaviors—to our surroundings, to the world around us. We may practice awareness intuitively or deliberately.

Sometimes, especially during times of individual and collective crisis, we lose control over our awareness. The mind runs wild. We obsess over things that tax us rather than teach us. Instead of monitoring our attention and focusing on thoughts and feelings that comfort us, we catastrophize and fixate on situations and emotions that cause us more stress. In a complex feedback loop, the brain shouts doom and gloom messages to the endocrine system that circle back to the brain. The chef and sous-chef's chemical soup sets off a rush of ancient sensations to increase the odds that we're up to the task of surviving whatever battle awaits. Unfortunately, those sensations also up the stress and anxiety levels when we've misread alarm signals by letting our brain take over our awareness.

In the introduction, I promised to offer a distinction between awareness and mindfulness. We often hear them used interchangeably. And while the synergy of the two practices form the foundation of meditation, we can place more emphasis on one than the other as needed to achieve the functional state that best serves us at any moment. Mindfulness can protect us from misguided attention. Like streaming a movie requires a stable, high-speed internet connection to keep from freezing the action, your awareness functions more smoothly when there's plenty of mindfulness bandwidth to buffer your attention.

Our body produces an amazing array of checks and balances. Mindfulness is one of them. Mindfully, we can restore the imbalance of control over attention run amok. Mindfulness—the word alone gives us a clue as to where the action takes place—is the angel on my shoulder that says, "Whoa! You're not about to fall off the end of the world. Don't believe your thoughts. Your attention tricked you into seeing only an emotional abyss that doesn't really exist." The success of virtual reality (VR) as a safe treatment alternative to real exposure therapy for facing our fears demonstrates how strong is our brain's impulse to believe feedback from our senses. How wrong that feedback can be.

Imagine taking your self-driving SUV onto one of the world's narrowest, steepest, most treacherous roads. The vehicle has lots of power under the hood, radar, cameras, 5G networking, and beefy tires ready for tough terrain. But if its computer system fails to recognize hazards, your mindful discernment and nuanced judgment must take over.

Daily life doesn't always present such cliffhangers. In the safety and sanctity of our tiny personal space behind an office desk or on a pillow on our living room floor, we can use mindful meditation to steer our awareness toward thoughts and intentions that keep us on track.

From long experience, Buddhist teacher and author Pema Chödrön knows that mindfulness offers us "a sense of clear seeing with respect and compassion for what it is we see. But mindfulness doesn't stop with formal meditation. It helps us relate with all the details of our lives. It helps us see and hear and smell, without closing our eyes or our ears or our noses. It's a lifetime's journey to relate honestly to the immediacy of our experience and to respect ourselves enough not to judge it."

Mind full of what? Your "mind chest" is stuffed with thoughts and thinking about thinking. You visit the past, elbow your way into the future. The one place you're not is in the present. There's a lot of unpacking you can do to make room in your mind chest for the moment. When you've consciously cleared space between your thoughts, you can take control and do more than turn down the volume. You can shut it off.

> Your "mind chest" is stuffed with thoughts and thinking about thinking. You visit the past, elbow your way into the future. The one place you're not is in the present.

That's the interesting part, because a key to living mindfully is learning how to be introspective without judgment and to use the overactive mind to do something it's terrible at doing: quiet itself and center in the moment. The mind wants to jump to how lousy your golf game was yesterday, ricochet off that to worry about finishing your Six Sigma Black Belt certification next week, then bounce around and shame you for gaining weight over the vacation with the kids. Researchers call that "monkey mind." What tones down the volume?

Meditation. Meditation doesn't mean you have to sit in a lotus position for hours or even forty-five minutes. Meditation can be a walk in the park. Yoga and breathwork are also great ways to bring yourself back to the present, as we'll see. It seems ironic, but mindfulness is about getting out of your head. That seems contradictory because we talk about going in to deal with the outer. When your mind fights quietude with clamor, you can distract it. We'll delve deeply into meditation beginning in Insight 3 and practice some of the healthy distractions in Insight 10.

> Meditation
> can be a walk
> in the park.

If your life is a racetrack, you may wonder if it's worth your time to add one more thing, like learning mindfulness techniques. Let me ask you a few questions. What's the benefit of sitting down to a healthful meal rather than scarfing pizza at 8 p.m. at your office desk? Or taking thirty minutes to read a bedtime story to your four-year-old rather than shuttle her off so you can watch reruns of David Carradine in "Kung Fu"? Or doing nothing for ten minutes rather than flipping on the late news?

Since awareness is the portal or gate to mindfulness, see for yourself how healthy distractions work. Try a few simple warmups and stretch your neurons. Pick an empty park bench or pull up the Chinese garden stool in the butterfly garden. Use your sense of sight, hearing, and smell to shift your awareness to children squealing with joy or the swallowtails rhythmically pulsing their wings against the lilacs. As you focus on your sensory awareness, you're detaching from concerns about yesterday and anxiety about tomorrow and immersing yourself in the present.

Listen Up, Don't Look Down

Does anyone tell you you're not listening or ask you to stop interrupting before you hear them out? Do you often give unsolicited advice or solve others' problems when they only want a sounding board? Do you consistently think about something other than what you're doing? You know what a "yes" answer to any of these questions means. It's a cue that you're not fully present in the moment. As soon as we really listen to others and focus on what they're telling us rather than what we're going to say next, we become aware of being unaware. That's an important step to living fully present in the moment.

Awareness needs to be practiced from a state of well-being. "To be in control requires tuning in to the level of consciousness that isn't perturbed by external forces." We can be aware that our mind resembles a chalkboard so scribbled with notations on Einstein's special theory of relativity, explaining the relationship between space and time, that we fail to see $E = mc^2$ written in the lower right corner.

Wayne Dyer acknowledges that "the most elusive space for human beings to enter is the gap between our thoughts." It's easy to see the dilemma: attempting to clear thoughts creates more thoughts and more thoughts clutter our clear vision and ability to focus our attention on a single aspect of the present moment. The volume is up in our surroundings—our homes, workplaces, and even centers of entertainment. Scientists know that our exposure to prolonged and excessive "decibel hell"10 is damaging to our health and well-being and contributes to anxiety and productivity losses in the workplace. In contrast to the rhythm of our heartbeat, the cacophony of sound reverberates in negative ways throughout our bodies.

Our senses are ceaselessly bombarded by unfathomable quantities of secondhand noise not of our own making. Unwillingly trapped next to someone's car stereo that's outputting 150 dBA (decibel level) is the equivalent of sitting in a lawn chair next to a Boeing 747 jet with its engines at full throttle. Exposure to 75 dBA for more than eight hours a day for prolonged periods can lead to hearing loss.

We think we've become desensitized to some of the world's environmental blather. The truth is that some of the noise pollution slips under our radar. Even the hum of our laptops now largely escapes our attention. That's why it's all the more important to listen to the sublime symphony created by our heartbeat and breath. In Insight 6, we'll learn awareness strategies to counterbalance distractions.

"The beauty of attention is that like a beam of light it can flood a space and penetrate deep into the threads of reality's tapestry,"[11] says

Adam Brady, martial artist, author, and Vedic educator associated with the Chopra Center.

We've seen that scientists credit the practice of awareness and mindfulness techniques with improved health and well-being. Did you know that practicing awareness can decrease fear? Our survival depends on our ability to change. We may need to adapt to a present situation as we see it more clearly. We may also need to make a shift in our thoughts and behaviors in the face of anticipated events. We're less fearful when we engage our full awareness and make choices based on valuable information from trusted sources, including interpretations of our own observations and accurate assessments of real and imagined outcomes.

Living mindfully doesn't require us to give up anything except self-defeating thoughts or habits that no longer serve us. Think of the Janus symbol of transitions and moderation we introduced earlier. Investing in our greater physical and mental well-being doesn't mean we have to make sacrifices. Journeying toward our best self doesn't require us to leave our lives and loved ones behind. In fact, you'll likely discover that the changes you initiate within yourself as you work toward living mindfully will enhance your relationships and your happiness meter will soar.

So far, the National Institutes of Health (NIH), a division of the US Department of Health and Human Services, has invested $100.2 million on research into the health and workplace benefits of mindfulness and functioning in the present.[12] The mental health benefits are the reason why the American Psychological Association (APA) endorses the practice of mindfulness. The APA's interest centered on positive effects such as "fewer depressive thoughts, significant stress reduction, better focus and working memory, and more cognitive flexibility." Some benefits of mindfulness meditation are abstract, and practitioners self-report experiencing a higher quality of life and increased empathy and compassion.

Getting a New Skin

Ophidiophobia. It's one of America's top ten fears—snakes. Where does that fear come from? The human race "grew up" alongside creepy crawlies. Anthropologists have hypothesized that life among slithery creatures helped primates develop sharper vision and larger brains to process danger.[13] Awareness was a key resource in our primitive survival tool kit. For certain, we made it this far because we developed a keen awareness of our environments and became mindful of how we interact with them, increasing the odds that we'd survive to pass our genes to the next generation.

For some of us—from the ancients to the present—snakes are an endless source of fascination. In many cultures, the snake is a sacred and archetypal symbol for initiation, transformation, renewal, and healing.[14] For millennia, the Egyptian circular ouroboros emblem of a snake swallowing its own tail has symbolized wisdom, wholeness, and infinity. In Mayan mythology, the Vision Serpent lay at the center axis atop the World Tree. In Fiji, the serpent who ruled the underworld made fruit trees bloom.

Each of these myths offers insight into humanity's innate need for transformation and rebirth. We adapt ourselves or our environment to be more, do more, have more. The snake does that ingeniously. When its insides have outgrown its outside, it sheds its restrictive skin. If it doesn't shed its skin, it will die. All animals, including us, shed their skins. Most don't do so as dramatically as snakes. Yet, we also outgrow destructive habits, toxic relationships, and self-defeating attitudes. As we become increasingly aware of our thoughts, flex and expand our emotional and physical resilience muscles, and visualize achieving bigger goals, we stretch our perceived limits and begin to live healthier mind-body-spirit lives in our new skin.

That's been my experience over the decades that I've worked with athletes, company employees, and those recovering from cardiac or other debilitating conditions. We can sit in an armchair contemplating a life of health and happiness in the fragile hope that commitment upturns inertia. Only when we're aware that our perceived fetters have no hold on us will we get up and out of our complacency, lace up our mental sneakers, and start the stretching exercises that help us to grasp our highest star.

{
You feel good not because the world
is right, but your world is right
because you feel good.
—Wayne W. Dyer, *The Power of Intention:
Learning to Co-create Your World Your Way*
}

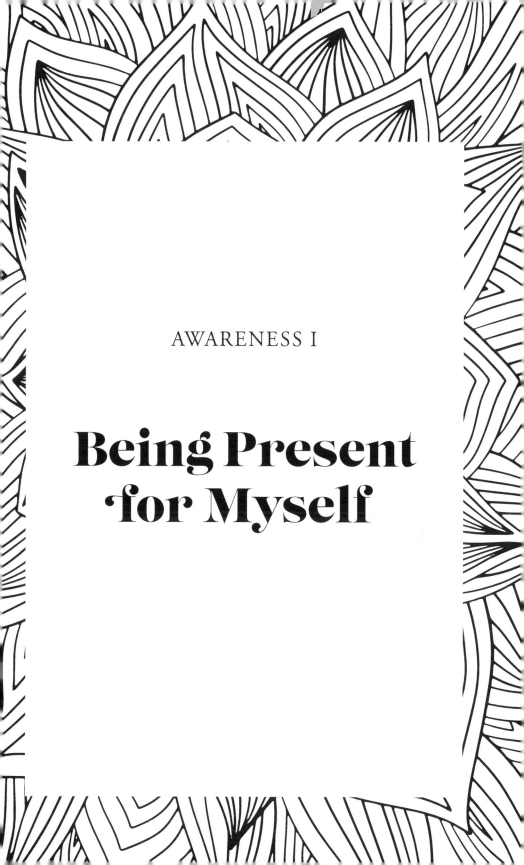

AWARENESS I

Being Present
for Myself

THREE

Create Your Creation

Everybody has a little bit of the sun and moon in them.
Everybody has a little bit of man, woman, and animal
in them. Everyone is part of a connected cosmic system.
Part earth and sea, wind and fire, with some salt
and dust swimming in them. We have a universe
within ourselves that mimics the universe outside.
—Suzy Kassem, *"Part Sun and Part Moon"*[1]

Insight 1: Accept the Miracle of You

I accept that I am the ultimate miraculous creation
of the Highest Power in the universe: Love. There is nothing
as incredible as the human being, spirit, mind, and body.

The He(art) and Science Behind the Insight

What a Piece of Work We Are

So Shakespeare's Hamlet effuses. "How noble in reason! How infinite in faculty, in form and moving how express and admirable! In action how like an angel! In apprehension how like a god! The beauty of the world, the paragon of animals!"

When was the last time you stopped to think what a piece of work you are? How often do you take a deep breath, still yourself, and feel in the moment how precious, extraordinary, and intertwined all life is? We've come a long way since we believed that we are at the center of the universe and everything revolves around us. We know that in the well-ordered whole that is our infinitesimally tiny part of the universe—our world doesn't revolve around us, we're not at its center, literally or figuratively.

Yet, we're far from being an insignificant part of the creation narrative, as those who contend we're just another complex animal would have it. Quite the contrary. Our ancestors' bodies and brains evolved in exceptional and distinct ways that permit us to put into words and communicate to others our conception of time and the real estate we call home. Through our wonderings, observations, inspirations, inventions, scientific discoveries, and insatiable quest for answers to yet-unanswerable questions, our species responded to the need for a story to unravel the secrets of heaven and earth. Archeologists reflect back to us the myriad ways in which our species has been dying to deify and demystify the ceiling of constellations, the lunar and solar phases that cycled above them.

> We are always, in some partial but essential way, its co-creators. In taking this perspective we make the most radical step of all. We begin to move away from a reflexive Copernicanism that made human beings irrelevant in the cosmos and recognize that there is vital place for us. . . . In the end, it is our dialogue with the universe that matters most. Acknowledging the intertwined evolution of culture and cosmic vision does not diminish the power of science; it allows us to see more clearly our role as participants in the universe.[2]

Earth is approximately 4.5 billion years old. We humans came on the scene several million years ago. Something about us persisted in changing, branching out. Consider the odds.

Stardust in Your Eyes

The pendulum that swung in the direction of our codifying humans as one "insignificant" species among 8.7 million species on our little blue planet also swings the other way. From the deep perspective of Sandra Farber, head of the former fabled Seven Samurai[3] team and award-winning astrophysicist known for her research on the evolution of galaxies, what we've become is no small thing. "We are the first generations of humans who are studying the universe billions of years ago as it formed. I think that's the most romantic scientific question you could envision."

> Recognize that we're on our own on spaceship Earth. We've been given the gift of time. We have at least a billion years in which our home, if we continue to take care of it, will continue to suffice. What a chance, right? So, far from feeling dwarfed by the vast reaches and energy of the cosmos, what we really learn is that we are the most remarkable and complicated product of cosmic evolution, and our potential is unlimited. In little localized pockets, the universe is capable of building some beautiful complexity. I'd really like people to understand that fantastic groundwork has been laid—a cosmic experiment has been running for 14 billion years, and it has gotten to an interesting point."[4]

Throughout his long and celebrated self-improvement career, Wayne Dyer reminded us that we are the same as our Source. "You are God. Because you come from God, you cannot be anything but God." Dyer's blend of spirituality, science, and psychology harmonize in a perspective that aligns with astrophysicists' findings: we are the stuff of the universe. "It's totally 100 percent true," says planetary scientist and stardust expert Ashley King. "Nearly all the elements in the human body were made in a star and many have come through several supernovas."[5] There's agreement that some of the elements that make us were formed along with the Big Bang some fourteen billion years ago. Massive stars formed from gases and dust and died violent deaths as supernovae. Each supernova explosion seeded the next stars and, in time, us, and we, in turn, seeded each successive generation of our species. It's pretty astronomical.

God is woven into all aspects of my life, yet I believe astrophysicist Adam Frank speaks a truth. "To see our vital, central role in the cosmos . . . there is no need to demand a deity exist or posit that it fine-tuned the cosmos to give us a warm, safe, cozy home."[6] We are co-creators of the universe we inhabit by sheer force of determination to dialogue with it. And that dialogue is reflected in our art—such as the recently discovered 45,500-year-old pristine cave paintings—culture, and science.

If that's not enough to make you feel special, here are additional complexities, adaptations, and qualities of our extraordinary spirit, mind, and body.

Our bodies are more than biomechanisms that make possible complex, ordered, and interdependent biological and biochemical processes. From Indian mystics to scientists to wellness coaches, we agree that our body has innate intelligence. Through mindful awareness, we can tune into our body's intelligence and let it tell us what it needs. Are we in spiritual, mind, and body balance? Or are we reacting to high stress— emotional triggers that cause disturbance and disequilibrium? Those emotions unleash a flood of hormones that manifest at the physical level. From our lifelong mind-body relationship, we know our feelings can be pleasurable or uncomfortable. But our true nature is pure bliss. Our bodies and minds can be trained to co-function to reach the space where we experience deep joy and restful awareness that nourish our spirit.

Throughout these insights, we'll practice integrating spirit, body, and mind, moving toward fulfillment and a sense of well-being.

Like a Candle in the Wind

So wrote Carl Sandburg and sang Elton John about our fleeting, fragile lives. While a flame, we light the way forward, yet aware of our inevitable, undefinable, unpredictable end. Driven by an invisible clock, we pushed our lust for ever grander achievements into high gear. Our ancestors bequeathed us jewels to stud the crown of human creativity and ingenuity. We recognize them as the royal tombs of the pharaohs in Egypt; the Taj Mahal in Agra, India; the Shah-i-Zinda, Samarkand, Uzbekistan; and the Castel Angelo, Hadrian's Mausoleum, Rome. Our celebrations of birth and death acknowledge the preciousness of an instant, of the time before breath ceases and the heart beats no more.

While it's true that some species react when one of their kind dies, scientists believe this response differs from human awareness of our own mortality, which requires forethought. Forethought, thinking or planning out some action in advance, is not the same as the instinctive activity of many animals that prepare winter larders, caching food during times of plenty for times of lack. Forethought, imagining the future, "gives a special intensity and poignancy to the time we are given to live and love. Without death, we would not have to search for meaning, and we would not have to search for purpose. And we need, first and foremost, even as we're dying, to celebrate the miracle of this day."[7] No doubt we are the only species who ponders, "if only."

When we whisper "if only," we have left the present moment to revisit something undone in the past. "Episodic memory," says Thomas Suddendorf, specialist in the evolution of the human mind, is our unique capability to increase our chances of survival individually and as a species by applying remembrances from our past to our future.[8]

Foresight, or mental time travel, as Suddendorf and colleagues refer to this human gift of future-oriented imagination, permits us to "set and pursue goals, prepare for threats, acquire skills and knowledge, and intentionally shape our future environment."[9] In the event plan A doesn't work, humans create plans B, C, D, and so forth. Contingency plans are like forethought on steroids. These complex thought processes involve controlling, monitoring, and adjusting the progress of each plan. When the goal is accomplished, we file away the experience as a memory and may revisit it many times or share it through story. The future becomes the present and then the present becomes the past.

We're Storytelling Animals

Since the evolution of language, humans have been hardwired to be storytellers. Stories rapidly advanced cultural evolution mostly because they permit listeners to "explore and simulate the future and test different outcomes without having to take real physical risks," explains Jonathan

Gottschall, author of *The Storytelling Animal: How Stories Make Us Human*. Our advanced capacity to control language contributed to our ability to conceptualize and relate stories, and storytelling contributed to our cultural evolution. Philosopher and author of *Consciousness Explained*, *Brainstorms*, and many other books that tackle tough topics like the evolution of our minds, Daniel Dennett has deliberated for decades over the slippery slope of our thinking about thinking and how thinking has affected our doing over eons. Dennett proposes that it is culture that makes *Homo sapiens* the "knowing hominid." From my own studies, I believe this to be true: cultural evolution "operates many orders of magnitude faster than genetic evolution, and this is part of its role in making our species special."[10]

Bioanthropologists, who study both the biology and sociology of human groups, have discovered another intriguing aspect of how we differentiate ourselves. Clothes not only make the man and woman, they also make us human.[11] Covering ourselves to survive cold and wet environments was a learned behavior. We can't pass along our genes if we don't take care of ourselves. But according to Emily Yuko Hallet, a postdoctoral scientist at the Max Planck Institute for the Science of Human History's African Evolution Research Group, and other researchers, we appear to have "put on the Ritz" and dressed to impress, not just ward off hypothermia.[12] The archeological record reveals tell-tale clues. One of them is the emergence of body lice. Genetic studies of those irritating critters show that they were one price we paid for donning animal skins, pelts, and woven garments as early as 170,000 years ago—before major migrations out of Africa—in a mild climate. Another clue—very special bone tools—points to the notion that some articles of clothing were fashion statements. The importance of these bone tools, Hallet explains, is that they were designed to carefully smooth leather without gouging it.

"Adornment creates a visual shorthand that tells others instantly who we are, who we want to associate with, and who we wish to be,"[13] says Pennsylvania State University paleobiologist and anthropologist Nina Jablonski, known for her study of the evolution of skin pigmentation. Skin of all colors may have been our earliest canvas. As early as 3300 BCE, Bronze-Age peoples added permanency to adornment with facial and body tattoos. Then and still, tattoos are visual stories that identify us as individuals and our place within a group.

Humans who have made life-sustaining discoveries benefit the collective group when they pass information along. For example, learning to soak some food sources to remove toxicity, cook food properly to make it digestible, and track game or drive a herd over a cliff helped to ensure the survival of our species.

As unique and clever as we are, we still share basic, instinctual minimum requirements with other species. These include the need to satisfy hunger, escape predators, seek shelter, and protect the clan. Once our most basic needs were met—or simultaneously with meeting them—we raised our sights. We don't know exactly when we became conscious of ourselves as beings in a relationship to a power we could not see yet sensed, but archeological finds keep pushing that date farther into the past. Did our aesthetic and ritualistic practices co-emerge? It's touching that we graced the burials of kinspeople and revered others with flowers and personal treasures. Our ancestors strung stories of their ever-evolving understanding of nature and themselves like beads on an infinite necklace to which we add our own contributions.

Our history of increasing complexity has intrigued scientists who study change in species. Among them is Uppsala University, Sweden, retired professor Börje Ekstig, who holds a PhD in physics. In his book *Mechanisms of Evolution*, Ekstig tackles a counterintuitive observation, "a most peculiar fact. The oldest of these [living creatures] are in general the most primitive whereas the most recent are the most advanced," he says. "We have started a new epoch in the evolution of life on earth, characterized by the emergence of advanced language, technology, religion, science, and art; faculties no other species has come close to."[14]

Center of Creation and Centering in Creation

"Obviously, we didn't create ourselves," responded author and teacher Sadhguru to a woman who asked about a supreme being that presided over the beginnings of everything. "This universe opens its doors only to those who pay enough attention. If the source of creation is throbbing within you and you did not notice it, are you not a tragedy? Everything is a part of you and you are a part of everything—not as a thought, but experientially—if you can experience everything around you as you experience the five, ten fingers of your hands, then you will see: life becomes tremendously beautiful."[15] Yes, it does.

"Just as the flower is a flowering of the field, I feel myself as a personing, a manning, a peopling of the whole universe," says Alan Watts, who extracted from Eastern religions ingredients from which he compounded a salve of awareness to Western wellness.

> I seem, like everything else, to be a center, a sort of vortex, at which the whole energy of the universe realizes itself, comes alive, a sort of aperture through which the whole universe is conscious of itself. In other words, I go with it as a center to a circumference. Each one of us—not only human beings, but every leaf, every weed—exists in the way it does only because everything around it exists as it does. In other words, there's a relationship between the center and the circumference. Without the center, no circumference; without the circumference, no center. So the individual and the universe are inseparable . . . but very few people are aware of it.[16]

Generation after generation, organisms have been able to build on genetic progress rather than start from square one. Evolutionary complexity and capability stand on the shoulders of the organisms that preceded them.

Let's Talk about It

We're seeing how miraculous are our bodies, minds, and spirits. While our brains evolved, our larynx adapted to enable speech. Of course, speech didn't suddenly switch on. Researchers believe our sociability—our natural tendency to seek relationship—accelerated our need to communicate quickly and effectively.

Linking our minds and being understood was as critical for our survival and well-being as banding together to combine our mutual strengths in hunting. When we speakers were able to relate life-and-death learning experiences, we imparted knowledge to listeners so they didn't have to go through the same experience. It's truly amazing how we repurpose information and ideas to bring us closer together and make our lives better.

We can wonder—as did Aristotle two thousand years earlier—at what point around the campfire did we, as rational beings and speakers, begin to embellish our hunting stories for our audiences who had heard the tales a time too many and were nodding off from boredom. Is that any different than our sharing the tale of the big fish that got away?

We can wonder when speech permitted the visionaries among us to share their prophetic dreams and sprinkle their telling with new words that crackled on listeners' ears like the popping fire. So keen did our awareness of other humans become that we began to interpret their gestures and utterances. By watching and listening, we developed the extraordinary ability to infer what others were thinking and feeling with some accuracy. We got the meaning of a furrowed brow, a puckered mouth, a lowered head, a broad smile. We use those skills daily at work, play, with our children, friends, and spouses. We connected and continue to connect our minds and spirits. And that serves us well and enhances our well-being.

It may be impossible to discover our turning points—when we reached intangible intellectual milestones. From our cultural evolution comes an impressive tangible inheritance: architecture, music, sculpture, paintings, literature, machines, medicine, science, technology, and more. Once out of the bottle, the genie of technology could not be put back. For example, seventeenth-century scientist Antonie van Leeuwenhoek was the first to detect individual living cells. He called them animalcules. In 1887, German microbiologist Julius Petri invented a shallow, circular glass dish, later fitted with a lid, for growing bacteria in a nutrient gelatin. Petri worked with "the titan of microbiology,"[17] Robert Koch, who was the first to prove in his London lab that bacteria was linked to infections and diseases such as cholera and tuberculosis. Today, we can create a variety of living organisms in a Petri dish, including a miniature heart. Perhaps the world is our Petri dish. But that, too, is a repurposed idea. From a 3D printer and a patient's cells, biomedical engineers have created a miniature human heart. What a miracle to one day give the gift of hearts to all those whose lives depend on replacements. But will those new hearts truly offer everything the human heart offers?

For all our unique intelligence to create the technology to make replacement parts for our bodies, we can't fully explain how our brain builds on past knowledge to create mind-shattering ideas. Through functional magnetic resonance imaging (fMRI), neuroscientists can see which parts of our brain are active because they receive more blood. They've discovered that for teens and adults the medial prefrontal cortex (mPFC)—just behind the forehead—is more active when we think about ourselves, and our self-perception gets increasingly complex over time. It's also more active when we think about others. Neuroscientists are able to see that thoughts can and do influence our brain's neurotransmitters. We're constantly flooded with signals from our environment and our past as memories, and a lot of that memory is accumulated knowledge. Thoughts trigger a corresponding chemical reaction in our body, an ecosystem of many communities and trillions of tiny organisms that get to work and do their job. Mitochondria, those little powerhouses within our cells, are like Energizer Bunnies that keep going and going and going, including when we use our brains to learn, feel, or solve complex problems. In fact, our brains use as much as a fourth of our body's energy.

Here's the conundrum. Even though the brain and the nervous system are part of our anatomy, explains Anil Seth, professor of cognitive and computational neuroscience at the University of Sussex, UK, "the mind cannot be found. When we range beyond the pure study of the brain, we enter the realm of the mind and consciousness. How it is that we are conscious—that we experience and know—is not something we will ever find in a brain scan."[18]

The mind has fascinated me since childhood. I've wondered how this powerful invisible force drives us from birth to death. The mind reasons and manifests thoughts and ideas formed out of the nothingness of our perceptions, emotions, and memory. As I studied the body, I became increasingly aware that while we cannot operate on the mind as we can the brain; mind operates on us. Professor Seth expands on the mind's creativity. "We are not passive recipients of a world that is being shown to us like a movie. Instead, we actively generate the world."[19]

Using simple optical illusions, neuroscientists such as Patrick Cavanagh, research professor at Dartmouth College and senior fellow at Glendon College in Canada, confirmed that the mind makes up the world as we go and enacts reality through the actions we perform. "It's really important to understand we're not seeing reality," Cavanagh says. "We're seeing a story that's being created for us. Most of the time, the story our brains generate matches the real, physical world—but not always. Our brains also unconsciously bend our perception of reality to meet our desires or expectations . . . they fill in gaps using our past experiences."[20] The stories our brains tell us seem real, even when they're totally fabricated. Making life up as we go, based on misperceptions, can be risky business.

Cavanagh lets us glimpse ourselves as creators of our own reality. The better we understand the trickster role of our minds, the more effectively we can use mindful awareness to gain clearer perspectives on our inner and outer worlds. And that's a tantalizing topic we'll return to in Insight 5.

Sleight of Hand and Swift Thinking

History and the arts have portrayed our real and archetypal heroes as victims of their own tragic or fatal character flaw. Mythical or flesh and blood, our heroes were driven by their prejudices, judgmentalism, egotism, and narcissism. Heroes' so-called weaknesses colored how they perceived themselves, others, and the world. The moral of the stories was that these weaknesses lead either to our heroes' awakening—an epiphany—or their downfall. Sometimes, both. The most common flaw? Hubris—excessive pride, inflated self-importance, self-involvement, arrogance, and even aggression. Aristotle called it a "form of slight." He saw it as slighting or disrespecting others or the gods. Hubris isn't the Achilles heel only of mythical characters. We see it as the unhealthy motivation for people we encounter on a daily basis. When we're aware, we see it in ourselves.

Ancient philosophers had a good handle on the link between the absence of humility and our actions. Aristotle had it right: character is voluntary. Modern psychologists have learned that hubris often masks fear, low self-esteem, and feelings of shame. Hubristic people often behave recklessly and impulsively with complete disregard for the well-being of others. What that has to do with the rest of us is that those whom we perceive as having a fatal flaw (which is difficult to see in ourselves) tend to evoke in us less-than-positive feelings.

Here's the extraordinary thing to which we alluded earlier. We have developed an amazing capacity to "read" others. No sleight of hand involved. Not only do we engage in varying degrees of mind reading, but we also have learned to understand more than a little about another's beliefs. Doing so is a uniquely human step toward developing compassion for those who seem to put up barriers to relationships. Eons of collaboration to survive and thrive have linked us in many ways. We see our friend stacking firewood, and we don't have to be asked to pick up an armload and add it to the pile. We seem to make that choice to help subconsciously. Our cumulative knowledge of the world permits us to reason abstractly and make assessments based on the feedback from our senses.

If we passively stand by as our friend runs back and forth from the wood pile to the stack, we'll likely become aware that his lips curl inward and his eyes avoid contact. We get it. He's thinking it wouldn't hurt us if we'd lend a hand.

We're not the only animals who recognize the intentions or goals of others in our species. Witness a pod of orcas joining an individual orca to successfully hunt and kill its prey. While chimpanzees can figure out a lot through individual and group dynamics, they don't know what other chimps perceive and believe, say Michael Tomasello and Katja Karg of the Max Planck Institute for Evolutionary Anthropology, Department of Developmental and Comparative Psychology. "Mind reading" is a distinctively human trait that tells us profound things about ourselves.

No animals have all the attributes of human minds; but almost all the attributes of human minds are found in some animal or other. Michael C. Corballis, author of *The Wandering Mind: What the Brain Does When You're Not Looking*, wanders into our amazing capacity to wonder and imagine the unimaginable.

Whether to deceive or inform, we humans seem to delight in making mental journeys into the minds of others, and indeed create fictional characters for the purpose. Young children, especially in the preschool years, often create imaginary companions, invisible friends with whom they share confidences. Together with the ability to travel mentally in time, travelling mentally into the minds of others provides the platform for one characteristic that does seem to be distinctively and universally human—storytelling.[21]

And among the stories we tell—based on evidence going back in time farther than our memory reaches—are answers to our mind's pressing questions. How old is the universe? What are the stars made of? How did we get here? What's our purpose? When will it all come to an end? What is our fate? That's one scientists can't answer. We are the only species with the capacity to destroy that which has taken billions of years to create. And, yet, we are the only species with the capacity to make a conscious choice to stop and reverse the course we've taken.

What a piece of work we are.

{ Yesterday I was clever, so I wanted to change the world. Today I am wise, so I am changing myself.
—Rumi }

Practice

Breath Observation with Relaxation

- Sit or lie down in a quiet environment.
- Get comfortable.
- Place your hands facing upward in your lap and touch your thumb to your index finger.
- Place the tip of your tongue against the roof of your mouth behind your upper front teeth.
- Let your breath out through your partially open lips.
- Begin a new breath through your nostrils, taking in air comfortably and relaxed.
- Follow the breath through your sinuses down your trachea. Lift your ribcage and allow your diaphragm to relax.
- Hold your breath for a moment, and then slowly release it through your partially open mouth, keeping your tongue behind your upper teeth.
- As you release your breath, relax your eyelids and eyebrows.
- Repeat the "in breath" a little fuller this time.
- On the "out breath," relax your jaw, cheeks, and lips.
- Repeat the in breath.
- On the out breath, drop your shoulders down and relax your upper back and chest.
- On successive out breaths, work your way down your body to relax each muscle group.

In the beginning, you may wish to practice this Breath Observation for three to five minutes and gradually work your way up to longer sessions.

Exercises

In your journal,

- ❧ List seven things that you believe are incredible about your body.
- ❧ List seven things that you believe are incredible about your mind.
- ❧ Describe that part of you we think of as spirit.
- ❧ What is its function?
- ❧ How does your spirit serve you?
- ❧ List seven things that you believe are incredible about your spirit.
- ❧ List seven things that you believe are incredible about all of life.
- ❧ My aha moment from this insight is

Inspiration

"Remember your greatness"
Before you were born,
And were still too tiny for
The human eye to see,
You won the race for life
From among 250 million competitors.
And yet,
How fast you have forgotten
Your strength,
When your very existence
Is proof of your greatness.
You were born a winner,
A warrior,
One who defied the odds
By surviving the most gruesome
Battle of them all.
And now that you are a giant,
Why do you even doubt victory
Against smaller numbers,
And wider margins?
The only walls that exist,
Are those you have placed in your mind.
And whatever obstacles you conceive,
Exist only because you have forgotten
What you have already
Achieved.
—Suzy Kassem, *Rise up and Salute the Sun:*
The Writings of Suzy Kassem

FOUR

Envision Beyond

Nothing is impossible.
The word itself says, "I'm possible."
—Audrey Hepburn

Insight 2:
Imagine the
"I'm Possible"

I know all things are possible through my Creator,
the Highest Power in the universe. I realize
my potential through thought, belief, and action.

The He(art) and Science
Behind the Insight

Drink from the Well of Empowerment

I love thinking that anything is possible. From scripture to Disney, the inspirational quote that "anything is possible if we just believe" rings of promise. The profound Matthew 19:26 verse, "With man this is impossible, but with God all things are possible" has evolved as a secular motivational expression affirming the power of positive thinking. You see it on memes, posters, T-shirts, book and song titles, you name it. Why have those few words so captured our imagination across cultures and time?

Telling ourselves or another person anything is possible is our acknowledgment that we don't know the unknowable. We don't have a crystal ball to reveal the outcomes of our individual and collective futures. Yet, we're charged with the electricity of hope that things work to our highest and best good. As a result, we act according to that belief.

Believing anything is possible doesn't mean that we're hunting for Aladdin's lamp and a genie to grant our every wish. Intuitively, we know that our beliefs and empowerment aren't a passport to a magical life. Belief in ourselves isn't a talisman that we carry with us as reassurance that as long as the Creator "is on our side," we're invincible.

Our thoughts—collected over time and from many sources—shape our personal vision and interpretation of the Creator, God, the Highest Power, cosmic or universal consciousness, or the intelligence in the universe. Believing in a higher power doesn't necessitate we associate with any religion or avow a deity. Being conscious of a higher power means we sense, know, or are inspired to believe that we're inseparable from an all-encompassing, incomprehensible energy that's impossible to explain scientifically or theologically, though we try. We may think of a higher power as a lifeforce that connects all things. For some cultures, that includes every rock, river, and rainbow. It's important to understand that we don't need to believe in a higher power or a Creator or God to recognize that we have more power than we know. We can merely act on that knowing. Sometimes, we need a little help from our friends to see more clearly, adjust our thoughts, and remove our self-imposed limitations.

Is "anything is possible" just another hackneyed phrase, or does science back this improbable claim? When we blithely append "anything's possible" to a wish or goal, we're usually thinking rationally of potentialities within the realms of nature, science, and human creativity for our time and reality. But our reality changes with our perception and theories about how to observe reality. What's real to us today may have been only an imaginative thought years or centuries or millennia ago. How likely are we to conjure up thoughts and images that will accurately depict our reality tomorrow?

Not very, according to Harvard professor of psychology Daniel Gilbert, a prolific lecturer and experiment designer with his colleague Timothy Wilson. Gilbert and Wilson's research makes startling revelations about our ability to correctly predict how we'll think, feel, and act five minutes or years down the road.[1] What this means for our future is that we need to be very clear about our perception of what's real for us now. How do we do that? We can learn to be aware that our past, which we thought we had laid to rest, drives us. Chances are that our past thoughts and beliefs are still shaping our decisions and actions. We're dynamic—not static—beings. Awareness can help us reassess whether old values, beliefs, and rewards for actions offer the state of happiness we're seeking. How we feel now and how we respond to any occurrence in the future is and will be colored by who we perceive that we are at any one moment in our brief history. I don't have a clue what will be possible for me in the next minute much less years from now. Here's what I do know. Goals are important, but so is leaving ourselves open to stumbling on happiness.[2]

One cannot divine nor forecast the conditions that will make happiness; one only stumbles upon them by chance, in a lucky hour, at the world's end somewhere, and holds fast to the days as to fortune or fame.

Willa Cather wrote this insight during her 1902 stay in Le Lavandou in the south of France. Her words—the epigraph for Daniel Gilbert's *Stumbling on Happiness*—form the matrix of research on self-knowledge: our thoughts, beliefs, feelings, motivations, and actions.[3] And they portend our capacity to experience happiness. As time passes, we're likely to stumble on it for smaller, yet grander reasons—such as awakening to a new dawn and the opportunity to live and love yet another day.

What is possible is impossible to know. It is a boundaryless question not for us to answer but to experience. Moreover, the outer limits of our individual experiences du jour are colored and shaded by our capabilities, conceptions, perceptions in each now. Tomorrow is unforeseeable. Yesterday gave us barely a clue.

Somewhere over the Rainbow

If bluebirds can, why can't I?

Most of us have daydreamed about how happy we'd be if we just landed that big promotion and raise. But studies similar to those conducted by Gilbert and colleagues show that when we do get that dreamed-of job, we're often disappointed because our expectations were unrealistic. That's called "affective forecasting," says Lisa Williams, professor of psychology at the University of New South Wales in Sydney, Australia. Additional research confirms that we're really poor at predicting how we'll feel at some time in the future when we get what we thought we wanted.

For many cultures, rainbows are symbols of hope and encouragement. Like the Janus figure, they mark endings and beginnings, the passing of a storm, something brighter to come. Our thoughts chase awesome rainbows to find our pot of bliss at its end. But chase a rainbow and it recedes. In fact, you and I won't see the same rainbow. Your rainbow is unique to you. That's because when the sunlight behind us strikes raindrops or mist or a waterfall in front of us at precisely a forty-two-degree angle, we visualize the refraction and reflection of light as a rainbow. Scientists have detected several hundred types, and they're all magical. A friend likes to think of rainbows as awesome reminders that magic happens, here and now, not somewhere on the other side.

That has profound implications for us. It doesn't mean that we shouldn't aspire to higher goals—less-stressful jobs, happier relationships, stronger bodies, better health. The metaphor invites us to be aware that we don't have to chase after pots of bliss; they may be at our feet. We may perceive the dream as infinitely better than our present. All too often, however, our emotions and rose-colored glasses make quick work of decision-making, and we leap before we look at the big picture. We can be unprepared for the dissonance between reality and where we imagine our happiness monitor would peak when we ride into the sunset of faulty predictions.

"People are generally not as happy as they expected they would be when they achieve their goals," says Elliot Berkman, associate professor of psychology at the University of Oregon. Why? Maybe we skimped on our due diligence because we were blindsided by the dazzle of the dream.

Maybe we didn't want to see the down and dirty parts of a new job. Perhaps we didn't think how hard it is in any leadership role to fire people or make budget cuts to programs that serve the homeless. Perhaps we forgot what it took to get where we are.

Please don't misunderstand. Change is good. It revitalizes us, stimulates us to learn new things and take on new challenges. But change for change's sake is chasing rainbows.

I know two dazzlingly bright, multi-lingual attorneys who entered law school starry-eyed, hearts ablaze with liberty and justice for all. In less than a decade, their law-firm candles blew out. They left behind their Juris Doctor to follow their newly recognized passions. One became director of a nonprofit that helped Indigenous people protect their water rights. The other moved to a Latin American country where he set up animal spay-neuter programs in poor urban and rural communities. Their lives are neither easy nor perfect, and the going did get tough, but both consider themselves happy, not just for a fleeting moment, but day to day.

Happiness might not have been impossible in their legal professions, but these two took the risk and embraced the unknown in their quest for meaning. In the case of the friend who helps small communities launch no-kill animal shelters that control the dog and cat population through donor-funded spay-neuter campaigns, the "impossible" dream came true. Not as a global stroke, but in one small corner of the world where he is changing lives because he is changing attitudes toward animals, creating caring and responsible stewards. Neither of these professionals abandoned their original goals. They merely reassessed them and figured out what they really wanted. Changing course wasn't a mark of failure; it was the act of courage that precedes success as a compassionate human being. And then there's the physician who left his practice to follow his creative bliss. His patience with busy gallery life and the zany art market remarkably reduced the stress that had worn him down and permitted two additional creative outlets: crafting novels and producing art of his own.

Brandon Stanton was a bond trader in Chicago when in 2010 he lost his job. "My two biggest lessons learned as a trader are take risks and get comfortable with taking losses and setbacks to help move you forward," he said in a CNBC interview. "I decided to forget about money and have a go at something I truly enjoyed." He had only a vague idea what it took to make a living as a photographer. When he sharpened his focus on building a portfolio of interesting people, he created a niche for himself. He called his decision absurd, but down deep, "I knew that I had the best idea of my life." The details? He'd figure them out as he went along.

Winston Churchill became a master at turning "failure up."[4] "Success is the ability to go from one failure to another with no loss of enthusiasm," he rallied. But it's more than that. A debriefing is in order to face the facts and learn from the mistakes.

What lights your enthusiasm fire when you wake up every morning? Making more than enough money to live well and paying it forward? Choosing a community that nurtures family and friends in a wholesome and healthy social environment? Following a meditative or yoga practice that tones body, mind, and spirit?

It's not possible to be who we aren't. We may not be current or historical heroes: a Nelson Mandela, Margaret Mead, or Neil Armstrong, yet it is possible to become who we want to be. Our bodies, minds, and spirits are all sculpted by a different set of genes and circumstances. We can mobilize our uniqueness and do what others thought we could not. We can take aim at mid-career malaise and cap that sapping feeling that life is passing us by. We can know that it's possible to be realistic in answering tough questions such as is this really what I want to be doing for the rest of my life?

Do you dream of traveling around the world? At seven, a friend announced to her father that one day she'd go all the way around the world. On her seventieth birthday, she got on a plane to begin the remarkable journey that turned her dream into reality. During the intervening sixty-three years, she never lost sight of her goal and the belief that she could achieve it. When she returned, she wrote a book about perspectives on life's so-called successes and failures.

Failure: Sometimes a Blessing in Disguise

Nana korobi, ya oki, meaning "fall seven times, stand up eight," refers to the Japanese concept of the power of resilience. The more times you've fallen, the closer you are to achieving your goal.

Mental resilience is a skill that can be practiced through meditation and mindful awareness. Resilient people get up and get back on the path to their goal. Ask really successful people and they'll tell you that they walked through the coals of failure. Failure helps us identify what we want by making obvious—sometimes painfully so—what we don't want as well as what works and what doesn't. Failure tests our mettle and builds strong emotional muscles. It teaches us how to cope. We aren't a failure; our process or perspective may have been. Failure shows us how we have to think, see, and do things differently. Job recruiters actually prefer applicants who nosedived off their professional bikes, bloodied their knees on the pavement, gotten up, straightened out their bike's frame, and peddled off. We may feel crash-and-burn incidents harm our resumes, but that's not true.

When everything goes smoothly, we're not always sure why. It may not even be because we did everything right. When we make a mistake, it's usually quite evident what went wrong. That saves a lot of trial and error and guessing. Those teaching moments help us focus on the right stuff and launch us into creativity and innovation. In 1969, NASA's scientists were intently and intensely focused on last-minute systems' checks and troubleshooting before the Apollo 11 mission launch. Transfixed to their computers, the team's anxious minds and bodies responded to the countdown as the lunar module Eagle, carrying astronauts Neil Armstrong and Buzz Aldrin, touched down at Tranquility Base. NASA's attention was fixed on the present and the error-free functioning of the computer system that achieved the first human walk on a celestial body. It's unlikely that in the heat of the flight, farthest from scientists' imaginings would have been to wonder what the future holds technologically. "Wow. We did this; what's next?" Computer scientist Margaret Hamilton led a team of engineers that programmed Eagle's onboard computer by predicting the types of errors humans would make in operating it in a present moment. There was a life-and-death immediacy about their every movement. She had to think like an astronaut, though her goal was to get them into space and home safely. That required her innovation.

Two decades before the world held its breath as it awaited "The Eagle has landed," *Popular Mechanics* magazine forecast that one day computers might weigh as little as 1.5 tons. Eagle's onboard computer weighed seventy pounds. We're no longer surprised that the smallest computer in the world fits on a grain of rice.[5]

A mere half-century after Armstrong and Aldrin made history, a staggering percentage of the world's population fixes its attention on one billion iPhones.[6] That's one hundred thirteen million in the US alone—plus all other brands of smartphones. Packed into any one of those elegant, slim cases is seven million times more memory than Apollo's Guidance Computer (AGC) and one hundred thousand times more processing power.[7]

That's interesting information, but what's it got to do with me? For all their mind-blowing artificial intelligence about taught strategies for defeating a human in the ancient Chinese board game "Go," computers can only make "inductive" predictions about the future with a degree of probability based on historical data fed to it. Computers will search for complex correlations among data sets and formulate "actionable insights." A prediction will always be derived from a continuous stream of data flowing from the past into the future. This is all well and good until reality changes dramatically. Worse, computers can't judge if the "correlations are real or ridiculous. Only human agents . . . can distinguish between meaningful and meaningless correlations."[8] Researchers at the Massachusetts Institute of Technology have designed algorithms modeled in part on the human brain in anticipation that deep learning techniques can teach computers to better predict the future by examining past behavior and events. The applications are a goldmine for industries such as healthcare, pharmaceuticals, hospitality, financial, aerospace, automotive, and manufacturing. Is it possible for computers to do what we do better and faster with greater reliability? DeepMind technology potential is rapidly building on our own and tackling abstract reasoning and inferences.

For now, our one-upmanship remains our ability not only to learn from our mistakes, but also to imagine a future where we don't make them. As the Center for Brains, Minds and Machines demonstrates, artificial intelligence (AI) does learn from its mistakes. What AI lacks is our motivation to eliminate them as a mechanism to decrease our stress and enhance our well-being. No emotional or physical pain, no gain.

Here's a puzzle. We still have the abstract reasoning edge. We're keen observers of others' body language—posture, gestures, and subtle facial expressions. Most of us can't read minds, but oftentimes we can infer what another is thinking or feeling and what they may do as a result of their thinking and feeling. But getting a good fix on ourselves? Not so much. Why? When we "read" others, we're observing them in real time. How they act this way or gesture that way in response to something happening in the moment.

Superimposing our current feelings, wants, and desires onto our future self is risky business. Don't bet the farm that we'll feel tomorrow the same way we feel this moment about the same or similar situation. There are just too many variables outside of us and inside. We may have little control over situations not of our making. Those inside of us . . . well, there can be a whole lot of changing going on. Personal growth and development, for instance. How we perceive ourselves and our relationships. How we align our values. How we make choices. Social media's flip-the-switch effect on us is one not-so-small example of thought and behavioral gamechangers. We can limit our exposure to such electronic noise. We can also give it no power over our lives. We can discriminate among all the messages, resonate with those that ring true, and discard those that don't. We can mitigate the risk of poor judgment by using another tool in our toolbox.

Thought Experiments

We step into a future of possibilities because we can. Before we do, we explore the future virtually. Simple thought experiments permit us to mentally rehearse a scene before taking it live. For eons and eons, our survival depended on our ability to envision the consequences of an act before we do it. If we can lash a very sharp, pointed-tip stone onto a sturdy, long pole, we might have a better shot at tonight's dinner. There's no doubt that thought experiments had to affect phenomenal evolutionary changes as we mindfully made our lives less perilous, warmer, cushier, more beautiful, and more bountiful. Thought experiments enabled earliest humans to imagine "what would happen if" they wandered ever deeper into the unknown territory of our little blue planet.

The Twelve Insights give you the opportunity to delve into relevant and ethical thought experiments. Each insight relies on your intelligence quotient (IQ) and emotional quotient (EQ) to decide what is true for you and anticipate and explore how changes in thoughts, beliefs, and behaviors have the potential to create positive effects in your life.

Hope Powers Resilience

"Hope is not only an attitude that has cognitive components—it is responsive to facts about the possibility and likelihood of future events."[9] Hope plays a major role in human motivation and is linked to intention and optimism. When we feel hopeful, we tend to keep pursuing a goal. False hope, on the other hand, leads to disappointment and disillusionment and can set us up for failure. Failure is seldom the end of the world, however. In fact, as I mentioned earlier, failure can be a powerful stimulus. It can revivify our drive and impel us to re-evaluate our goal. Failure can influence our perspective of the goal's meaning and the benefit from achieving it. It can confront us with a yes or no question: Is the price to be paid too high? When we look at so-called failure from different angles, we can re-envision what success looks like.

In the workplace, hopefulness is a prerequisite for resilience. People who feel supported and know that someone is there to help them, who believe tomorrow will be better than today, will persevere under difficult circumstances. Hope fuels our willingness to try the impossible.

If we missed boarding the Eurostar train from London to Paris, we can find another way to get there. But the question is why did we miss the train? Not achieving success on the first round may be a consequence of not being clear about what we want and how badly we want it. When we want something badly enough, we're willing to make sacrifices, like getting up in the wee hours of the morning, or spending a little extra for a ticket on the later train.

What we think we want may not be our real goal. If we're too vague about our goal, it's difficult to previsualize what it feels like to have already achieved it. Once we crystalize our goal, we can cross the threshold of what we'd like to see happen and enter the action space of doing what it takes to make it happen. What's possible? Well, what is it that you really want? Imagine it concretely so you can make it real. "Consciousness doesn't dangle outside the physical world as some kind of extra. It's right there at its heart."[10]

Yes, the laws of nature, or constants, are immutable—at least until some other theory supplants them. They're the sea across which we make our infinite voyages: real or imagined. But what is reality? And why is it relevant? Our perception of reality impacts our beliefs and actions. Thinkers—from the ancients to contemporary scientists—have proposed theories to explain the inexplicable. With new concepts about the nature of reality come new words: multiverses, holographic universes, parallel universes, many worlds, many minds, collective consciousness, and more.

We don't need to study quantum mechanics or the theory that the universe is pure, abstract information to strengthen our relationship to ourselves, others, and the world. But we may heighten our awareness of each of these relationships when we understand that, as scientist Luis de Queiroz puts it, "ultimately, reality as we experience it seems to be the result of human consciousness interfacing with the quantum levels of existence that are pure waves of energy."[11] Granted, most of us aren't sitting at the breakfast table contemplating what is and isn't real in the Platonic abstract.

We probably aren't looking over our cup and professing, "I agree with de Queiroz that reality is an 'intangible substrate of absolute coherence and mathematical geometry from which the physical world is derived and formed.'" Maybe it's enough to now and then become mindful that the love energy we are is infinite, without beginning or end. We might think of it as a resilient energy similar to American theoretical physicist David Bohm's concept that "everything that exists contains the information of everything else that exists."

What is the "anything" in anything's possible, anyway? That's seems pretty broad and unfocused. We don't need to do everything or have everything or be everything to be happy. In fact, it is impossible to do all, have all, and be all. So, rather than think we can achieve all things, let's consider which of those things are most important to us. I don't know about you, but my "anythings" are actually states of being. The interesting thought to ponder is that in looking at what I want to be more of—something that seems in the future—I'm actually working on qualities of my present experience. Each moment, starting now—not tomorrow—I want to be more creative. Inventive. Compassionate. Empathic. Open. Inspirational. Motivational. Courageous. Energetic. Mindful. Aware. Happy.

And the more appreciative I am of the awesome qualities or traits that I work on daily, without judgment, the surer my progress. So, I may never be as courageous as I'd like to imagine myself to be. Or as inventive. But, I'm pretty darned good at motivating people, being mindful, and being aware that there are things that I'm OK about never being able to do. I'm actually relieved. It's kind of freeing not to feel compelled to try all sorts of things simply because they may be possible. I've been a successful entrepreneur many times and not so successful other times. I've made money and lost money.

If money is important to you and acquiring a lot of it is one of your goals, the qualities above are useful tools to till the fields you've sown with optimism. Have you asked yourself how will more money enhance your happiness? Will it enable you to have more free time? Buy more things? Make you more powerful? Empower others? How much money is more and how much is enough? How do you measure when you've reached your goal? What happens when you've reached your goal? Will you want to pursue more or change your goal? What does your gut tell you about your goal?

Trust Thyself

"Trust thyself," urged the eternal optimist Ralph Waldo Emerson. Yet, we don't always. Participants in my lectures have told me, "I don't trust my own judgment." I've heard that when they do believe in themselves, others don't. Do the opinions of others matter to you? Do they affect how you see yourself and what you think you're capable of? Only you know for sure. No one knows you like you know you. You've been your constant companion for a lifetime. If you believe that you don't know yourself well, then begin now to explore the person who resides in your body. Books can't tell you who you are. Here is Emerson's insight:

All persons are puzzles until at last we find in some word or act the key to the man, to the woman; straightway all their past words and actions lie in light before us.

Perhaps you already keep a journal. If not, I invite you to. It can be as simple as a spiral notebook to jot down your responses to the exercises at the end of each chapter. Or it can be as luxurious as a leather-bound keepsake in which to write and save your dreams, goals, and experiences, record your awarenesses and inquiries. Whatever format you choose, let your journal be a travelogue of your exploration into mindfulness. This is your time.

Emerson kept detailed journals of his thoughts and actions. To the famed philosopher, transcendentalist, and poet, "experience is the only teacher. To finish the moment, to find the journey's end in every step of the road, to live the greatest number of good hours, is wisdom."

Adopting secondhand thoughts and beliefs as our own is like trying to jam our foot into Cinderella's glass slipper. When we outgrow the childlike qualities of trust and innocence, we may trade uncensored, vivid pictures of our bright futures for fear, doubt, hesitancy, cynicism, and judgmentalism. We become unsure of our own thoughts, parrot ideas we think will impress, and try to squeeze ourselves into a shoe that doesn't fit.

Believe in your own dreams, own and internalize them, Emerson tells us. "Speak your latent conviction, and it shall be the universal sense; for the inmost in due time becomes the outmost."

The Powerful Doctrine of One More

If you've ever felt that you don't make a difference in this world, think again. We've learned that throughout history small changes can make a huge impact. Sometimes, all it takes is just one more of something. When we turn up the heat by one degree on 211-degree hot water, it boils and can power a train. That one extra degree helped to launch an industrial revolution. Add a degree to ice and it melts. Quitting too soon can result in failure. Giving something one more try can take it to the tipping point. One step at a time makes big strides. With a total of twenty-eight Olympic gold medals, Michael Phelps II is the most decorated athlete of all time. His secret? Instead of training six days a week as most competitive swimmers do, Phelps added a seventh. "If I swim seven days a week," he said, "that's 52 days I gain on the next guy."

Most of us are familiar with Apollo 11 Commander Neil Armstrong's 1969 quote about a history-making event: "One small step for a man, one giant leap for mankind." The "doctrine of one more" applied to the efforts of every NASA team member to push the technological envelope and put a person on the moon. A better predictor of achievement than even aptitude and talent, perseverance is vital to the mastery of any skill. Whether the "one more" is a small step or a giant leap, it inspires us to surpass obstacles, limiting beliefs, and fear.

For years, our daughter, Makenna, tried to face her fear of the playground monkey bars. Fear always won. How often I heard, "Daddy, I can't. I'm afraid." She watched her schoolmates from the safety of the ground; their calls beckoning her to try. One afternoon when she was nine, she rushed home from school, flushed with excitement.

"I did it! I did it!"

"Did what? I asked, thinking she had aced a spelling or math test.

"I crossed the monkey bars."

My heart swelled and I felt her joy as my joy. For years, I had watched her as she tottered nervously on the top rung of the ladder. She'd wrinkle her little forehead as though she was in pain and clung to the vertical supports like they were the interplane struts of a biplane flying at five thousand feet.

"Keep reaching out," I'd tell her. "Just one more." But she couldn't muster her courage to stretch enough and bridge the gap to the first crossbar.

"Daddy, I can't."

"Yes, you can, honey." But leaning into the center, clenching the steel, and swinging out to grab the next bar was battling the abyss.

"Keep reaching out," I coaxed time after time. But she always climbed back down.

This day, I could imagine her up there; her schoolmates watching and cheering, Makenna probably repeating to herself, *Keep reaching out.*

Now, full of victory, she threw her arms around my middle and squeezed me tightly.

"I'm so proud of you. What did you do different?"

"I had to let go of all my fears."

Her prophetic words slid out so matter-of-factly, as if she'd practiced doing just that in every aspect of her life. Perhaps she had. Or maybe she became aware, as did I, that the first time we attempt the impossible will be far from the last.

> How should we be able to forget those ancient myths that are at the beginning of all peoples, the myths about dragons that at the last moment turn into princesses? Perhaps all the dragons of our lives are princesses who are only waiting to see us once beautiful and brave. Perhaps everything terrible is in its deepest being something helpless that wants help from us.
> —Rainer Maria Rilke

Susan Jeffers learned a lot about feeling the fear and doing "it" anyway. In her 1987 bestseller, *Feel the Fear and Do It Anyway*, the much-needed message seemed impossible to get out. Publishers felt the fear and ran the other way. Rejection letters piled up. Visionless publishers had their secretaries type out quick and very dirty assaults to her ego. But Jeffers would have none of it. A few years before her 2012 death, she shared "the worst one": "Lady Di could be bicycling nude down the street giving this book away and nobody would read it." To the publishing house Harcourt Brace Jovanovich, that was bunkum. It courageously published the wisdom of the "Queen of Self-Help" and sold more than two million copies. *Feel the Fear* was translated into thirty-six languages and distributed in one hundred countries.

> He who is not every day conquering some fear has not learned the secret of life.
> —Ralph Waldo Emerson

Get Out of Your Own Way

Sometimes we have to get out of our skin and step outside of fear to slay the dragons ready to devour our hopes and dreams.

I don't know what's possible for me, much less for you. That's for you to spend the rest of your life pushing boundaries to discover. Like I urged Makenna: "focus on just one more" bar, step, breath. Put behind you one more rejection letter. Audition for one more script. Take one more course. Play one more game. Soothe one more patient. Talk to one more elderly person. Get out of your own way and let what's possible be.

> Those who are comfortable taking chances know that the best way to grow is to reach beyond their grasp. Their sense of direction comes from the heart. They don't shy away from surprise; they might even seek it out. And they seldom die with regrets. In the end we regret not what we have done but what we have not done.
> —Mark Goulston

Practice

The Box Breath

Breathwork has long been used to bring us into the present moment and focus mindful attention to our breath. Box breathing is also known as equal breath, *sama vritti pranayama*, and four-square breathing because the technique involves slow, deep breaths repeated in an even cadence.

Box breathing is a powerful stress reducer and can heighten performance and concentration. This technique has been taught to athletes, US Navy SEALs (Sea, Air, and Land Teams), police officers, nurses and many others who need to easily return to a peaceful state. When we hold our breath, CO_2 builds up in our blood. This increase in CO_2 activates the parasympathetic nervous system as a counter response to the fight-or-flight sympathetic nervous system.

According to the Mayo Clinic, there's sufficient evidence that intentional deep breathing, such as box breathing, can reduce stress, lower blood pressure, and improve mood. As a result, box breathing has become a healthy, effective method to mitigate depression and control disorders such as anxiety, panic, and post-traumatic stress. Intentional breathing techniques also can help relieve insomnia and help manage pain.

If you're new to box breathing, you may experience a slight dizziness after a few rounds. This is normal. If you feel dizzy, return to normal breathing while sitting quietly for a minute. Then resume box breathing. As you practice, you'll notice dizziness disappears.

To enhance the mindfulness experience of box breathing, find a quiet environment. It doesn't have to be dimly lit, but that may be helpful as you begin. You may wish to slow your counting by saying, "one thousand one, one thousand two" and so on.

Step 1: Slowly Exhale

Sit upright. Close your eyes. Place the tip of your tongue against the roof of your mouth behind your upper teeth. Exhale through your mouth to expel all the oxygen from your lungs. Mindfully place your attention and intention on the act of breathing.

Step 2: Slowly Inhale

Inhale slowly through your nose to the count of four. This may require a bit of attention, as you may automatically want to breath in through your mouth. Fill your lungs. Inhale more air and notice that your diaphragm contracts and moves downward to permit your lungs to expand further.

Step 3: Hold Your Breath

Hold your breath to a slow count of four.

Step 4: Exhale

Exhale slowly through your mouth to the count of four. Be aware of releasing all the air in your lungs.

Step 5: Leave Your Breath Out

Leave your breath out for the same slow count of four.

Repeat the box breath for four repetitions or until comfortable.

Consult with your physician about holding your breath after you inhale if you have any of the following: low blood pressure, heart or lung disease, any condition of the eye or recent eye surgery, sinus infection, problems with your ears, or if you are pregnant. Simply inhale and exhale to the count of four.

Exercises

In your journal,

- ❧ List seven important things that you want to accomplish or achieve. They can be physical things that you'd like to acquire (a house by the ocean), a professional goal (get that promotion to general manager), physical or mental-health milestones you'd like to reach (increase my running distance to 10 miles), an event in which you'd like to participate (run a marathon), states of being that bring you harmony (learn how to reduce work stress before it affects my mood), whatever is important to you.

- ❧ Rank these seven in order of importance.

- ❧ List ten (yes, you can) things that you can do in the next days and weeks to help you achieve your No. 1 priority.

- ❧ List any fears that you believe currently block achievement of your No. 1 goal. Ask yourself if this is a realistic fear. Does it have a basis in fact? If so, what can you do to "let go" of the fear?

- ❧ My aha moment from this insight is

Inspiration

You were born with wings, why prefer to crawl through life?
—Rumi

FIVE

Project a Healthy Future

What lies behind us and what lies before us
are tiny matters compared to what lies within us.
—Ralph Waldo Emerson

Insight 3: Check In With Myself

**I maintain awareness of my thoughts, beliefs, and actions
by being mindful and living in the present
while always projecting my highest and healthiest future.**

The He(art) and Science Behind the Insight

A Case of Mistaken Identity

You've been there, done that thousands of times. Maybe you were networking at a Chamber After Hours event. If so, you might have introduced yourself like this: "Hi, I'm Logan, and I'm a structural engineer at my all-green firm." At your nephew's bar mitzvah, you might approach new people more breezily. "Hey, I'm Tony, the uncle."

Consider how many times since you were a toddler that you've told people your name. That's a lot of self-reference. Dutifully, you print your name and sign it on documents from opening a bank account to acquiring a home loan, from applying for a job to registering for a university certification program.

How do you respond when the human resources (HR) director interviews you and says, "Tell me about yourself"? Where do you start? Of course, if you're applying for a position, you've done your research, and you've got a strategy for reeling off your skills and competencies, how they benefited your current or former employer, and how they transfer to the new company. But are those skills and competencies who you are? Are they your highest potential?

You're "honey" to your significant other. "Mom" or "Dad" to your kids. "Nana" and "Poppa" to your grandkids. "Shorty" to your former marine buddy. "Lefty" to the softball team. Our tombstones—provided we choose that memorial—etch in stone even our middle names and two dates. Maybe also the words "Beloved Mother" or "Bravest Firefighter."

Names are merely labels or pointers to us. They don't give the slightest clue to the question, "Who am I?" Yet, names are vital to us because they're the mental cues that link a memory about a person to the now, a person about whom we did have a clue and maybe even with whom we shared a lifetime of experiences. We whisper the name of someone special; we flock to the Vietnam Veteran's Memorial and other such places and trace the names of friends and family members as one more remembrance.

We are the myriad characters with roles in life's innumerable plays identified with unforgettable names. For this audience we are so-and-so. For that, we answer to whomever we are for that moment in time. Yes, you read that correctly. If you think who you are all the time is consistent, perhaps you ought not to bet at the races.

Let's take a closer look at the thoughts and beliefs we have about ourselves. Or our *Self*, to be more precise. When we respond to the question "Who am I?" we go to our brain's file cabinet—the *Self*—and pull open the drawer labeled concepts about me: *Self-concepts*.

Self-concepts are the mental constructs we form about ourselves colored by our perceptions and valuative judgments. The drawer is divided into categories: Kind, Compassionate, Trustworthy, Conscientious, Competent, Stupendous, and so on. Depending on how organized we are, we file folders that label our identities behind each category. There's an identity folder for me labeled "Entrepreneur." Another, "Father." Yet another, "Fitness Coach." Then there's "Wellness Advocate." I label each folder according to how I think of myself, and how I believe others think of me. We all do this. The labels identify a different aspect of ourselves that contributes to our self-concept.

Our identity folders contain the good, the bad, and the ugly aspects or characteristics that we've praised or condemned, showcased or hidden. We've probably stashed away beliefs about ourselves that experiences have long proven untrue. It's hard to replace old self-concepts with more accurate ones.

Self and identity—though we often use the words interchangeably—aren't the same thing. Neuroscientific and psychological studies confirm the distinction. The "I" that I am happens to also be a father. But I am much more than that. You are much more than your job, title, and even name. As I explained above, all these attributes, characteristics, and roles are pieces of the puzzle that is you. But they are not the totality of the puzzle.

You Are Not Every Tom, Dick, and Harriet

Whatever our birth certificates read, who we are is spelled out in the arrangement of the letters A, G, T, and C, the four types of bases found in all our genomes—or DNA—our operating manual. "Genomics is . . . what makes each of us different and what makes us the same."[1] As we saw in chapter 1, your genome is 99.9 percent identical to the seven billion people around you. But it's that tiny 0.1 percent difference that affects many of the ways you're unique. Even identical twins don't share 100 percent of their genetic material. Sometimes the differences between twins raised in the same household can be startling.[2] And that's because we're more than our DNA.[3]

Who we have become is a clay vessel turned on the pottery wheel of life. Parenting, where we came from, where we strive to go, age, gender identification, education, religion, profession, avocation, health, opportunity, and much more, are the speed at which we turn the pottery wheel. Our self-concepts and identities are the hands that mold its shape.

"Self-concept and identity are highly malleable and can even be dynamically constructed in the moment, so stability is more seeming than real,"[4] says Daphna Oyserman. Research conducted by Oyserman, dean's professor, Department of Psychology, University of Southern California, examines how small changes in context can shift our mindsets. Her exploration confirms that what we think and feel about ourselves and our world impacts our health, motivation, and behaviors—our well-being.

To be sure, what we think and believe and how we act are determinants of our future that are under our control. And we can control our perception of and response to situations outside of our control. Yes, terrible things happen to people. Devastating events break some people while others are resilient. The foundation of survivors' resilience is a basic belief in their ability to maintain some control and to rebound. We've seen that "even the most bitter memories can foster endurance, self-efficacy, and contentment in the present juxtaposed to the past."[5]

Some survivors of traumatic and life-changing events are able to create a new image of themselves and find contentment in the now. People have told me that they experience a palpable feeling of well-being that sends a positive vibration all the way to their core—to their essence. The intrinsic human essence represents attributes such as self-evaluation and self-reflection that make us what we fundamentally are, without which we would lose our identity as human beings.[6] It is our essence that is the purest part of us, indistinguishable and inseparable from love.

> Love is the only way to grasp another human being in the innermost core of his personality. No one can become fully aware of the very essence of another human being unless he loves him. By his love he is enabled to see the essential traits and features in the beloved person; and even more, he sees that which is potential in him, which is not yet actualized but yet ought to be actualized. Furthermore, by his love, the loving person enables the beloved person to actualize these potentialities.

These powerful insights above by Austrian psychiatrist and philosopher Viktor Frankl (1905–1997) remind us that we can project our highest future only under two critical conditions. We must know who we are, and we must remain mindfully aware of our thoughts and beliefs about ourself and our relationship to others and the world. Through honest self-reflection, we see through the façades—our own and those others erect out of self-defense, fear, or unwillingness to explore the inner. Frankl witnessed the power of an individual "to choose one's attitude in any given set of circumstances, to choose one's own way." How do we achieve our highest potential in the future? Relegate to File 13—the trash—thoughts and beliefs that aren't congruent with our desire to be self-actualized.

We've said that achieving our potential means different things to different people. In 2020, the world added four hundred twelve additional billionaires. There are now close to thirty-three hundred. They might equate fullest potential with wealth: ownership of McMansions throughout the world and a multi-billion-dollar superyacht, one of which is equipped with its own missile defense system and a bulletproof master bedroom suite. If I feared needing such defenses, I haven't reached my highest potential.

For most of us, our ordinary lives are a soup of environmental and societal stresses that don't include expenses equal to the Gross Domestic Product (GDP) of small nations. Yet we can taste well-being even though we may feel fear or face failure. There are intangible, existential perks to working toward our highest potential: revealing the spiritual nature of who we are. Spiritual perks are priceless. Living with joy, peace, and love in our hearts costs nothing. Meeting each new day with the knowledge that we've achieved a value alignment among our thoughts, beliefs, and actions doesn't require an expensive college degree.

Getting to Know You

Throughout our lifetime, we've formed intimate relationships. The most intimate relationship possible is with ourselves. As we're learning, we often erect a smoke screen between the various aspects of who we are. Our self-concept is shaped by our self-image, the view we have of ourselves; our self-esteem, the worth or value we place on who we are; and our ideal self, the who we long to be.

Up to now, we've talked about the benefits of mindful awareness to relieve stress and instill harmony when chaos runs amok in our bodies and minds. Through breathing exercises, focusing on an object, observing people from a park bench, listening to birdsongs, or the hum of bees, we disconnect from the hustle and bustle to reconnect with our higher selves. Mindful awareness helps us to adjust our perception of reality, get unstuck from the past, and become grounded in the present moment.

Mindful awareness puts us in touch with our true self. We can take that experience farther and deeper. We can "collapse" the world around us and sense even for an instant that we are not only a small part of a whole, but that the whole also exists in us. We are one with a vaster, grander scheme than we let ourselves imagine.

Many scientists propose that, on the smallest, fundamental particle level, it's possible that all matter has a kind of awareness. Some few attribute a consciousness to all things that's beyond our understanding. "What if consciousness is not something special that the brain does but is, instead, a quality inherent to all matter?" asks philosopher Philip Goff.[7] Goff proposes that such a concept helps explain our sense that we're "tapping into universal wisdom" or "a higher consciousness." This awareness may arise as a fleeting awakening. For those who discover that moment, they find themselves transcending the din and entering a special, quiet place.

The Sound of Silence

What if we could voluntarily lower the volume? What if we could switch off the cacophony of sensory distractions, including the sometimes-infernal internal chatter whenever we need to? We can. And many of us do. And when we do, we purposefully listen to the sound of silence. We're intentionally switching on our mind's ability to be contentless—without content. Sixties' anthropologist Carlos Castaneda's Yaqui brujo, Juan Matus, called it stopping the world. Neuroscientists Patrizio Paoletti and Tal Dotan Ben-Soussan of the Research Institute for Neuroscience,

Assisi, Italy, studied the effects of inner and outer silence. They call this state of consciousness without content the place of pre-existence. "Willingly staying in silence as it occurs in many meditation practices is actually advantageous for mental and physical well-being," say Paoletti and Ben-Soussan. In that space, we can bypass the filters of time, emotion, and memories and reach "a sense of peace and quiet."[8]

Paoletti and Ben-Soussan call the first of three states of awareness the Narrative Self. That state of awareness derives its narrative—or story—from the past, remembrances. It also borrows story from the future, imagination. We've shaped the Narrative Self story, as you can guess, from our perception of our personal identity. More on identity shortly. The second state of awareness, called the Minimal Self, centers attention on the here and now. As the name implies, in the third state, Overcoming of the Self, "self disappears" as the practitioner achieves contentless consciousness.

Perhaps an easier way to wrap our heads around a contentless state of mind is to think of it as though we're immersed in all content. Yet, our intent is to focus on no particular content. An analogy may help. Imagine you're at a ball pit many times bigger than those at McDonald's or the Discovery Zone. You dive into the one million crayon-bright balls and swim around, having a great time. You're not focused on the red one on the other side of the pit, as there are thousands of red balls among the yellow, blue, and green ones. You aren't focused on the balls at all. Your awareness is on the experience of floating or swimming freely among so much content that it disappears.

There are a number of approaches to achieving contentless consciousness—a concept thousands of years old. Ancient sages have explained that our highest state of awareness doesn't just come and go. It's always present in our mind. In Buddhism, this always-there essence is called Buddha Nature. In Hinduism, it's the True Self. In Zen Buddhism, a parallel technique to contentless consciousness is called *shikantaza*, "just sitting." Indian philosopher and teacher Jiddu Khrishnamurti (1895–1986) called it "choiceless awareness."

In that tradition, contemporary teacher Shinzen Young calls it "do-nothing" meditation. Sounds like an oxymoron, doesn't it? We do nothing to improve our mindfulness and focus when we're doing something. The principle may seem elusive, but its effectiveness is well-founded. Experts consider "do-nothing" meditation an advanced practice. It's challenging, but not impossible for beginners. I'm introducing it to you because "do-nothing" meditation is one way for beginners to stop beating themselves up for their over-active monkey mind. Unfortunately, newcomers to mindfulness meditation sometimes experience a sense of failure at not being able to quiet monkey mind. And that's stressful. We can't muscle our way to mindfulness meditation and achieve a relaxed state.

Here's how you might try it. During meditation, instead of redirecting our wandering attention back to our breathing, focusing on the rhymical in and out of breath as we usually do, we stop being intentional. If we intentionally redirect, we're not doing nothing, which is the goal. Contentless awareness asks that we sit silently yet aware of our surroundings. What's new is that we're not micromanaging our thoughts, feelings, and sensations. In mindfulness meditation, when our mind strays, we return to awareness through the hall monitor of focus on the breath.

During choiceless attention, we let go even of our attention to the act of meditating, always without force, without judgment, without frustration. There is nothing to push back against, nothing to resist. We let go and let flow, like a leaf drifting on a stream. The leaf floats without getting caught up in branches and rocks. Whatever happens, happens. If we notice we're focused on a sensation or thought, we simply stop. No chiding. No refocusing. Only "no focusing." We're shutting down intention.

> Thoughts, feelings, and sensations are not different from the space that is mind. Silence is another kind of space. When everything is quiet and suddenly there is a noise, we ordinarily say the silence was shattered. But it's more accurate to say that we forget the silence and listen only to the sound. I started to listen to the silence, around me and inside me. I became aware of another dimension, an infinite internal space that had to do with my ability to experience my body. This dimension had more the quality of depth: it seemed to go down forever. There was no bottom. There was no me there.[9]

Among Harvard's many studies on awareness and mindfulness, one was particularly unnerving. Psychologists Daniel Gilbert and Matthew Killingsworth discovered that 47 percent of the time their large test group wasn't paying a bit of attention to what was going on in front of them. Focus is a human frailty. Unless we're passionate about some activity, it's difficult to become engrossed in it. When we do something we love, our involvement can be all-consuming. As we discussed earlier, we lose track of time. Where we are disappears. Everything else fades into nothingness. We're intent. But can we be intent on more than one thing at a time?

Massachusetts Institute of Technology (MIT) neuroscientist Earl Miller says no and debunked another myth: We're super multitaskers. Wish it were true. That doesn't mean we can't walk and chew gum at the same time. But our brains just can't focus on two things at once. What we think is multitasking is really rapid "task switching," and it's exhausting. To burst another bubble, when you think you're getting more done by multitasking, you're actually 40 percent less efficient.[10] Science has proven that we get more done by doing less, not more.

That's one rationale behind introducing you to the "choiceless attention," the "do-nothing" meditation exercise at the end of this chapter. But it goes much deeper than that. We don't want to waste energy by resisting thoughts with intention or getting mired in beliefs that—to use a term I've used before—no longer serve us. We want to be in the present and yet not *of* the present. That's non-attachment, most often called detachment. Detachment is a necessary step toward achieving our growth, but it's a much-misunderstood term. It does not mean that we do not care about or are unmoved by a thing but that we understand why we have such attachment to it. We can also practice detachment from outcomes. In this sense, I'd like for you not to attach feelings to any perceived success or failure as you try "do-nothing" meditation. At its best, the do-nothing state gives our bodies and minds needed relaxation by releasing us from the need to be in control. To clear the way for our Highest Self, we need to get out of the way. It isn't easy. But it's necessary.

> This being human is a guest house.
> Every morning a new arrival.
> A joy, a depression, a meanness,
> Some momentary awareness comes
> as an unexpected visitor.
> Welcome and entertain them all!
> —Rumi

Secular Meditation to Thrive in the Moment

In the late 1960s, Chögyam Trungpa, a Tibetan meditation master and Oxford University scholar, gave up his monastic vows to work as a lay teacher and introduce meditation in terms beyond Buddhism to non-religious audiences and help people integrate the practice and other contemplative activities into their daily lives. "Meditation is not a matter of trying to achieve ecstasy, spiritual bliss, or tranquility, nor is it attempting to be a better person," he taught. "It is simply the creation of a space in which we are able to expose and undo our neurotic games, our self-deceptions, our hidden fears and hopes."

Insight 3, "Check In with Myself," urges me to be aware of my thoughts, beliefs, and live in the present. So, why the discussion about differentiating our true self from our identity and losing ourselves when we're immersed in a pleasurable task? How are those related and relevant?

First, I can't check in with myself if I don't know who myself is. Who will reveal the unique individual that I truly am if not the one who knows me best? By looking at who we are not—the case of mistaken identity—we peel the façade and begin to reveal the hidden self.

Second, if I haven't met my most profound and extraordinary self in the quiet of contemplation or meditation, how can I project a highest future for a self I do not know? How can I see myself clearly if I don't look behind the mirror? How will I project my highest future when I'm consumed with the image of myself that the world reflects?

Third, when we're doing what we love, swimming in bliss, unafraid of the depths, we are our true selves, wholly in the present. Yesterday is superfluous. Tomorrow rushes us and calls us away from our passion in the moment. This is how a painter feels when every brushstroke is inspired. Or how the poet feels when her verse flows from a source unknown. Or how the grandfather feels when he's constructed his first grandbaby's cradle in his own workshop.

The present, by its very nature—every now succession of instances—demands that we're mindfully present. We were there—in the past—but now we are here. Being in the moment requires us to pay attention. We can't pay attention to the past or to the future. Neuroscientists and psychologists have given us many reasons to be here now. The top two are our improved mental and physical health.

As in everything, moderation is key. For Rick, Ilsa, and Louis in *Casablanca*, the past is inescapable. Memories flood the oasis. For some of us who are survivors of tragedy, memories can be a launchpad from which we project new thoughts, beliefs, and actions. Tenacity, resilience, and adaptability enabled those who are survivors to forge new lives with a "singleness of purpose," as Henry Kissinger called it.[11] We can't dismiss the importance of connectedness and giving, which we'll discuss in Insight 7.

Astrophysicists discover the existence of exoplanets outside our solar system by the slight gravitational wobble of their nearby star. They can't yet be observed directly. Similarly, we discover the self through "its relationship to people . . . and the world around you and within you. Relationship is the mirror in which the self is revealed. Without self-knowledge there is no basis for right thought and action," wrote Krishnamurti, who at age eighty-five met theoretical physicist David Joseph Bohm (1917-1992). Bohm had contributed significantly to neuropsychology and the philosophy of the mind. For years, the pair engaged in meaningful exchanges about the essence of things.

To Aristotle, the literal translation of essence is from the Greek expression "the what it was meant to be." When I was young, the "Who am I?" question asked at the opening of this chapter—phrased less philosophically—was one that gave me momentary pause. Who is the "I" that is Daniel Johnson, and what is it that I am to be? As I've related, I tested wearing this and that identity—shoe-shine boy, entrepreneur, consultant, trainer. After learning to meditate, I understood "to be" differently. My myriad identities began to look like window dressing. I sensed my true nature had to be foundational, and my core self had to be guided by my higher thoughts, in a way different than I was guided by my faith, which is considerable. So, what was this quality that I was sensing during mindfulness meditation?

Cosmic Consciousness

In their famous published dialogues, Krishnamurti and David Bohm pried apart the subtleties of mind and its seeming compartmentalized functions. Among their explorations was the slippery slope that is our perception of intelligence. Not intelligence as we think of it,[12] but a deeper, perhaps even cosmic intelligence, a consciousness so sweeping that it is, perhaps, related to love. Not the "I love you" but the larger, all-encompassing love capable of breaking down the wall. What wall? The limitations of the human mind, the barrier that our minds erect. The obstacle through which we can't see what is True with a capital "T." Bohm dropped a bombshell. The wall is an illusion. "Knowledge deceives the mind," he said

And it can pollute. Our "individual stream of consciousness is loaded with all the traces left on it by positive and negative thoughts, as well as by actions and words arising from those thoughts," said Matthieu Ricard, who traded the white lab coat of a molecular biologist for the maroon robes of a Buddhist monk. Purifying the stream means cleaning up our thoughts, which we'll explore further in the next several insights.

"Positive emotions don't disturb our mind," Ricard said. "They reinforce it and make it more stable and more courageous. An emotion is negative if it destroys your own and others' inner peace."

We wouldn't be where we are today if we ignored all thoughts that weren't positive. Much invention trickled from brain to brawn because we were miserable in our current state. Imagining a drier, safer cave arose from the thought that our current digs were cold, damp, and stinky. Figuring out how to transport the morning fire to the night's next camp without burning our buns or toasting our backs was the ember of an idea sparked by pain and hunger. We thought. We survived. We projected our ideas, hopes, wishes, and dreams onto the future and developed creatively. You know the expression, "She's lost in thought." She's exploring a virtual reality—that gift I mentioned of being able to test our ideas with brain cells before taking action. As long as the links in the chain of thought, belief, and action are unbroken, we can thrive as an integrated entity: body, mind, and spirit.

Jordan Poppenk, research chair in cognitive neuroscience at Canada's Queens University, found that we generate about six thousand two hundred thoughts per day.[13] That's the conservative estimate. Other researchers push that mind clutter to as many as sixty thousand thoughts per day. Naturally, some thoughts are important; others, impotent. Is it any wonder that ancient Chinese philosophers associated our restless, capricious inner chatter to monkey mind, as we've been calling it?

There's so much contamination and trash among the gold and gems that we need to take care not to trust every thought as sacrosanct. It's practical to "show me the evidence." Uncover the lies. Sit as judge and jury to those that don't ring true. This sounds like it's in contradiction to the advice about not judging the material that comes up through awareness and mindful meditation. The key is discrimination. We'll know it when we feel it.

The more we practice mindful meditation, the more physical changes to our brain's prefrontal cortex and parietal lobes occur. Research at Germany's Max Planck Institute for Human Cognitive and Brain Sciences discovered that different meditation techniques also positively affect other parts of the brain. After eight weeks of mindfulness practice, the amygdala—the brain's primal computer that converts fear and emotion into preparation for fight or flight—changes. The amygdala shrinks while the prefrontal cortex, which is responsible for awareness, focus, and decision-making, becomes thicker. Another study demonstrated the effectiveness on reducing the stress hormone cortisol by 51 percent when participants faced meditative partners rather than meditating alone. The fascinating thing about this finding is that social stress is the key stressor in most of our lives.[14] Yet we, social beings, felt comforted by the presence of another when there was no competition and the goal was mutual support.

Joshua Grant, a postdoctoral researcher at the Max Planck Institute, found that expert meditators were able to remove or lessen the stressful nature associated with pain, strong emotions, and memory. These practitioners altered the connectivity between two brain regions that normally communicate. Rather than block the experience of pain, "it seems they refrained from engaging in thought processes that make it painful." Grant also found that the change in perception was permanent, and the pain-lessening effect was no longer dependent on achieving a meditative state. Scans showed that the resting brain of these meditators appeared much the same as the brains of ordinary people who were meditating. The prefrontal cortex no longer needs to be larger to affect mindful awareness and concentration, as those states become the default conditions. The brain-body response has now become automatic.

Life Is Just a Bowl of Cherries

Sometimes, however, it feels like the pits. But there is a way to feel whole.

"I'm really excited about the effects of mindfulness," says Adrienne Taren, researcher at the University of Pittsburgh. "It's been great to see it move away from being a spiritual thing towards proper science and clinical evidence, as stress is a huge problem and has a huge impact on many people's health."[15]

Research has shown that negative thoughts stir up raw emotions that trigger our stress-response system to produce fight or flight hormones. It takes one and a half minutes for the effects of an emotion to come and go. The longer we run on the hamster stress treadmill, the more adrenaline and cortisol floods our system. Adrenaline increases our heart rate and elevates blood pressure. Cortisol increases glucose (sugar) in our blood stream. Over time, these stress hormones put us at risk for anxiety, depression, digestive problems, headaches, heart disease, sleep problems, weight gain, memory and concentration impairment, and possibly some autoimmune disorders, says the Mayo Clinic.

Like lightning, negative thoughts tend to follow familiar paths. They send us cowering in a tiny, dark corner of that vast essence, which, as we've discussed, is the reality of who we really are. Through mindfulness practice, we can light a lamp and walk into those dark places. We can check in with our true selves and become aware of the false narratives that block our way to our highest and healthiest future. We can choose to open the door of awareness. With that door flung open, we're free to go higher and down deeper. What an extraordinary paradox.

Remember this. The identities that we thought of as us are merely transitory constructs. When we strip to bare reality and cast off the cloak of misperception, we uncover our true and radiant self. Mindful meditation heightens our awareness of our inseparableness from the whole. Through that opened door, we discover the united self: the oneness of body, mind, and spirit. "In that process lies the whole story of answering 'who am I?'"[16]

Practice

The powerful "Do-Nothing" Meditation

- In a quiet place, sit very straight. You may use a cushion on the floor or sit in a chair.
- Relax and loosen your jaw. Remind yourself to relax your jaw periodically during meditation. Be aware if you are tightening back up. If so, relax, let the thought and tension go.
- Accept the present moment.
- You don't have to control your breathing. Let go of shallow breathing easily and naturally.
- Pay attention to the feeling of doing nothing.
- As soon as you're aware that you're doing something—thinking about your bank balance or if you backed up your computer at work—let it go and effortlessly release it.
- Effortlessly release concentration.
- If an emotion surfaces, let it go—effortlessly release it.
- If you feel like you're struggling to do nothing, let it go—effortlessly release it.
- Keep relaxing without giving doing so any effort or thought.
- Let go of feeling guilty for sitting down and doing nothing.
- Let judgment go. You are making progress. Like going to the gym, you'll build mental strength.
- Monkey mind is normal. Your mind is going to purge a lot of old thoughts. Let go of resistance.
- Let yourself have twenty minutes of "just sitting" with contentless awareness.
- If you feel doing nothing isn't working, if you're falling asleep, or if your mind is swinging through the jungle canopy, return to focusing on breathing for three to five minutes.

Exercises

In your journal,

- List as many false identities as you can that you thought were really you when you were a child. Now, do the same for your adult self. If you're stuck, these articles may help: https://www.psychologytoday.com/us/blog/compassion-matters/201711/are-you-living-accidental-identity and "Creating a False Self: Learning to Live a Lie," *HuffPost*, November 17, 2011. https://www.huffpost.com/entry/creating-a-false-self-lea_b_269096 by Tian Dayton, PhD.
- List as many of your positive attributes as you can. Underline those that are most important to you.
- List as many negative thoughts as you can that you've become aware of since this morning that are based on beliefs that aren't true. Underline those that are recurring, or habitual thoughts.
- What does it mean to you to project your highest and healthiest future?
- List as many times and situations as you can in which you need to be most present in the moment.
- List seven negative thoughts that you play over and over in your mental tape recorder that you'd like to erase. Underline your top two priorities.
- What can you do today to wipe those off your mental slate?
- My aha moment from this insight is

Inspiration

If you realized how powerful your thoughts are,
you would never think another negative thought.
—Peace Pilgrim

SIX

Count Your Blessings

The optimist lives on the peninsula
of infinite possibilities; the pessimist is stranded
on the island of perpetual indecision.
—William Arthur Ward

Insight 4:
Leverage the Power
of Optimism

I choose to be an optimist, knowing that my thoughts
and words will come to be. I expect to discover
gifts of joy within my body, mind, and spirit.

The He(art) and Science
Behind the Insight

Oblivious to the Rose

Khalil Gibran, the internationally celebrated poet and author of *The Prophet*, contemplated the perspective of two common and opposing points of view. "The optimist sees the rose and not its thorns. The pessimist stares at the thorns, oblivious to the rose."[1]

It may surprise you to know that more people than not are born optimists. Others have to work at it. "Humans," writes neuroscientist Tali Sharot, "do not hold a positivity bias on account of having read too many self-help books. Rather, optimism may be so essential to our survival that it is hardwired into our most complex organ, the brain."[2]

We all know people for whom optimism not only doesn't seem hardwired, it seems short-circuited. For these folks, Martin Seligman, professor of psychology and director of the Positive Psychology Center at the University of Pennsylvania, wrote *Learned Optimism: How to Change Your Mind and Your Life*. The success of *Learned Optimism* arose as a counterpoint to Seligman's prior investigation and book, *Learned Helplessness: A Theory for the Age of Personal Control*. The nucleus of his early research, "pathologies that disable the good life, which make a life not worth living," revealed that once people feel that they have no control over their situation, they tend to give up rather than fight for control.[3] Even more debilitating was patients' feelings of emptiness once therapy reduced or alleviated their anxiety, depression, anger, or fear. Happiness didn't rush in to fill the void. Curiously to Seligman and other researchers, "curing the negatives didn't produce the positives." In the late 1990s, frustrated with the glass-half-empty approach to enhancing patients' well-being, Seligman picked up the gauntlet that had been laid down after World War II by scientists who saw promise in focusing on positive psychology.[4] Seligman pivoted his research, fully aware that "happiness is a scientifically unwieldy notion." He was right.

Happiness is like the wind. Sometimes you feel it; sometimes you don't. But it's an ever-present force. Wind is the motion of air around us. Happiness is the emotion of well-being within us. Wind just needs something to stir it so we can recognize its presence. You've probably heard someone refer to their mood as being in the "doldrums." Technically, the doldrums are equatorial calms, seemingly windless weather in which sailing ships get stuck and go nowhere. Not surprisingly, the term doldrums also defines a psychological state of inactivity and stagnation, even a spell of sadness and depression.

Over the many years, I've observed the mind and body effects of chronic pessimists who are challenged to feel the wind fill their sails. When they're caught in a storm, they forget to rely on the storm sail and steer into the waves to maintain control.

So what's the big deal whether our explanatory style, as scientists call the way we view our life, is positive or negative? As it turns out, plenty. Optimistic thoughts and beliefs help us to live healthier and happier lives. Negative thoughts that nothing will work out, that we're incapable, incompetent, or attract only bad luck undermine virtually all roads to living in joy and achieving success, whatever our endeavors are. Optimists set realistic goals. Pessimists either don't set goals or give up on them when they appear unachievable. That makes pessimists vulnerable to sadness and depression.

Maybe you remember these lyrics from childhood: "Nobody likes me, everybody hates me. Guess I'll go eat worms." Please don't eat the worms. Don't eat the daisies, either.

Sunnyside Up or Over Easy?

The most upbeat and satisfied people with whom I've worked, congruent with Seligman's research, think differently. Persistence and resilience seem be their middle names. "I quit" and "I can't" aren't in their vocabulary. Their thoughts aren't stuck in the past. Clear and honest evaluations of past lessons inform the present, and now is good. If it's not great, well, tomorrow will absolutely be better, even if it's not perfect.

Living optimistically is like running a marathon. It isn't about finishing first. It's about finishing. It epitomizes the proverb *nana korobi, ya oki*—fall down seven times, stand up eight. Blisters, skinned knees, and throbbing muscles are the grit of character development. That said, we can't discount times when it's wise to stop doing what we're doing if doing it harms us or someone else in some way. That's not failure. It's reassessing the facts and choosing to change the situation. Failure isn't a lack of success. It's one step on the road to success. A setback isn't a life sentence to more setbacks.

Bumper stickers remind us that sh*t happens. It's a cliché: bad stuff happens to good people. We know that, so we aren't blind to reality. For example, after a long day's hiking, we're raring for s'mores. If we're not willing to wait out the sudden downpour, start a fire with dry wood and tend it until the embers glow, then we can't roast the marshmallows. Time for plan B: the bag of trail mix in the SUV. The oversimplification reminds us that the optimist doesn't abandon the quest. The optimist adjusts the goals.

Using positive psychology isn't about approaching every terrible, horrible, painful occurrence in life in a touchy-feely way. Far from it. Instead, we learn to cultivate our individual strengths and virtues and build on them, creating resilience. We can build the body, and do, but, often, the real work is inside—on the mind. Our thoughts are under our voluntary control. We have the power to shape, discard, disbelieve, or believe them. The superficiality or depth of our happiness depends on our choices. Let's not conflate being a Pollyanna with being an optimist. "Optimism is not an exercise in fantasy, but a reality-based belief system that leads us to be active and effective in our lives, working toward good outcomes while avoiding bad ones," said professor and psychologist Christopher Peterson.[5]

Before you get the impression that positive psychology and positive thinking are one and the same, let me clear that up. Within the scientific field and practice of positive psychology, positive thinking is but one of our mindful and intentional strategies for changing our behavior or managing stress. It's as though we're saying that a baseball pitcher has the option to throw a curveball, fastball, slider, or something else. The pitch isn't the game. It's an action that moves the game along. There are many rules and plays within the sport. In the game of life, optimists tend to use positive thinking to perceive the world around them as a happier place.

Just as we describe the world around us, happiness has three dimensions. Weaving the virtue ethics of ancient philosophers with modern motivation theories, Seligman parses our experiences of happiness in three broad categories: the Pleasant Life, the Good Life (also called the Engaged Life), and the Meaningful Life.[6] They bear a slight resemblance to Abraham Maslow's hierarchy of needs.

Each of the three dimensions builds on the needs and desires of the previous dimension. Successive dimensions recognize an individual's happiness is tied to an increasing commitment to self through personal growth, and then to others. Ultimately, individuals experience the greatest happiness from living a meaningful and purposeful life in which they apply their highest strengths toward altruistic acts and in service of a higher good.[7] Life's thorny. As we flourish among the roses, we're bound to get stuck now and then.

What Are the Odds?

Hands down, the optimist's point of view—positivity—leads to healthier, happier, and longer lives. In 2019, the Proceedings of the National Academy of Sciences reported on the results of longitudinal studies—from ten to thirty years—conducted on men and women who were considered optimists. "Previous studies reported that more optimistic individuals are less likely to suffer from chronic diseases and die prematurely. Our results further suggest that optimism is specifically related to 11 to 15 percent longer life span, on average, and to greater odds of achieving 'exceptional longevity,' that is, living to the age of eighty-five or beyond."[8]

I'm heartened by this and similar studies that conclude the reason for "exceptional longevity" is that optimists are better at stress management than pessimists. That gives optimists the edge to greater resilience, coping skills, resulting in better mental and physical health. However pessimism and paranoia negatively impact our health. Pessimists believe that bad things happen to them and blame others or themselves. Or they consider serendipitously good occurrences as flukes that will probably never happen again.

Optimists are confident that they can beat the odds, regardless of what life throws at them. As we'll see, they are wise to also incorporate realistic assessments of their situations so they don't delude themselves into thinking they're bulletproof. Optimists are more likely to consider themselves successful than are those who are pessimistic and don't see the lessons in the failures. Professionally, optimists' histories demonstrate that they have ridden storms and can pull together the emotional and physical resources to survive them again. These attitudes help them reduce the influence on their bodies of harmful stress. As the longitudinal studies demonstrate, optimists have stronger immunity. They experience lower rates of hypertension and heart disease and a lower risk of diseases such as cancer.

And, worth mentioning, Stanford University studies show that optimists have a better love life. Much goes into having a positive attitude in close relationships, not the least of which is the feeling that when there are disagreements, the process of working them out will be fair and the outcome will make the relationship stronger.

There's more to optimism than telling ourselves everything will be all right. Sometimes it won't. That's the point. The optimist isn't blindsided by hard knocks or by times of great good fortune. That's denial. Optimists know they have more control over a situation than might be apparent. And when they take control where it's possible, they believe the outcomes will be better than if they gave up and let others—or fate—control their lives.

Then there are realists. They tend to see things as they are without passing judgment. Most of us swing back and forth between optimism and pessimism, but we tend to lean more one way or the other.

How do we become an optimist? One way is for our parents to have given us good optimism genes. We can thank them for about a quarter of our perspective that the world is basically a beautiful and safe place. However, as we grew up, a lot of the world rubbed off on us. We may have learned to make harsher judgments based on our changing thoughts and beliefs about today and what tomorrow will bring. That still leaves room for us to mindfully be here now and stop worrying about the future. Which brings us to another way to become an optimist: learn. Practice. Mindfully change our thoughts and beliefs. But, you might say, "I'm paranoid for a reason. There are scary things out there." My response is this: What are the odds that we'll be right, that our future will turn out as we worried it would? How many times have we been right in the past about what our future would hold? Researchers have confirmed that social integration and optimism went hand in hand. Be around happy people and practice anticipating the positive.

If you find you're leaning toward pessimism, you have the power to change that. You can become aware of your negative thinking.

Just as you can work on any habit that you want to change, you can put your mind and body on alert about negativity. You could set a mental alarm clock that awakens you each time you need and want to take control. For example, "Every time I have a negative thought, that thought is going to trigger an awareness. I'm going to stop and recognize that my thought is most likely not true. I'm going to review the facts, which probably don't support my negative thoughts and feelings. Then, I'm consciously going to replace the negative thought with positive affirmations."

If a little optimism is good, a lot is better. Right? Not necessarily. Turns out that our brains can tend toward "optimism bias," aka the "illusion of invulnerability." Basically, that's too much of a good thing. In more of us than you might imagine, unrealistic optimism can put us in harm's way. That bias can lead us to think that our chances of experiencing a positive outcome the majority of the time is pretty high. Now and then, we overshoot our goal, and life is good. But life can also be good when we've fallen short. Here's Khalil Gibran:

> Your living is determined not so much by what life brings to you as by the attitude you bring to life; not so much by what happens to you as by the way your mind looks at what happens.

Throughout the *Twelve Insights for Mindful Living*, you'll hear me encourage striking a balance. That's the realism component that helps protect us from rose-colored-glasses syndrome or the polar opposite— walking under that perpetual cloud of doom and gloom. Over optimism can lead us into risky behavior that can be dangerous and jeopardize our physical or emotional well-being. If we never think about what could go wrong, we can't prepare for it.

What's the goal? A healthy mind. The fitness trainer in me thinks of it as strengthening our "mental muscle," just as my goal is to help others to strengthen their heart muscle. A good mental weight-lifting exercise is balancing realism with optimism. With anything, moderation is key and using wisdom is our due diligence. If we exaggerate the positive, we can overlook warning signs that something's not quite right. We were born with the capacity for fear for good reason. We can be the unprepared and untrained fools who rush in where angels fear to tread. We're rational beings and we owe it to ourselves and our loved ones to use the mental capacity gifted to us.

Be happy. See the bright side. But look before you leap: double-check everything before wingsuit BASE jumping[9] or whatever adventure rings your chimes. Optimism leads to "exceptional longevity" only when we use our brain to accurately assess the information it receives. Don't let social media and advertising drive you to do things that are high risk just because you think you've been lucky so far. Be wise and know that being optimistic isn't a safety net to jumping into danger. There's nothing heroic about foolhardiness.

Adjust the Sails

A friend told me a story about her mother, who really disliked hearing her daughter whine about this or that not being right and nothing was happening the way it should. Her mother would look her straight in the eyes and say, "Don't just do something, stand there!" That meant the opposite, of course. If you don't like something, change it. If you can't change it, get a better attitude. Ironically, the mutation and the original are both pertinent to us.

Sometimes, when the going gets tough, we just need to meditate on things and stop the world. Whether focusing on breathing or using the do-nothing meditation we learned earlier, we can sense when to back off, let events run their course, and take care of ourselves. That gives us the space to let momentum carry the situation to its natural end without our intervention. We may not like the outcome, but it's possible that it could have been worse if we hadn't taken our hands off. You know the verse: "Grant me the serenity to accept the things I cannot change, the courage to change the things I can, and the wisdom to know the difference." Know when not to be an optimist—such as in the face of negative information or dangerous situations. Your life, health, or emotional well-being may depend on your being a realist and knowing the difference.

Our capacity to learn is one of the unique gifts we share.

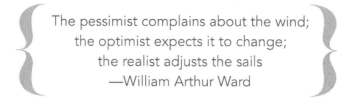

> The pessimist complains about the wind;
> the optimist expects it to change;
> the realist adjusts the sails
> —William Arthur Ward

Anticipation Can Be Better than the Real Thing

Speaking of gifts, there's a beautifully gift-wrapped box on the table. It's for you. But you can't open it until your birthday. The box is surprisingly big, way bigger than the thing you've wanted most: tickets to your magic place. But maybe that's part of the game. The anticipation piques pleasurable tension. Dopamine—the messenger chemical—surges in your brain,[10] explains Joanna Schaffhausen, PhD psychologist who studied neuroscience. "If everything is as nice as the brain predicted, dopamine levels remain elevated. If things turn out even better than the brain hoped, dopamine levels are increased. If, on the other hand, the activity is less pleasurable than we thought . . . dopamine levels plummet."

You go through the week feeling excited about what's in the box, mentally planning your long-anticipated trip. In the present, you relish the vicarious experience of something pleasurable to come. But researchers from the Netherlands found that for study participants, taking a trip or vacation didn't make them happier. The anticipation did. The bottom line is that even if the reality leaves a lot to be desired, we can enjoy the run-up beforehand.

What's in your anticipation box?

Most of us experienced numerous dopamine peaks during our youth. In adulthood, not so much. There seem to be more valleys than peaks. Novelty, newness, and uncertainty drive them.

Since our earliest history, anticipation helped us survive. In fact, anticipation of the future plays a role in our well-being. Our brains reward us now, in the present, for planning and anticipating positive and desirable events in our future.[11] Notice the word "planning."

Perhaps you read *The Secret* or saw the movie. If you weren't introduced to the Law of Attraction concept there, you've likely run across it in references to making our dreams reality. The idea is that you pin to your vision board images that represent whatever you want to manifest. So, if your bucket list includes exploring the ancient metropolis once known as Constantinople, you pin up photographs of Aya Sofya, Topkapi Palace, Blue Mosque, Süleymaniye Mosque, and the Grand Bazar. Your attention is the great time you're having just as though your desire is manifesting. Presto! Your trip is as good as assured.

Russian occultist Helena Blavatsky, founder of the Theosophical Society and—for a time—a spirit medium, appears to have used the term "Law of Attraction" in print for the first time in 1877 in reference to New Thought philosophy. Unlike magnetism, in which opposite poles attract, the Law of Attraction states that like energy attracts like energy: positive thoughts manifest positive experiences; negative thoughts manifest negative experiences.

In his 1937 bestseller, *Think and Grow Rich*, Napoleon Hill repeated the emotional elixir: believe in yourself and the universe will be at your beck and call. Many self-help luminaries since Hill have proposed that we enlist cosmic laws to deliver to us the lives of our dreams. As they put it, whatever we focus on necessarily grows, so focus on big things. Based on these theories, our homework is merely to use creative visualization and proper focusing to manifest whatever we want more of in our lives. According to the law, if we're destitute—lamenting (focusing on) our destitution—attracts only more poverty, not wealth.

There's an implication in the Law of Attraction that greatly concerns me. Their "when I manifest the little red sports car, the management position, the McMansion, the dreamy spouse, or the island in the sun, I will be happy" fixation can inflict a crushing blow when the universe doesn't deliver. We'll return to this later. Participants in my presentations have shared with me their self-doubt when what worked for the luminaries who tout the Law of Attraction brought nothing into their lives but more stress. They believed the flaw was theirs, not the law. Maybe they didn't believe strongly enough in their ability to manifest their dreams. Or they weren't "doing it right." Or they didn't focus hard enough. To me, the worst part was that these people with good intentions developed the misconception that happiness is "out there," in some distant future. That mindset is antithetical to the advice known since the ancients—live in the present, be here now. Fixing our attention on our desires distances us from our capacity to be content with what is. Love the moment we're in—imperfections and all. Find joy in the small stuff in our present. Discover purpose and meaning as we explore who we are, right where we are.

Regardless of our faith or religious persuasion, we can be sure of this: the universe isn't at our beck and call, much less ready to bend spoons at our will. Thinking about red Lamborghinis won't bring us a red Lamborghini, contends Neil Farber, MD and PhD at Arizona State University. Writing for *Psychology Today*, Farber reminds us that it's easier to think than to do, to wish than to prepare. "Action boards are for achieving. If you don't look at and plan for potential obstacles, you will be unprepared mentally, emotionally, and practically for facing real challenges."[12] Farber and countless psychologists and scientists urge us not to let the pseudoscience of the Law of Attraction distract us from our real work. Our energy is best spent being "realistic optimists" who recognize that happiness is an everyday feeling when we choose to live mindful, meaningful, and purposeful lives.

When things don't go our way, it helps to recognize that not everything we wish for is good for us. We can be sure that in each of our lives there will be outcomes that appear to be negative but which turn out to be blessings in disguise. When the storm has passed, it's our work to find the silver linings in the clouds.

The quote in the introduction "All experience is preceded by mind, led by mind, made by mind"[13] is often misinterpreted and reduced to "We are what we think." The danger inherent in taking this extrapolation to heart is believing that manmade laws of convenience that pander to our desires are more powerful than those of the universe. Buddhist scholars who have paid attention to the abuse of this phrase as a maxim reveal its fallacy. "Our thoughts constitute part of our actions," but not all of them. We are not what we think. Further, what we think can cloud the truth for us of our experiences and mask the wisdom and well-being that already reside in us. Do we need to be mindful of our thoughts? Absolutely. As I've said, our mind tricks us. It lies to us. We flourish when mind, body, and spirit are in congruence and are one in truth.

A workshop participant once asked me if we can be both an optimist and pessimist at the same time. Of course. We can be generally optimistic but face a situation over which we have no control and for which the outcome is likely to be in someone else's favor. Is that view pessimistic, or is it realistic? We can take a view of optimistic realism.

Silver Linings, Revisited

London-born Golden Globe recipient Thomas William Hiddleston chooses to meet each morning as an optimist. "There is a lot of darkness in our world; there is a lot of pain, and you can choose to see that or you can choose to see the joy. If you try to respond positively to the world, you will spend your time better."[14]

Although we've said that, it bears repeating. Meanwhile, let's reap the rewards of anticipation and overall optimism. Have them at the ready in your repertoire, because your role is starring in a happier, healthier life. Leave magic-bullet laws to those who aren't ready to do the real work.

Close the umbrella and look up for the silver linings that are always among the clouds. They may not be instantly apparent, but you won't see them unless you look. And if you don't like the thorns on the roses, clip them.

Practice

The Relaxing Breath

Years ago, I adopted and introduced workshop and seminar partici-pants to physician and integrative medicine expert Andrew Weil's "4-7-8 Breath," also called the "Relaxing Breath," that you can use anywhere and in any position. However, sitting with your back straight is best. Some beginners of this practice feel a little lightheaded at first, but that sensa-tion will pass.

Workshop participants often tell me that inhaling through the nose and exhaling through the mouth feels awkward at first. It requires a little practice. Try this. Gently press the tip of your tongue against the roof of your mouth behind your upper front teeth and keep it there. You'll get the knack of exhaling around your tongue.

To complete one breath cycle,

- ❧ Exhale completely through your mouth, making a puffing or whooshing sound.
- ❧ Close your mouth, keeping your tongue in position. Inhale slow-ly through your nose, pulling air in by using your diaphragm to fill your lungs to the count of four.
- ❧ With lungs full, hold your breath to the count of seven.
- ❧ Open your lips slightly, tongue still in place. Exhale to the count of eight if you can. Push out every last little bit of air using your diaphragm again.

Once you're comfortable with this practice, you can try exhaling with a burst of air with a sound, counting to eight. Release.

Repeat this cycle three more times for a total of four breaths. Once comfortable, you can build up to a total of eight breaths. Feel free to practice these four cycles as often during the day as you wish.

Maintaining the 4:7:8 ratio is more important than the time you stretch out this exercise. If holding your breath that long is difficult, speed up the inhaling and exhaling without changing the ratio.

Exercises

In your journal,

- Do you consider yourself more optimistic or pessimistic?
- Are you optimistic about certain things and pessimistic about others? What are the circumstances?
- Scientists believe that our brains have a built-in optimism bias. Describe a time when you were overly optimistic and would have benefited from being more realistic?
- List at least seven things you feel optimistic about right now.
- List as many things as you wish about which you feel pessimistic. Which of these are out of your direct control?
- List as many things as you wish that have tested your optimism in the past twelve months.
- What do you say to yourself when the chips are down?
- How is your attitude of gratitude related to optimism?
- My aha moment from this insight is

Inspiration

Sometimes when you're in a dark place you think
you've been buried, but you've actually been planted.
—Christine Caine

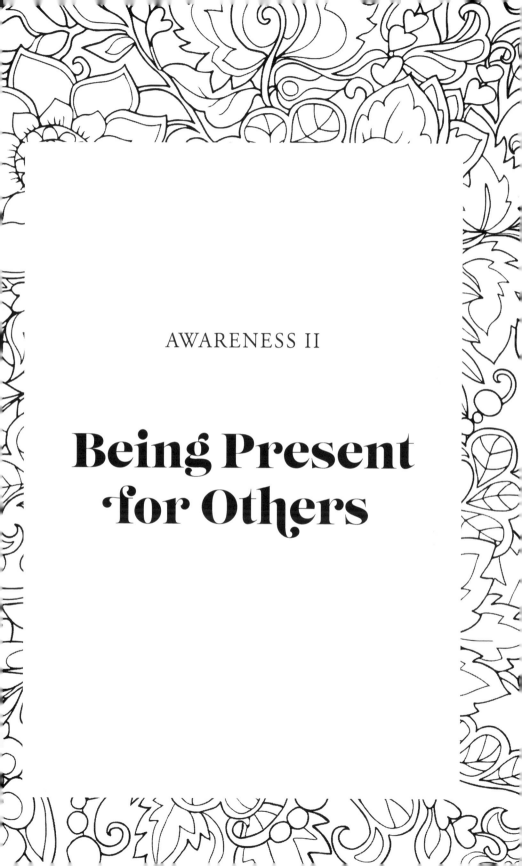

AWARENESS II

Being Present for Others

SEVEN

Align Behaviors with Values

A value is a way of being or believing that we hold most important. Living into our values means that we do more than profess our values, we practice them. We walk our talk, we are clear about what we believe and hold important, and we take care that our intentions, words, thoughts, and behaviors align with those beliefs.
—Brené Brown

Insight 5: Walk My Talk

I align my behaviors with my beliefs to maintain permanent and positive motivation. Feeling confident about my security, survival, and recognition advances my health and harmony.

The He(art) and Science Behind the Insight

We Are More than We Think

Many of us are born doers. Our wants and needs are powerful motivators that get us off our duffs. So does our altruism, even when it isn't convenient. We may volunteer at a shelter because it feels good to help assure that homeless people get a roof over their heads and healthy food in their bellies. Perhaps we mow the back forty before our daughter's garden wedding because her joy melts our heart. When we're driven by positive motivation, we anticipate the benefits, internally (intrinsically) or externally (extrinsically).

Avoiding something distasteful or undesirable can also be a strong motivator. We do one thing to avoid the consequences of doing another thing or of doing nothing. Negative motivation can drive us to finish a progress report to avoid our team's missing a deadline. We may feel that if we pull the right levers or push the right buttons, we'll escape the electrical shock. A negative motivation can also be paralyzing. When the fear of failing is overpowering, or a positive outcome seems hopeless, we might erroneously conclude that it would be less painful to do nothing.

"It is not a question of which type of motivation is more important, but instead, awareness of where we lack the necessary balance to create the ideal catalyst for goal achievement," explains Beata Sounders, specialist in positive psychology, about the relevance of context in motivation.[1]

Perhaps the most powerful motivation for me to change behaviors was the prospect of being a husband and father. Choosing to accept those responsibilities was the most dynamic thing I've ever done. My parents' toxic marriage and the personal trauma I experienced as a child at the hands of both my biological and step fathers, as well as my mother's alcoholism, had warped my perspective of what a family could be. I couldn't imagine the potential for me to be in a truly loving, meaningful relationship. And I developed an almost extreme fear of bringing a child into the world and then not being the parent I would have chosen to raise me. For more than a dozen years, my beautiful, intelligent sweetheart, Melinda, and I did our due diligence, living and growing together, all the while assessing if there really was a future for me as a life partner who could break through the patterns of the early traumas and be all I hoped to be as a husband and father.

It wouldn't be too strong to say that I was scared to death. Alongside the commitment to marriage and then to parenthood, I committed to change my behaviors. Already fit, I kicked habits that could interfere with my optimal health and safety, particularly risky pastimes like rock-climbing and other sports that put me in harm's way. I sold my motorcycle. Staying awake behind the wheel of my vehicle used to be a real challenge that changed the day Makenna was born. When I saw our newborn daughter, every ounce of effort I had invested in becoming worthy of her was rewarded in the tiny treasure entrusted to my care. Over her growing years, I watched in awe as she became a self-actualized, self-efficacious, self-motivated, compassionate, talented individual. My contributions were only to love her unconditionally, protect her, encourage and empower her, and release her to the world. Through mindful awareness, I was able to observe how two of my core values—to cherish and protect life and maintain a positive attitude—drove my motivation and set the course for changing my beliefs and behaviors.

Motivation ebbs and flows. We can experience the gamut. The motivational gravity that turns our tide is different for everyone. Although motivation and energy aren't the same thing, they're closely related. When we're super motivated, energy seems to be there for us. We can focus intently on something we love to do and discover that we've been in the flow for hours and hours.

When our motivation is low and we're in a slow fade, overcoming inertia to just get started feels like a chore. Worse, we can experience burnout, feeling no desire to do things that normally brought us pleasure. Our minds and bodies aren't equipped for twenty-four seven demands. Even short mental shifts in mindfulness can make a big difference in our recovery and restoration.

"What you do with your downtime matters," says social psychologist Heidi Grant Halvorson.[2] It's a common misconception that the counterbalance to burnout is relaxation to feel restored. Surprisingly, we can achieve greater benefits by engaging in an activity that's fulfilling and meaningful to us, not to someone else, but that taps into and allows expression for our values.

For me, as you've read, golf is a mindfulness interlude in nature with friends that not only advances my health but also brings my body, mind, and spirit into harmony. For several hours, the workplace recedes. When the morning game's over, I'm freshly motivated to step back onto the exciting path that my focus on wellness and mindfulness have taken me.

To psychologist Beata Sounders, "finding ways to increase motivation is crucial because it allows us to change behavior, develop competencies, be creative, set goals, grow interests, make plans, develop talents, and boost engagement." Furthermore, motivation is a vital resource "that allows us to adapt, function productively, and maintain well-being in the face of a constantly changing stream of opportunities and threats."[3]

When we lose our motivation, we can lose our momentum. That's a signal to raise our awareness that something's out of balance. We've reached a threshold of sorts and need to check the alignment of our beliefs with our behaviors or actions.

Over the years that I've developed approaches to help myself and others achieve our highest physical and mental fitness potential, I've explored the dynamics of mindful awareness as it applies to all aspects of our lives. It's unassailable that we can't generate enthusiasm for our actions without positive motivation. We just go through the motions. That's not flourishing.

Psychologists have named dozens of components of motivation. This one lists six, that one suggests there are ten. I work with my clients and workshop participants based on three primary and comprehensive motivational factors: security, survival, and recognition.

Security and survival we understand as a very basic motivation, as in Abraham Maslow's hierarchy of needs, that's both intrinsic and extrinsic. Maslow's pyramid progresses from the most basic physiological human needs to sustain life and assure survival. After food and shelter, we require personal safety and security for our survival. These include financial security, health, and well-being.

Beyond listing physiological needs, Maslow's hierarchy describes psychosocial needs and self-actualization. We can sum these up as recognition. We recognize our need for love and belonging, and, ultimately, develop a sense of self-worth that grows into our actualized and highest potential to love others and behave altruistically. We recognize our shared humanity. In the understanding that we do not exist in isolation, we open up to our wisest and most gifted selves to make significant contributions to the well-being of others.

Security is more than just a pseudo-assurance that you're protected from a twenty-first-century saber-tooth tiger. As Deepak Chopra explains, we accrue security by reducing our vulnerability[4]—that is, we don't give away our power by ignoring what's true for us and behaving, instead, as we think we must to fit in.

Go beyond through discovery and exploration. This leads to insight. Your inner vision clears. Understand that life is full of awe and wonder. From this you see a reason to revere your own existence. You have been placed in a world where you can be devoted to something, and your worship gives you a sense of worth.[5]

There is a more subtle but vital recognition that's more difficult to digest—social media and advertising's claims to the contrary. It's "the recognition," Chopra says, "that you are not your body and you're not even your thoughts."[6]

Thoughts alone have no power. We empower them with our preoccupation and focus. Michael Neill, neurolinguistic programming expert, recognizes the need to head thoughts off at the pass before they solidify as beliefs that drive behavior.

"It's not the thoughts that pass through your head that impact your life," contends author and inspirational speaker Omar Itani, "it's the one you take possession of and think about all day long. Once we agree to give our attention to a thought, it becomes more and more real to us over time and has more and more power over our life."[7] But, thoughts don't have to be indelible.

Psychologists such as Jennice Vilhauer, former director of Emory University's Adult Outpatient Psychotherapy Program in the School of Medicine, have long understood the behavioral implications. "We act in ways likely to bring about what we believe is true. That is the very definition of creating your reality," she says.[8] We take back our power when we become aware that some of our behaviors are motivated by beliefs based on flawed perceptions of who we are and what we value.

Values—the Matrix for Motivation and Behaviors

In previous chapters, we devoted considerable energy to uncovering and understanding who we are. That is, our true self, not the identities that we assume to do what has to get done in our lives. We learned that we are not our identities. We see that our thoughts propel our beliefs (or congeal into beliefs), and they are the motivation that kicks us into gear. Let's explore how our motivations are bound up with our values.

When we recognize our true selves, we're seeing through the fog to our most elemental, positive core values and letting them be our motivation—a permanent, not temporary motivation. As we get older, some values can and do change. Those that we drop or replace were likely secondary or tertiary values—perhaps those we adopted or were forced on us—not core values that drive our highest and brightest moments.

After our mental and physical health needs are met, we can extend our gifts to making the world a better—safer, more loving, more just, gentler, kinder, greener—place. Only when we have integrated all the aspects of our true self, when the things that we do spring from the values we hold, when they become the motivation for our rising in the morning, have we achieved harmony and can walk our talk.

Values such as compassion, commitment, courage, integrity, perseverance, discipline, and accountability are broad motivations that can serve as the basis for goals, according to a team of Polish researchers.[9] Other values are service, hope, trust, honor, honesty, and faith in something higher than ourselves. Notice that the values mentioned are the ether that hovers at the highest level of Maslow's pyramid of needs—self-actualization. Self-actualized people live life with meaning and purpose. Austrian neurologist Viktor Frankl had no doubt that human behavior is motivated by their search for a sense of life purpose.

We can see motivation not as a single factor that drives action, but as a chameleon. We would like to think of ourselves as being steady as a rock, but we're dynamic beings who are motivated by different values in different situations. We may apply one value at work and another at home. At work, we may need to take trust with a grain of salt. Yet we may trust our family members implicitly. We may value the service performed by those who offer their time and energy from the heart, yet feel offput by the celebrity who shows up at the shelter for the publicity. We recognize authenticity in others. In ourselves, we feel the congruity between our values and behaviors.

Many of our behaviors aren't conscious decisions played out; they're backstage dialogues beyond our awareness. Despite myriad values that shape a nearly infinite number of motivations for why we do what we do, most all behaviors stem from two primary motivations mentioned above: intrinsic and extrinsic.

Extrinsic motivation is made more powerful by external rewards. The promotion for landing the big contract, for example. Intrinsic motivation is doing something for its inherent satisfaction. The reward is that it's fun, engaging, endorphin-producing, and we feel warm and fuzzy inside. Studies show that those with intrinsic motivation are more likely to succeed at specific goals or tasks. Family—providing for loved ones—is now considered a third motivation. Here's an interesting sidenote: extrinsic and intrinsic motivations can morph into one another, and they're not mutually exclusive.

Professor Mihaly Csikszentmihalyi, who famously coined the psychological state "flow," describes it as an optimal experience in which we engage in a behavior purely for its own sake—an autotelic activity. The motivational factor is the doing; the rewards are in the present, not earmarked for some distant future. Autotelic personalities thrive on immersing themselves in their passions. In *Flow: The Psychology of Optimal Experience*, Csikszentmihalyi deepens the connection between motivation, harmony, and happiness:

Whether we are happy depends on inner harmony, not on the controls we are able to exert over the great forces of the universe. Certainly, we should keep on learning how to master the external environment, because our physical survival may depend on it. But such mastery is not going to add one jot to how good we as individuals feel, or reduce the chaos of the world as we experience it. To do that we must learn to achieve mastery over consciousness itself.

Teaching you how to master consciousness isn't the goal of this book. Rather, our task is to bring to your awareness the fact that you have conscious control over your perceptions of the situations that arise in your life. Living mindfully aware of opportunities and bringing disparate thoughts and beliefs into harmony with our actions are both under our control. We understand that when we focus our attention on our thoughts, those thoughts influence our emotions—how we feel. Our emotions influence how our body responds chemically, which triggers certain behaviors, and those actions shape our reality.

Symphony of Inner and Outer Harmony

Eckhart Tolle, author of *The Power of Now*, feels that "If you get the inside right, the outside will fall in place." Tolle is talking about what he calls the "Deep I"—with a capital "D"—rather than the "surface I." The concept goes back to our sense of identity as distinct from our real self. That's the part of us that is difficult to understand conceptually. All we know "is there is an underlying sense of presence, of being-ness, that is at once still, alert, and vitally alive." At this point, Tolle explains, we become aware of awareness. "When you realize yourself as the 'Deep I,' it enables you to have a compassionate attitude toward everything that makes up the 'surface I'—your physical form, your personal identity (or the historical person), the thoughts and emotions you experience. It gives you an access to true creativity and true intelligence."[10]

How do we get the inside right? No need to eke out an hour's worth of quiet and stillness to focus on being aware of awareness, unless you wish to. I invite my seminar participants to gift themselves a few minutes here and then to step out of thinking, as Tolle puts it, and sense the "Deep I." Becoming mindfully aware of our true self can have a profound effect on our attitudes toward and interpretation of the challenges that sometimes surge tsunami-like into our experiences. It isn't that we suddenly believe everything that happens to us is all right or OK. But wonder of the "Deep I" does bring into perspective the things that happen to the "surface I." Tragedies, illness, loss, grief. They're not small things. They're painful, wounding. Yet, they can't touch or diminish the "Deep I," our spirit, and our core values.

Values are a matrix for the formation of our thoughts, which congeal into beliefs. For many of us, our personal values are deeply rooted in the soil of our upbringing, fertilized by the positive or negative reinforcement that we received from our caregivers and our environment. They become embedded as innate character traits that we know as goodness, honesty, integrity, humility, trustworthiness, and much more, which set a high bar for our judgments about everyday experiences and the choices we're called upon to make. As we grow, our experiences, religious or social laws, education, politics, the arts, and so much more shape and reshape our doctrinal and aesthetic values. They loop around to become common values that shape society, laws, institutions, customs, and just about everything we do individually or collectively. We see them as social norms that may little reflect the virtue of our "Deep I" values, which are non-negotiable. These can neither be forced on us nor taken away.

When our core values are congruent with our identity—our "surface I"—our motivation comes from a place of choice. We act autonomously from our highest potential. We cut the strings that others pull. We're free to set goals and look at experiences as opportunities to fulfill them. But sometimes values conflict, especially among generations. Each of us has a set of taboos established by those around us that define the dos and don'ts of our social, cultural, and work environments.

Beliefs—assumptions or convictions that we hold as true about people, places, or things—give meaning and purpose to our lives, drive motivation and behavior, and attract or repel us. When we act according to our beliefs, we advance our health and harmony and have a powerful, positive effect on those around us because we're living authentically.

Without values, beliefs are rudderless. You've heard them called our moral compass. Together, our beliefs and values undergird the way we see ourselves and others. We recognize that the values we hold sacred may not be shared by someone else. That can be a trigger for conflict. Yet, much of humankind seems to share core principles or commandments that are inviolable. Understanding the correlation between our values and beliefs and how they drive our motivation is a prerequisite to creating a life of balance, harmony, and joy.

Out of Thin Air

Where do our beliefs come from? Do they suddenly appear out of the blue, like cirrus clouds over mountains? Or are they a long time in the making? Scientists tell us we inherit some beliefs. Others we adopt from those who have authority over us or we look up to. Some are remnants of memories about experiences long gone. Even were we a monk on a mountain, our beliefs would fly the flag of our values. We can choose which beliefs to hold or discard. Interestingly, our habits reinforce beliefs as much as the other way around. Research has shown that when someone challenges our beliefs, we're often hard-pressed to defend them, as many have no basis in fact. MIT Sloan School of Management and Harvard University point to the spread of misinformation and fake news and their role in manipulating opinions.[11]

As we're seeing, our beliefs are the bricks and mortar of the stereotypes we form. Biases and prejudices are the mortar that cement them in our thoughts and trigger behavior such as hate crimes. But our beliefs don't have to control us if we are aware and have a clear concept of who we are and who we want to be. In other words, if our values—and moral virtues—are strong, we can rein in deleterious thoughts and empower motivation with those that contribute to our own harmony and well-being.

The three main types of beliefs are synonymous with the three aspects of awareness into which I've divided this book. They are the belief or awareness about ourselves, about others, and about the world and life.

An Attitude of Gratitude

We can tell a lot about a person from the way they externalize their inner attitude. When people stand straight and hold their heads high or place their hands on their hips and frown, we quickly form positive or negative impressions about what's going on inside. But can we trust our perception of reality?

As psychologists and the US Marines who train new recruits know, the bonds are strong between values, beliefs, attitudes, and behavior. Awareness of the mind's power to create reality could defuse potentially explosive behavior and provide critical time to process the unexpected. Lives could depend on it, whether we're strategizing in the trenches or on the boardroom battlefield.

A behavior is our response to what we're feeling, thinking, or have been taught. The challenge is that my behavior can affect your behavior. When we behave in a way that's contradictory to our beliefs, we experience cognitive dissonance. The anxiousness we feel motivates us to change our attitudes and beliefs to conform to our actions. A better way is to develop a positive, permanent behavior by marrying the values held by our "Deep I" to motivations formed of true beliefs, not fictions.

What motivates you? God? Nature? Loved ones? Achievement? Security? Peace? Tranquility? Health? Fitness? Happiness? Seeing the good in yourself and others? Service to a Highest Power? Service to others? What attitude do you adopt as you rise each morning?

For me, the attitude of gratitude brews before my morning tea. As I silently contemplate big and small things that I'm thankful for, the list lengthens. One awareness triggers another—happiness precipitates more happiness. At work and at play, I see my attitude of gratitude rub off on others. Not every day is perfect. I appreciate the hard lessons that also bring my thoughts and beliefs into harmony with my behavior.

Once you've gotten the hang of being in harmony, it's like riding a bicycle. You'll never forget.

Practice

Mindful Walking

Getting out into nature provides the healthiest benefit, but if that's not possible, you can engage in mindful walking in any environment—even stepping out of the office in the city for a while. Wherever you are, include these actions:

- Place your focus on one or more of these three senses: sight, sound, and smell. Gradually increase your awareness to engage in all three together.

- Observe the ground (whatever surface you're walking on while maintaining your safety, whether you're in the city or in nature), plants, birds, animals, water, or sky. Notice the different textures of hard (concrete, steel, glass) and soft (earth, foliage and flowers, bird feathers, fur of your own or others' pets as they walk by). What do you smell? If you're in the city, attune your sense to smell beyond vehicle exhaust. Is there the aroma of bread from the bakery nearby? The garlic and ginger smell of the Thai restaurant? The sweet scent of blooming roses or the distinctive fragrance of freshly cut grass? What do you detect? Is the sky gray? Deep blue? Milky white? Is the sun backlighting the clouds? Is there a rainbow?

- Be aware of each step, its length, speed, how much weight you bring down on each foot. Now, consciously walk naturally, but lightly. How does it feel to walk lightly upon the earth? Is the sensation different than when you hurry, and your feet hit the ground hard in a rush?

- Slow down to the slowest pace possible. Observe your balance. Mindfully roll from your heel to the ball of your foot to your toes. Get in touch with your body's relationship to your environment.

Notice the different muscles being used in your calf as you slow and the surfaces beneath your feet change.

ﾑ Before you end your walk, think about how this walk felt like none before it. Was there any awareness about yourself and your body or the places you walked that was surprising to you?

Exercises

In your journal,

- ❧ List seven of your behaviors that align with your beliefs.

- ❧ Create seven affirmations appropriate to this insight, "Walk My Talk." Here are a few starters: "I'm proud of the person I'm becoming." "I'm truly happy in this moment." "I'm creating the life I want to live." "I leave the past and choose to live in the moment." "I find silver linings in storm clouds." "I'm aware of my thoughts and bring them into harmony with my desire to live in joy."

- ❧ How do you think your friends see you? What adjectives would they use to describe you to someone else if they knew you weren't listening?

- ❧ When you pass a mirror, stop and look into your eyes. Give yourself the gift of a compliment. Offer one of the affirmations you created above.

- ❧ My aha moment from this insight is

Inspiration

Be purposeful in your actions.
Be mindful to keep your behavior in alignment with your goals.
Remember, you can refine, improve, and enhance yourself;
all other control is illusory.
—Steve Maraboli

EIGHT

Seize Optimal Health

To ensure good health: eat lightly,
breathe deeply, live moderately, cultivate cheerfulness,
and maintain an interest in life.
—William Londen

Insight 6:
Accept Responsibility

I am responsible for my lifestyle and self-care.
I will live long and strong by being proactive about
my preventative exams and age-appropriate health screenings,
and I will respond to any signs or symptoms
that are not natural for me.

The He(art) and Science
Behind the Insight

Live, Love, Laugh

. . . and be happy,[1] so the song goes. Children laugh about four hundred times a day, but we adults? Not so much; only about fifteen times a day. That's too bad, because laughter is "the most radical act anyone can commit," says Patch Adams. Scientists agree. "Patch" is really Hunter Doherty Adams, the legendary physician who founded the Gesundheit! Institute and clowned his way to healthier and happier patients, young and old. But the insight that laughter is good medicine came to him the hard way. Suicidal as a young adult, Adams had an epiphany: "You don't kill yourself; you make revolution." His target would eventually become healthcare reform, but at eighteen, Patch first had to reform himself: he committed to being happy, funny, loving, cooperative, creative, and thoughtful. "These six qualities allow me to be an instrument for peace, justice and care for all people and nature." This unorthodox approach to wellness so impressed surgeon Bernie S. Siegel, later author of *Healing Laughter and Miracles* and other books, that he vowed "to carry back Patch's message to my workplace and use his tools in my everyday life."[2]

A quarter century ago and still, Patch believes that there is no separation not only between mind, body, and spirit, but also none between the health of the individual, family, community, and world. Best of all, you don't have to be a kid to benefit from Patch's wellness regimen. I practice it, and I'm committed to weaving his six qualities into my daily life—plus a few more—and introducing them to my clients and workshop participants.

Patch didn't bottle the power of laughter, but the elixir of finding and expressing joy is a magic potion that delivers good medicine to every body and mind, regardless of gender, size, shape, ethnicity, or age. The side effects? None. And it's free. There's also no hocus-pocus or pseudoscience here. Laughter triggers the release of the body's feel-good chemicals called endorphins that can even relieve pain. In the process, laughter decreases stress hormones and strengthens our immune system by increasing infection-fighting antibodies. Neuroscientists and psychologists know that if we want to relax our bodies, we need to relax our minds and vice versa. Giving ourselves permission to wind down with laughs and smiles is an often-overlooked tool in our self-care health kit.

Long ago I decided to stretch my services beyond fitness training because I felt that wellness was more holistic and involved all aspects of ourselves, who we are, not just the physical. We're understanding more and more about how the mind and body are inseparable. What affects one affects the other, and for me, helping others build strong, healthy bodies also means helping them build strong, healthy minds. My first prescription—for those ready to take the leap of faith that health and happiness are theirs for the small fee of being mindfully aware—is to joyfully seize opportunities to laugh through the tears and smile through the sorrow. The second prescription for self- and other-care? Hugs. I dispense them freely and urge you to do the same. The late Leo Buscaglia, professor and author of best-selling books on loving and human relationships, affectionately known as "Dr. Hug," believed that love leads people gently back to themselves. The foundation bearing his name is grounded in a handful of Buscaglia's words to live by: "Only when we give joyfully, without hesitation or thought of gain, can we truly know what love means." Give a hug without expectation.

We've been particularly hug-deprived in recent times. Hugs are addictive, but you can't overdose on them. One ten-second hug is powerful enough to trigger the brain's release of dopamine, which makes us feel good; serotonin, the antidepressant that elevates moods and helps to control anxiety; oxytocin, which reduces stress, helps fight disease, promotes heart health, lowers blood pressure, boosts self-esteem, and can even enhance weight loss. More hugs help advance healing, decrease the negative effects of cortisol, and lift our spirts and affirm our sense of safety and security. When the gas pedal for this vital "fight-or-flight" hormone gets stuck, too much cortisol can lead to high blood pressure, headaches, brain fog, concentration problems, and fatigue.[3]

Health is the soul that animates
all the enjoyments of life.
—Seneca

Early in my career as a fitness trainer, I became aware that health wasn't simply the absence of disease: our thoughts, habits, and ability to cope with stress played an inseparable role in our wellness. Incorporating mindfulness techniques, I began to harness the power of the mind and body connection. A particular client brought this relationship into sharp focus.

An overweight, late-middle-aged man in poor health asked me to be his personal trainer. His goal was to live a healthy and strong life. My cardio-fitness program included resistance and flexibility training. He worked on building strength and endurance and proudly reached the capacity to row vigorously for sixty minutes. I could help him build greater resilience, but I couldn't change the stress of his personal life, which was in shambles. Extreme emotional distress triggered two heart attacks that he would not have survived had it not been for his motivation and tireless efforts to get in better shape. The silver lining? He lived another ten healthy years.

Three days a week for about eighteen years, I served as a personal fitness trainer to a woman in her early forties whom I'll call Sonja. Tragically, Sonja's fiancé died in a plane crash the day before the couple's wedding. When she came to me for help, Sonja was aware that she had put her health on a back burner, and she was ready to change her habits and take responsibility for her self-care. In her early weeks of training, she hated the workouts. Not surprisingly, as I see this all the time, her adrenaline-pumping sessions began to grow on her. If she skipped a workout, she felt something was missing. For her mother's sixtieth birthday, Sonja's daughter granted her one wish from a long bucket list: skydiving. Jumping out of a plane required absolute mindfulness, even more than her attention on body, mind, and spirit states during the rigorous workouts that changed her life. With her skydiving goal accomplished, Sonja set new goals. Today, she is among the happiest, healthiest, self-made, and self-actualized women I've had the privilege to work with.

There's something momentous about sixtieth birthdays. Psychologists have seen it, and when they themselves hit the big 6-0, they feel no differently than the rest of us. How did we get there? Except for feeling we've gained a little wisdom and perspective over the decades, our minds still feel like vibrant, energetic teens, and we're somehow invincible. Is sixty the new forty? Whatever the slogan, I like it. We're living longer, healthier lives, and working longer, too, as we'll see, thanks to awareness of better healthcare practices and the benefits of nutrition and exercise. There's more to it than living longer—there's staying younger longer. It's never too late to start getting fitter than you were yesterday.

For highly motivated, adventuresome people, their "where there's a will, there's a way" drive sometimes has to be tempered with common sense. A few years ago, a good friend gently but firmly said "no" to his mother whose ninety-third birthday request also was to skydive. Mother and son compromised on indoor skydiving. She suited up for her wind-tunnel, mock zero-gravity experience and laughed like a child in pseudo-weightlessness. A year or two prior, at her son's request, she reluctantly gave up cross-country RV vacations and finagling campground hookups like she had for more than half a century. Years had neither aged her mindful awareness of nature's benefits nor sated her desire to deeply immerse herself in memorable experiences that involved many of her senses simultaneously. But for the sake of her well-being, bucket-list expectations needed a bit of adjustment.

What are age-appropriate activities? That depends. Age truly is in the eye of the beholder; add a few clichés about mind over matter—or body. Always appropriate are regular healthcare exams and screenings. Talk with your doctor about a baseline health exam and regular checkups. If you're eligible for Medicare, check its website for details about coverage for physicals and wellness exams.

Happiness is the highest form of health.
—Dalai Lama XIV

Attitude, Attitude, Attitude

John Steinbeck understood that "A sad soul can be just as lethal as a germ." That knowledge charted Patch Adams's entire career course. We can't blame ourselves for laying the groundwork for unhappiness and less-than-desirable health. Longitudinal studies have shown that healthy—or unhealthy—lifestyles can be passed down to children from parents and early caregivers because they are our first teachers. As they think and do, little impressionable minds usually think and do. It takes more than a little maturity, experience, and discernment to learn how to break harmful mental or physical habits introduced to us accidentally or intentionally.

There's a point at which self-care is our responsibility. Self-care is honoring the gift that we are and is not synonymous with being selfish, self-indulgent, or self-centered. Self-care is as smart as upkeep on our homes and maintenance on our vehicles. When we keep our vehicles lubed, oil changed, new tires installed, they keep us safe and serve us well. Neglect a vehicle and see if you can depend on it. Our bodies are no different. Our road wear is the stress of home, work, environment, finances, children, parents, neighbors, politics, and more.

Religions and literature have called our bodies temples, holy and miraculous vessels. At the not very least they carry around our vital organs that keep us going and going and going. Our hearts beat an average of seventy times per minute and pump two thousand gallons of blood every day. The most complex organ of all—a 1.4-kilogram mass of tissue called our brain—is the yet mysterious receiver of electrical impulses from our sensory organs and transmitter of messages. Extraordinarily, it's the cathedral and altar of our hopes, dreams, knowledge, memories, love, hate, fear, courage, reason, interpretations, perceptions, and so much more.

All of the insights in this book recognize, honor, and center on the wisdom of the mind in collaboration with what scientists now call our "second brain," our heart. I find that I can't express enough gratitude for that miraculous organ, my heart. Consider this small act for yourself and, perhaps, incorporating it in your gratitude routine.

Thinking, feeling, and acting from our hearts as a metaphor dates to antiquity, but scientists are finding that heart intelligence is real, wired with forty thousand neurons that have a hotline to the brain. The "little brain in our heart" appears to have cellular memory.[4] Since Christiaan Neethling Barnard's 1967 successful heart transplant, prominent cardiologists began to study the memories, altered personalities, thoughts, behaviors, and tastes of transplant recipients. The decades of research raise the already mystifying and controversial issue: what exactly is our mind and where is it? The mind—bounded by our skulls—was thought to be the center of human consciousness, but we now need to look at the mind and consciousness differently. Georgetown University pharmacologist Candace Pert explains scientists' revelations.

The mind is not just in the brain, but also exists throughout the body. The mind and body communicate with each other through chemicals known as peptides. These peptides are found in the brain as well as in the stomach, in muscles and in all of our major organs. I believe that memory can be accessed anywhere in the peptide/receptor network. For instance, a memory associated with food may be linked to the pancreas or liver and such associations can be transplanted from one person to another.[5]

Cardiocentrism goes back to the ancient Egyptians who believed that the heart was the house of thought and the soul. Aristotle and other Greek philosophers accepted the theory that lingered and even merged with a cerebrocentric physiology. Consider our contemporary language. Many idioms still reflect our cardiocentric notion. Here are just a few examples: hard-hearted, soft-hearted, wearing our heart on our sleeve, follow your heart, broken-hearted, heart-to-heart talk, our heart is set on it.

You've noticed that a recurrent theme in the *Twelve Insights for Mindful Living* is the importance of maintaining a positive attitude. Not a Pollyanna disposition, as we've discussed, but a solid belief that we can and must take responsibility for all our actions and decisions. We're at the helm of the ship that is our mind, even when it's tossed by storms or because our misinformation and misperceptions threaten to run it aground. Plato believed that the body is a "prisoner" of both mind and soul, which still has psychological relevance. Runaway thoughts place us in peril. All the metaphors aside, Deepak Chopra brings home a basic understanding: "Every negative belief weakens the partnership between mind and body." We've seen that a positive attitude gives us the edge in dealing with whatever life brings us. We're not all cut from the same cloth as Patch Adams, but we can all benefit from wholesome, hearty laughter.

Mind Your Ps, Qs, and DNA

Most of us pay no mind—or little—to the biologically complex organisms we are. Sure, we know that our hair and eye color are determined by our genes. Instructions for how we look and how we function are packaged as DNA, short for deoxyribonucleic acid. Those beautiful, twisting, paired strands of DNA molecules are made up of just four different chemical units called nucleotide base pairs. The sequence of these more than three billion base pairs, most of which reside in the nucleus of our very rough estimate of 37.2 trillion cells,[6] forms a mind-boggling code that is our unique genome. Our genome is the blueprint that makes me me and you you. The fact that these trillions of "cells can cooperate for decades, giving rise to a single human body instead of a chaotic war of selfish microbes, is amazing."[7]

Along with genes that determine how tall we are and whether our hair is black or red, we also inherit genes that predispose us to some diseases. Unfortunately, bad things can and do happen to good genes. Our environment, diet, and lifestyle—everything that we put into our bodies and how we treat them—affect our health. Stress, lack of exercise, exposure to chemicals and toxins, smoking, too little or too much sleep, and a high-sugar, low-fiber diet are some of the factors that influence our health. But researchers want us to know the good news: our genes are not our destiny. The results of numerous studies, particularly one published in the *Proceedings of the National Academy of Sciences*, found that patients who changed their diet, walked thirty minutes a day, and practiced mindfulness techniques such as breathing and meditation to manage stress, actually changed their genes.[8]

Our biological complexity is staggering. We grew one hundred billion times larger and six billion times heavier than the single cell—smaller than a grain of salt—that would become us in our mother's womb. Every day since our birth, approximately fifty billion to seventy billion new cells are born, and every minute, three hundred million cells die. We're a constantly renewing wonder. And while we can't be dealt a different deck of chromosomes, we do have the power to upregulate or downregulate at least some of the genes in our hand.

At the dawn of agriculture, around 8000 BC, we numbered five million. Now, imagine we 7.9 billion people on planet Earth each have blood vessels—arteries, veins, and capillaries—that if they were strung out end to end would circle the Earth more than twice for a child and about four times for an adult. No two of us have identical fingerprints or retinas. That's a lot of DNA instruction. The United Nations projects that by 2057—a generation and a half—our world's population will reach ten billion. To thrive, not just survive, we need to learn to cope with new stresses, practice self-care, and discover happiness in leading emotionally and physically healthier lives.

It is health that is the real wealth, and not pieces of gold and silver.
—Mahatma Gandhi

Age Is Just a Number

How does mindfulness fit into self-care? When we marry or partner in a committed relationship, we enter into either a legally binding or emotionally binding contract. We vow to love, protect, honor, respect, and cherish that other person. How many of us are committed to love, protect, honor, respect, and cherish our bodies? Maybe some of us had put self-care high on our list of priorities since we started junior high school or college athletics. Others of us finally hear our bodies' alarm go off and, in a panic, jump into a fitness or wellness training program. Better late than never.

During my time as Senior Olympics racquetball tournament director, I was continually awed by participants such as a one-hundred-four-year-old runner who was more fit than many people half her age. Stories like hers are rare and inspiring.

At one hundred nine, Fauja Singh became the superhero of the true story *Fauja Singh Keeps Going*, by professor Simran Jeet Singh.[9] Born unable to play cricket and run with his friends because of a disability, Fauja, the little boy from Punjab, began the slow process of learning to walk. At eighty-one, he put on his first pair of running shoes. "All my life, people set limitations on me," he revealed in the book's foreword. Encouraging patience, the centenarian reminds us that not only are our bodies different but so, too, "are our experiences with disabilities." Fauja's formula for a long healthy life? He daily challenges himself "to think, exercise, eat healthy, and pray."

Fauja's rubric works for many yogis and Hindu monks, like Swami Sivananda from Varanasi, India, who was interviewed at a sprightly one hundred twenty and showed off his old passport to prove his age. Swami Sivananda's recipe for a long life—yoga, bland food, and no sex—isn't likely to be palatable to many westerners. Thank heavens there are many recipes for optimal wellness, but the basic ingredients are the same: feeding our bodies the highest-quality natural foods we can afford, being proactive about our healthcare, exercising regularly, and listening to our bodies and minds. No one knows us better than we know ourselves.

Like Austin-based healing practitioner Andrea Marz, I invite and coax clients to get in touch with their bodies, "learning to hear the whispers before they turn to shouts," especially learning to listen to our deep, visceral responses to physical and emotional trauma that have the potential to sabotage our health and happiness. Here is mindfulness in practice:

> I believe that everyone experiences trauma in different ways, and that healing is possible. That for me, healing happens when I go into my body. [S]ometimes, I can even ride the wave of destruction. Watching, as the dominos of my existence rupture. I am learning to listen to the nuances that lie beneath the surface of my skin. Sometimes I feel like an expert. Sometimes I feel like that little girl. Either way, I let myself feel loved and cared for in a way that only I can do for myself.[10]

I admit that listening to my body took much mindfulness practice. I had to learn to tune out the noise and become aware of the sound of my body's intelligence, a wisdom that emerges from a cellular level, the unspoken language of body-mind-spirit integration that reaches into the far past and into the far future, but which is rooted—ever so present—in the now.

Why Women Live Longer than Men

It's complicated. You expected I'd say that, didn't you? The fact is girls are more likely to survive to their first birthday than are boys. "This advantage continues throughout life."[11] On average, a woman's lifespan is 8 percent longer than that of a man. But it wasn't always that way.

At the beginning of the 1800s, no country in the world had a population whose life expectancy—a measure of premature death—was longer than forty years. That changed over the next century and a half as healthcare vastly improved in the world's richest countries. Today, in every region of the world—including in underdeveloped nations—people can expect to live more than twice as long as their ancestors. By 2018, life expectancy for the entire US population was 78.7 years.[12] By 2019, the life expectancy in Spain, Switzerland, Italy, and Australia exceeded 83 years. But people of the Central African Republic barely reached 53 years.[13]

While access to healthcare has much to do with longevity, so does better and more equitable distribution of food, particularly quality food. In almost every society, women now outlive men, but the spread in ages is most prevalent in developed countries. Recent statistics show that males in the US have a 60 percent higher mortality rate than females.[14]

Why do women celebrate more birthdays than men? I used to joke that men take a duct tape and Super Glue approach to their health. But, tragically, ignoring early warning signs and symptoms is no joke and too often leads to premature and unnecessary death.

"Paradoxically, while women have lower mortality rates throughout their life, they also often have higher rates of physical illness, more disability days, more doctor visits, and hospital stays than men do. It seems women do not live longer than men only because they age more slowly, but also because they are more robust when they get sick at any age."[15]

Here's what research reveals, including some surprises:

- ✍ Increases in blood pressure occur earlier and at a faster rate in women than in men, according to Susan Cheng, a cardiologist at the Smidt Heart Institute at Cedars-Sinai, who conducted a study on cardiovascular health differences between the sexes.[16]
- ✍ Women go to the doctor more often than men, but in some countries the age spread is wider than in others.[17]
- ✍ Infant and childbirth mortality decreased.
- ✍ Chromosomes and hormones more positively affect longevity in women than they do in men. As men age, the hormone testoster-

one is linked to a decrease in their immune system's ability to fight disease and an increase in the risk of cardiovascular disease.

❧ Males develop more visceral fat surrounding their organs, predictors of cardiovascular disease. Women tend to store subcutaneous fat under the skin.

❧ Smoking is more prevalent among men than women, although the gap has been narrowing.[18] According to the results of neuroimaging studies, smoking seems to activate the reward pathways in men more so than in women, giving rise to increased rates of smoking among men.[19]

❧ Men tend to work at more hazardous jobs, which can make them more susceptible to life-threatening, work-related injuries. While women athletes are more prone to common sports-related injuries,[20] more men are injured in extreme sports.

❧ Medical technology and treatments of infectious diseases have helped increase survival rates for women, including from cancers.

❧ According to a Harvard study, women tend to connect more with each other than do men. They're more candid about revealing personal information, securing support for seeking medical treatments, and socializing in ways that increase their sense of well-being and overall happiness, even if the work or home situations are untenable.

❧ The positive effects of education on long-term memory are more pronounced in women than among men.

❧ A recent complex study on the effects of genetics and aging on our immune systems published in *Nature Communications*[21] found that after the age of sixty-five men lose antibody-producing B cells in their blood, but women don't experience the same loss.

❧ Women are more risk-averse than men. Accidents, risky behavior, suicide, excessive alcohol-related conditions, such as cirrhosis of the liver, tend to increase mortality rates in men more than in women.

In interviewing one hundred twenty-eight people in their eighties for her book *Eightysomethings*, eighty-five-year-old psychologist Katharine Esty confirmed my duct tape and Super Glue theory about men and self-care. Aging women really do tend to put in more effort to stay healthy, while men will still order steak and French fries.[22]

The gap in longevity will continue to widen. The US Census Bureau projects that women's life expectancy will reach 87.3 years by 2060, compared with 83.9 years for men.[23] Our genetic and biological differences can be mitigated by changes in lifestyle. Giving up when confronted with challenges doesn't have to be an option. We can power through our issues, even if the pace is slower. Holding on to health is holding on to great wealth. Infirmity doesn't have to be our destiny. We can help our genes along.

Saying "I Do" and Living Longer

Research on the health benefits of marriage has been hampered by the lack of viable current data, but there is still plenty of evidence to support the tenet that men benefit from long-term relationships more than do women. According to the Census Bureau, 36.5 percent of men self-identified as "single, never married," compared to 30.4 percent of women. Over the years, cohabitation is up and marriage is down. Despite the efforts of the Census Bureau to understand the changing nature of households, questionnaires can't sort out the myriad nuances of who is and isn't in a lasting relationship with whom and the potential of that relationship to increase health and life expectancy of one individual over the other.

As many of us know, a piece of paper doesn't make a marriage, but decades ago, researchers noticed that married men lived longer, healthier lives than unmarried men because there was someone to look after them, urge them to seek preventative healthcare, follow up on issues, and, as we can guess, oftentimes urge healthier alternatives to steak and French fries. Of course, the face of marriage and family has changed dramatically. There isn't quite a pendulum swing, but scientists and statisticians are noticing that never-married men are now living longer and many more are proactive about their self-care and mind-body well-being. Still, despite trendy gyms, Zen-like health spas, and yoga classes scheduled at hours convenient to working adults, the Mars vs. Venus longevity gap is wider now than it was a century ago, according to the National Center for Health Statistics, as reported by *Harvard Health Publishing*. And the statistics about being widowed are sobering, a topic too sweeping to cover here.[24]

No matter your relationship status, you can and need to take responsibility for your self-care. Living long and strong may be a gift of your genes, but only if you treat them with TLC.

Fit as a Fiddle

We're made to move. Counter to our best health interests, many of us are stuck all day behind desks or at stand-in-place jobs. Exercise is our nature and a natural and powerful tool to maintain physical and mental health for people of all ages. My clients and workshop participants hear me say that it's never too late to get in the habit of fitting even thirty minutes of physical activity into each day. Let feeling so much better be your motivation. Do whatever moves you: walking, running, hiking, swimming, water aerobics, cycling, yoga, tennis, workouts at the gym if you're able. If you're sedentary, start slowly. If you have limited mobility from an injury, illness, or disability, there are exercises that keep mind and body in gear. Talk to your doctor about a safe, healthy exercise routine to strengthen whatever parts of you are mobile.

Your doctor may prescribe working with a physical therapist or specialized fitness trainer knowledgeable about exercises appropriate for where you are. Expect days when you want to shuck the routine. Remind yourself that the benefits far outweigh the effort. Here are a handful of benefits: lose those unwanted pounds; manage blood sugar and insulin levels; lower risk of heart diseases; strengthen muscles and even potentially increase bone density; reduce the risk of lung, breast, colon and uterine cancer; restore or put more zing in your sex life; sleep better; feel better. As we've learned, mental health goes hand in hand with physical health. The release of endorphins when we exercise relieves stress and promotes a sense of well-being. But regular exercise does so much more. It enhances memory, decreases depression and anxiety, elevates mood, and triggers changes in the brain that can alleviate symptoms from conditions such as Attention Deficit Hyperactivity Disorder (ADHD) and PTSD. The biggest benefit of exercise has been the focus of this chapter: mindfully and responsibly creating a lifestyle that contributes to a calm, harmonious, longer, higher-quality life.

When Life Doesn't Go as Planned

A debilitating injury, temporary or permanent disability, or serious illness can turn our world upside down. Serious health issues can seem like they burst upon us out of thin air, shattering dreams, plans, daily patterns, and our entire lifestyle. We may feel anger, denial, fear, despair, hopelessness, loss, grief. Sometimes, we feel incapable of coping with the changes in our life brought on by this new situation or diagnosis.

However frozen or numb you may feel, please understand that you're not powerless. You can create effective coping skills. Don't expend valuable energy trying to fake being cheerful and breezy. Studies show that it's healthier to be aware of and accept your true feelings. Pretending everything is normal only adds to stress, increases pain levels, and hinders healing and recovery. It's natural to be fearful or sad. No need to sweep emotions under the rug. Observe them without judgment. Begin—if you haven't already—to incorporate mindfulness techniques into your daily regimen to heighten your awareness of all the people and things that support you. Live authentically, open to loving support. Here are strategies to help you cope with unexpected health issues:

- Learn the facts from your doctor, not from the Internet. Don't assume the worst.
- Listen to your body's whispers. Lovingly thank your body for having served you faithfully for however long it has. Bless the beautiful gift that is your body.
- Acknowledge your emotional tsunami and the waves of feelings that ebb and flow. Ignoring them delays recovery and can actually impede interventional treatments and therapies.

∾ Give yourself permission to be sad or to grieve. However, don't linger in that space long. Let mindful awareness and meditation bring you to calmer states of mind.

∾ Eat nutritious foods that nourish your body, mind, and spirit. Your physician may have recommended a specific diet. Discover ways to make it fun so you're less inclined to crave taboo food and drink.

∾ Maintain optimal fluid levels. Avoid caffeine and alcohol as well as sugary or artificially sweetened colas and soft drinks.

∾ Mindfully center in the moment and find meaning, purpose, and beauty even in the smallest things. Do the things that bring you joy. Be mindful of the things that make life worth living.

∾ Laugh often and unabashedly. Bring happy people into your life that make you laugh. If you love animals and it's safe to be around them, bring their unconditional love and joy into your life.

∾ Exercise your mind and body in safe and appropriate ways. You'll benefit more from your medical treatments when you're physically and emotionally strongest.

∾ Give yourself a chance to receive the best care by being open to the options. Seek second and third opinions as you feel the need.

∾ Adopt an optimistic attitude and a realistic outlook. Set goals for yourself that are achievable and a few that are extra challenging. Nurture yourself when you feel anxiety or fatigue.

∾ Ask for help. Ask for and give long hugs. Enjoy relaxing massages appropriate to your body's needs.

∾ Make a point to surround yourself with a nurturing environment, one that is calming, soothing, tranquil, peaceful, beautiful.

∾ Recognize that loved ones have feelings, too. Anxious about you, they may be going through their own emotional tsunami and may not always be mindful of their words and actions. Forgive them freely. Accept that they may trip and fall and need to get up again to be there for you. Emotional support is a two-way process. Fill your heart with love. Let your spirit soar.

- ❧ Be patient and gentle with yourself. Healing and recovery take time. Visualize the parts of you that are getting better, even if progress is purely emotional.

- ❧ If you're up to it, volunteer at your favorite charity. Join or start a support group if it's nurturing and furthers your growth and development rather than fosters stress and anxiety.

- ❧ Practice relaxation and mindful meditation. If your mind wanders, gently bring your attention back to your breath. Focus on this amazing breath—the breath of life. Every second, minute, hour, day, week, or month is a precious gift.

Our bodies vie for our attention amid the clamor of our noisy lives, repeatedly sending messages that something's not right. If we're not aware of our body intelligence, we may close our mental ears and scuttle away from our intuitions, both of which are foolhardy. Imagine an aircraft maintenance engineer brushing off a pilot's expressed concerns about a mechanical issue and clearing a preflight inspection without performing repairs.

Not many years ago, a thirtysomething father of two young children whom I'll call Jeremy, an employee at a large utility, boasted that he hadn't seen a doctor in years. Jeremy felt fine, and it seemed that his body was quietly functioning as it should. Heart disease has been called a silent killer. That silence can be deadly, warns the Mayo Clinic. Jeremy's progressive employer provided a $500 incentive to get a physical. Thanks to that inducement, Jeremy got a checkup. His doctors discovered Jeremy had a life-threatening heart condition that they treated just in time; and two children didn't lose their father. The concept of employer wellness incentives isn't new, but it's still revolutionary. With or without the fiscal inducement, we each have personal incentives to be proactive about our self-care. The payoff is huge.

Practice

Five Senses Countdown

This practice will help you increase your self-observation and observation of the spaces around you. The intent is to fully engage your five basic senses: touch, sight, hearing, smell, and taste. The beauty of this practice is that awareness of and the deliberate mindful engagement of each sense send messages loaded with information to the brain that enables us to perceive and understand ourselves and our world better and more accurately. It's simple and fun—child's play with a very adult way to continue to increase our brain's elasticity. Ready?

- Look for five things with vivid colors or particularly unique structures in nature or people. Let yourself experience an "Oh, that's an interesting impression."

- Listen for four things that you seldom pay attention to such as the ticking of a clock, the chime of the church bell, the rustle of tree leaves, the gurgle and trickling of running water, the laughter of children. When was the last time you really listened to sounds?

- Touch three things with keen mindfulness of their texture, firmness, warmth, or coldness. You might assess each of these three by the characteristics of how they feel when you have your eyes closed.

- Smell the abundance of different aromas and fragrances; then focus on just two. They can be flowers, lotion, the crisp, fresh-linen smell of clean clothes. Slowly breathe in that scent and give it your mindful attention. How does it make you feel?

- Taste one thing with full awareness. Is it sweet, sour, salty, savory (umami), or bitter? Is it smooth like custard? Crunchy like a chocolate-chip cookie? Meaty and chewy?

Take your time with each of the above. You can do the countdown or observe them individually. But I encourage you to repeat them often. What do you notice about your body and mind during this exercise? Did you forget that your plantar fasciitis had been bothering you? Did you stop breathing shallowly? Did your heart rate slow? For a few moments, did you stop worrying about something at work or about the bills?

Exercises

In your journal,

- ❧ List seven current lifestyle or self-care approaches to wellness that you would like to improve.
- ❧ What do you believe are your responsibilities for your self-care?
- ❧ What health and wellness milestone would you like to see yourself attain in the next thirty days? In six months? In one year?
- ❧ My aha moment from this insight is

Inspiration

Your mind, emotions, and body are instruments,
and the way you align and tune them
determines how well you play life.
—Harbhajan Singh Yogi

NINE

Connect and Feel Courageous

Make a conscious effort to surround yourself with positive, nourishing, and uplifting people, people who believe in you, encourage you to go after your dreams, and applaud your victories.
—Jack Canfield

Insight 7: Offer and Accept a Hand

I connect and surround myself with
like-minded people for support and to be supportive.
I find purpose and joy through helping others.
I take someone's hand every day and caringly
offer a hand to those in need.

The He(art) and Science Behind the Insight

Innocence of Young Children

In the previous chapter, I stated that we're born to move. We're also hard-wired to be helpful without having to be taught. Studies have proven the notion that children are innately selfish is a myth. Why is this chapter opening with commentary about children when this book is clearly for and about adults? Well, it seems many of us have forgotten what it's like to be a child, even those of us who are parents. And while we hear people all the time say, "act like an adult—be more mature," we may have skipped a few pages in the book about living to our highest potential. Children have attributes that many of us have lost, forgotten, or supplanted by situational behaviors that we've come to believe enable us to survive day to day.

Felix Warneken, a developmental psychologist at Harvard University, focuses his research on the cognitive and motivational bases of altruism, cooperation, and cooperation in children from fourteen months to five years. His revelatory conclusion is that "human infants have a biologically based predisposition for altruism. Young children are about as helpful and giving as human beings ever get." A child's willingness to help and be kind is innate.

Young children will even stop playing to help someone pick up things that have been accidentally dropped, or try to create equity where the odds are unfairly stacked in someone else's favor. They're acutely attuned to fairness, and they act or react to situations in helpful or altruistic ways without the motivation of reward—what's in it for me.

But our innocence only lasts so long, finds Maria Plötner of the Max Planck Institute for Evolutionary Anthropology. As early as five, children begin to experience a psychosocial shift researchers call the bystander effect. This is important because being helpful is a key behavior in social cohesion and group cooperation. Psychologists call it prosocial behavior. As we grow and integrate into communities, we learn certain helping behaviors that are not simply woven into the fabric of social norms; they're expected. Some of us had parents who taught us to open doors for older adults or carry their groceries to their car. The proverbial image of the scout helping an elderly woman across the street does seem quaint today, so where has all our empathy gone? Long time passing?

Is There an Empathy Deficit?

The truth is that we haven't necessarily become less empathetic in adulthood.[1] We're simply more discretionary about where we expend our emotional and physical energies. We make different choices based on complex thought processes. Often, we seem to walk about with blinders, our attention is fixed not on views or a friend. Instead, we act like cellphone zombies, dissociated from people and places and unable to respond to natural beauty and wonder or connect civilly to our brothers and sisters on the sidewalk or beach.

What happened to nodding an implied "good day," or the gesture of smiling into the faces of strangers when faces look up and eyes meet? Social psychologists who study the negative effects of technology on our interactions—or lack of them—call this void space an "absence presence." The Catch-22 is that for those of us not absorbed in pseudo-communications—the average Instagram caption length accompanying an image or video has increased to 405 characters, roughly 65-70 words[2]—our cloak of invisibility raises our level of stress and is "deleterious to health." So concludes Stephen L. Carter, professor of law at Yale University and clerk to US Supreme Court Justice Thurgood Marshall.

Decades ago Carter authored *Civility: Manners, Morals, and the Etiquette of Democracy*.[3] Carter defined "civility" well beyond good manners, but "as the sum of the sacrifices we make for the sake of being together." If we expect better from those around us, "a good place to start might be saying hello on the street. If that's too big a change, how about if we all look up from our screens a bit more often and enjoy the view."

When we're hurting or dealing with tough issues, we want to know that someone cares, that we matter to someone who understands what we're going through. We need empathy in times when it's the hardest for others to give it. Now and then, we need someone to see life from our perspective. We may even need to be rescued from economic, political, social, psychological, and physical assaults.[4]

Psychologists John Darley and Bibb Latané first observed the behavior mentioned above in 1964 and labeled it the bystander effect, also known as the "Genovese Syndrome."[5] Darley and Latané learned that bystanders gauge the degree of responsibility they feel to respond based on factors such as whether they feel a person is deserving of help, or if the perpetrator is actually present. Bystanders also evaluate the potential of endangerment to themselves if they intervene or if they believe someone else in the crowd might be more qualified to help. The larger a group of bystanders who are strangers to each other, the less likely is any single individual inclined to help and the more likely is social paralysis to set in. If the group is cohesive, however, members are more apt to intervene in a perceived emergency.

Counterintuitively, people go into rescue mode more often if there are few or no others to intervene. We see this behavior play out time and again on TV newscasts. Sometimes, you see a few brave souls march in to help someone with whom they identify, even in situations where others fear to tread. They're responding to the ways in which we make a decision to get involved. We tend to feel less personal responsibility the larger the group. As many social variables affect how bystanders respond to someone in distress, it's challenging to generalize helpfulness. Bystanders may feel safer recording violent assaults and posting them on social media, which has "a powerful influence on the bystander effect," particularly among adolescents.[6]

"Very young children don't go through this complex reasoning," discovered Harvard psychologist Warneken, whom we introduced above. Often, "they see the situation and just go ahead and do something." Adding years to our experiences and having a greater capacity to assess the cost does change how we perceive and respond to helping others. Psychologists and social media experts are increasingly calling for parents, caregivers, and institutions to encourage us to become like very young children in the sense of behaving in a prosocial nature by becoming helpful "active bystanders."

New studies with results published in the *Journal of Adolescence* show that while we tend to judge adolescents and young adults as smartphone junkies, we may be unfairly generalizing. In fact, many teens responded positively to the warm, fuzzy feeling attached to demonstrating kindness, generosity, and helpfulness toward strangers and those outside their circles. The payoff was that, long term, these young people developed a higher level of self-esteem and a greater sense of well-being. The opportunity? Parents and caretakers, help your kids get involved in volunteer or charitable work to benefit those they may never see again. It also gives them one more building block for developing compassion, empathy, and purpose—a "why" of life.

In chapter 7, I opened my heart and showed you two significant "why" influences in my life: my wife and my now-grown daughter. Let's identify yours.

> Surround yourself with people
> who talk about visions and ideas, not other people.
> —Akin Olokun

We cleave to those who bring meaning and purpose to our lives and feel a sense of responsibility and affection toward them, behaviors and emotions philosopher Friedrich Nietzsche well understood.[7] When we know the "why" of our existence, we can bear almost any "how." Identifying reasons to carry on when life hangs emotionally or physically by a frayed thread brought psychiatrist Viktor Frankl, author of *Man's Search for Meaning*, to an important understanding. The "inner hold" that keeps us from giving up to excruciating physical and emotional pain differs for everyone. A yet-achieved goal, sweetness of our child, closely knit group of friends or family, preservation of treasured memories, bravery and raw courage: these and countless other "whys" dredge up "hows," the strengths to climb out from our dark abyss to meet if not greet another dawn. In that daybreak, we find the reasons life is worth preserving. Perhaps someone has reached out not only their hand, but also their strong arm, grasped us firmly and yanked us from the precipice. Perhaps our rescuer was the sheer will to cling to a value—the belief that all life is precious, including our own.

And when we ourselves are strong enough—and even sometimes when we feel we have nothing left to give—we reach out to grasp not only to that outstretched hand but solidly lock onto the arm and pull hard. An interesting thing occurs at the moment we give when we believed we had nothing to offer. That fight-or-flight response kicks in with its rapid chemical chain of hormonal events: the release of adrenaline and endorphins. In times of crisis and extreme danger, people have mustered the heroic strength and endurance to lift cars, fight off bears, and thwart brutish, armed attackers.

Had we stopped to think before we reacted to help another, a life might not have been saved. Had we not saved ourselves first, another life might have been lost.

Prickles and Goo

Long, long ago, in 1969, in the land of International Business Machines (IBM, nicknamed "Big Blue") and the growing family of mainframe computers, Alan W. Watts lectured as part of a series on the Tao of philosophy to its Systems Group. Watts spawned smiles from the "Big Blue" audience when he proclaimed that there are two personality types: "Prickles" and "Goo." Prickly types act like "intellectual porcupines" and go out into the world surrounded by protective spikes, sharp-focused, and pointed in their vision and goals orientation. That's not all bad. There's virtue in having a precise and clear point of view. Prickly types accuse Goo types of being vague, ill-defined, mystical, romantic, a bit fuzzy around the edges. In reality, life's "neither prickles nor goo exclusively; it's gooey prickles and prickly goo."[8] Which type and sub-sub-type any of us are depends on our quite personal point of view, our unique "magnification" and perspective of the people, places, and things surrounding us.

So, let me share a little parable told in various cultures and modernized over the years. Even if you've already heard it, let a little goo awareness trickle into your prickly side again.

A man pulled into a gas station and asked the attendant, "What are the people like in the next town up ahead?"

The attendant looked him square in the eye. "What were the people like in the town you just came from?"

"They were awful people. Rude, cold, hostile, abrupt and unfriendly. They wouldn't give me the time of day."

"Well," said the attendant, "I'm sorry to say it, but you're going to find exactly the same sort of people in the town up ahead."

A bit later, another driver pulled in from the same direction as the first. "What are the people like in the next town up ahead?" the visitor asked.

"What were the people like in the town you just came from?" asked the attendant.

"Wonderful people," the second man responded. "Friendly, warm, helpful, patient, and kind. They went out of their way to help a stranger."

"Well," said the attendant, "I'm happy to tell you that you're going to find exactly the same kind of people in the next town up ahead."

One traveler saw the world as a friendly place where people were caring and compassionate. The other had a quite different perspective. Moral of story? We often find what we expect to find. Usually, people respond to us as they perceive we respond to them—prickles or goo. In encounters with others, we set the vibes in motion.

Wisdom of the Two Mr. Rogers

When Fred McFeely Rogers died in 2003, the world's moral compass point wavered. From 1968 to 2001, the ordained Presbyterian minister and child development specialist hosted the critically acclaimed *Mister Rogers' Neighborhood*. For those tireless, positive thirty-three years, Mister Rogers bathed millions of children of all ages and many cultures in core human values and showered them with the acknowledgment that each human is a priceless gift. He exuded authentic, unconditional love, compassion, and appreciation for all people, as his words show.

> All of us at some time or other need help. Whether we're giving or receiving help, each one of us has something valuable to bring to this world. If you could only sense how important you are to the lives of those you meet; how important you can be to the people you may never even dream of. There is something of yourself that you leave at every meeting with another person.

Fred Rogers received more than forty honorary degrees, including the Presidential Medal of Freedom. He taught us, our children, and children's children real-world strategies for living purposeful, meaningful lives through empathy and kindness, and he offered counterweights for coping with anger, shame, and fear.

> It's not the honors and the prizes and the fancy outsides of life which ultimately nourish our souls. It's the knowing that we can be trusted, that we never have to fear the truth, that the bedrock of our very being is good stuff.

Standing distinguished in his tuxedo before a worldwide audience at the televised 1997 Emmys, Fred Rogers received the coveted Lifetime Achievement Award. During his acceptance speech, and true to his nature, he asked everyone to take ten seconds of silence and focus on the people who helped us become who we are, who have cared for us and who wanted what was best for us in life. "Whomever you're thinking about, how pleased they must be to know the difference you feel they've made."

Tell them.

A very different character, but a moral compass nonetheless, was William Penn Adair Rogers. In 1928, journalist and satirist H. L. Mencken shared his wonder: "Look at the man [Rogers]. Millions of Americans read his words daily, and those unable to read listen to him over the radio. I consider him the most dangerous writer alive today." So sweeping was Will Rogers's influence.

While Will Rogers wrote that he never met a man he didn't like, the feeling wasn't always mutual, especially among pork barrel politicians and bureaucrats at whom he took smart and truthful jabs. Ben Yagoda, who authored Rogers' biography in 1993, called him "a decent man who knew how to communicate decency masterfully."[9] He's a man after my own heart.

"You never get a second chance to make a good first impression." We repeat Will Rogers's famous quote—one among many familiar to us. One-quarter Cherokee and the youngest of his prosperous rancher father's eight children, Rogers left the family homestead for show business. Before long, his acting career morphed into a position as reporter and, eventually, he settled into the role as a writer who dispensed folksy humor and no-nonsense wisdom at the drop of his cowboy hat.

Those witticisms and truisms about everyday morality and the integrity of working people earned the guest of presidents and foreign dignitaries a reputation as a cowboy philosopher. Sadly, Will and his wife lost the son whom they named Fred Rogers—an interesting coincidence, but no connection to our Mr. Rogers above—when the toddler was just two. The cowboy philosopher formed opinions on everything, including that learning occurs one of two ways: "one by reading; and the other by association with smarter people." Associating with smarter people: that's been my lifelong practice since I was a shoeshine boy whose great fortune was stumbling upon an "executive coach." Our brain and heart are the executive who guides our thinking and action.

He isn't a Rogers, but Abhijit Naskar is one of the young thinkers who has something in common with Fred and Will. The neuroscientist, humanitarian, and best-selling author from Calcutta, India, is an advocate for a gentler humanity. Naskar focused his research on the potential for our self-awareness and self- and other-acceptance to create a path toward a consciousness overflowing with "sweet harmony." The goal: leave no room for prejudice, hate, extremism, and discrimination. His pithy tweets and book excerpts sound like twenty-first century takes on ancient wisdom. Look down on no one and lift others up, he urges. Naskar appeals—as did Abraham Lincoln in his first inaugural address to the nation—to the better angels of our nature. But our brain's divisive and tribalistic tendencies—a self-preservation mechanism—get in the way of our recognition that we are all members of the human race. Naskar admits that "it takes a lot of resolve and ceaseless, civilized self-correction to break free from that tribalism."[10] But we must.

We've learned that self-serving beliefs and behaviors are not the totality of who we are. Scientists have yet to and may never discover the nature of our consciousness and the source of our empathy, compassion, and altruism, and their links to our prosocial, humanitarian behaviors.

We are neither of the two Mr. Rogers nor a neuroscientist bent on rewiring our hearts and minds, but all of us can nurture the better angels of our nature.

Birds of a Feather Do Flock Together

Opposites do attract—if you're a magnet. Relationship researchers have proven otherwise. Yet, the majority of people asked still buy into this false notion that in romantic relationships, there's a magnetism between totally different personalities. I remember hearing "Jack Sprat could eat no fat/ His wife could eat no lean/ But together both/ They licked the platter clean."

The rhyme is early seventeenth-century political satire, but the largely unfounded notion that opposites attract and complementary personalities are the cement of great relationships is still with us hundreds of years later. In the real world of me getting to know you and you getting to know me, we are more likely to hang out together if we've got more in common than less.

The more someone looks and acts like us, the more we're attracted to them and the more trustworthy we believe them to be. Not only are we drawn to like-minded people, but we also tend to create others in our own image if we desire them in our circle. Our bias paints them as appearing like us. Studies also have shown that when someone we trust endorses someone new to us, another's acceptance can be sufficient for us to perceive the newcomer as physically and intellectually similar to us.[11] These findings have far-reaching consequences as we strive to become more inclusive. We misrepresent their outcomes if we use studies on attraction as an excuse to exclude anyone. Our memory is short if we disregard that we are all more alike than not. Why don't we think of our 99.9 percent genetic likeness as a bridge to span the chasm of seeming differences? I'm continually heartened by the array of faces in my audiences because I know that the negative effects of stress, illness, injury, and heartbreak don't discriminate any more than do the positive effects of joy, happiness, health, peace, and contentment. The old saying, "beauty is more than skin deep," recognizes that when we've become seemingly blind to another's substance and character, we may need to close our eyes and open our hearts. We can metaphorically peel the layers of social and religious dress codes and cultural traditions to reveal the values we share. We can apply the Platinum Rule—treat others the way they want to be treated—and see ourselves as members of a global team whose goal is to be good stewards of the earth.

Throughout *Sesame Street's* fifty-year history, there's been a reason why Cookie Monster is blue, Kermit the Frog and Oscar the Grouch are green, Big Bird is . . . well . . . a big, funny-looking character with a big, loving heart. And, Big Bird's big friend is the endearing and species-un-specific Aloysius Snuffleupagus, or Snuffy for short, who loves opera and daily attends rehearsals at the Metropolitan Opera House in New York City. Today's Muppet cast includes Julia, who has autism, and a Black father and son. These "groundbreaking" *Sesame Street* shows, as professor Naomi A. Moland, author of *Can Big Bird Fight Terrorism?* describes them, are carefully created to mirror life. And, increasingly, they do. The ever-expanding ethnically diverse, motley crew shows us ourselves with all our warts and foibles, idiosyncrasies and misconceptions.

Moland's research, which has focused on the influence of media on international education, peace, conflict, and cultural diplomacy, reveals that around the world adults frequently watch *Sesame Street* with the children in their care. The internationally and country-specific show that transcends celebrating human diversity also tackles complex topics, including racial discrimination and fear of HIV positive people, in child-friendly ways.[12]

Sesame Street episodes send the messages that it's more than OK for blue and green monsters to be friends, accepting of each other, and mutually supportive. *Sesame Street*'s Muppets' and human community begs big questions that begin to form in childhood and churn in our brains and control our behaviors as we become adults. In what ways are we alike? What makes us unique? What draws us together? How do we collectively celebrate the many traits, beliefs, and values that we share? How do we become more tolerant? How do we see ourselves in another and open ourselves to being seen? How do we begin dialogues that start with shared visions: to love and protect our families; to give our children the best possible education; to protect the planet's life-giving and life-sustaining natural resources; to establish and protect the right to worship as we please; to participate in our governance; to be free from those who would enslave us? How do we humanize each other? Where do we start? How about with ourselves. Here and now. Becoming mindfully aware.

Let's look beyond what it takes to become global friends and neighbors to see how people choose to relate when it comes to romantic interests. More than two hundred forty studies conducted by social scientists since as early as the 1950s affirm that opposites may attract, but enduring relationships are usually among people whose personalities are cut from the same cloth. Love interests who are intellectuals gather to banter over topics and seek support for their points of view. Nature enthusiasts mostly find soulmates among those with whom they share foot paths. Extroverts tend to band with other extroverts. Oops! Or do they?

That's a tricky question, because the personality-trait labels extrovert and introvert are subjective and open to a broad range between extremes. When does an introvert become an extrovert and vice versa? We're complex beings for whom labels are usually superficial, confining, and situationally appropriate at best.

In her bestseller, *Quiet: The Power of Introverts in a World That Can't Stop Talking*, Susan Cain challenges "the omnipresent belief that the ideal self is gregarious, alpha, and comfortable in the spotlight." The misguided notion is that we can measure introversion by the ruler of this so-called ideal. Cain and others have learned that "introversion is about where your energy comes from and less about how you put it out."[13]

Sometimes you feel like an extrovert. According to exhaustive research, most times you don't. Does that make you an ambivert? Perhaps you're flexible, adaptable, changeable with varied situations, and actually enjoy being a non-conformist. "While extroverts tend to be known as the 'life of the party' and introverts are seen as the 'wallflowers,' ambiverts can be considered 'moderators.' In social settings, they keep the conversation going in such a way that everyone feels comfortable giving equal input. As an ambivert," Cain says, "you might also feel like you have a good grasp of how extroverts and introverts feel, because you've also been in their shoes."

Introverts are happiest exploring their rich inner world of thoughts and feelings, sifting through the debris of life's chaotic events for meaning and flying under the workplace radar. Extroverts are energetically collaborating in an open-space meeting, the team lead quickly scratching out ideas on a whiteboard as members talk over each other. Two major differences between the types? The degree of social stimulation that defines their comfort zone and methods of working. Harvard psychologist Daniel Gilbert describes introverts as "those who change the world instead of tweeting about it."[14]

Where do you fall on the extrovert-introvert spectrum? If you said more "introvert," you're in the company of a long list of historical, scientific, and literary greats. If you responded, "depends," you may be an ambivert.

I have three reasons for bringing up this narrow range of personality types. First, I believe, and many psychologists and social scientists agree, that labels are often dangerous and detrimental. Yes, of course, they help us with identifications and enable us to speak about categories of people, places, and things. But in the context of people, they can be self-limiting and misleading. Second, we are complex body-mind-spirit beings who are never all this or all that all of the time. Now and then we need a sphere of people in which to immerse ourselves and feel alive. At other times, we need a deep forest on a quiet morning to recharge our spiritual batteries. Third, we are who we are. We have no need to pretend we're anyone else. We expend the wrong kind of energy when we kid ourselves and try to be who we are not. That doesn't mean we shouldn't aspire to our fullest potential. All great and successful people have their heroes. From birth, we learn by emulating. Emulate those worthy of you. No need to judge those whose lives and values are different than yours. Simply surround yourself with people who uplift you and bring out the best in you.

Usually, because few of us have taken legitimate personality assessment tests, we're the ones who label ourselves extrovert or introvert. We think we know ourselves best, and we've discussed this in depth. In truth, our self-assessments of personality traits and preferences are colored by perceptions that may be inaccurate. In other words, we may be fooling ourselves. Ever notice that when we look in the mirror the first thing we do is lift our chins a bit and smile at ourselves? We may stand a bit straighter, shoulders back, tummy sucked in.

How did we behave as the speaker at our last presentation? Confident? Projecting? Outgoing? Enjoying the applause? Is that who we are when we step down from the podium? Do we become a different person on stage than off? Are we the leader or follower?

Creatures by default of the Technological or Information Age, we join digital hands around the world out of our deeply seated desire to connect. As we do, we leave behind digital footprints, clear pictures of our personality traits and tastes every time we go on social media. The Stanford digital-footprints study ferrets out nuances of our personalities that—under other circumstances—we consciously or subconsciously keep veiled. Our social selves are often emboldened to express opinions and share information inadvertently. Friends and ads tempt us to flutter from site to site.

Studies show that these digital footprints are more accurate clues about who we are than all our self-reporting or researcher observations in lab settings. When we know we're being studied, we stop behaving naturally and change our responses and behavior, says Michal Kosinski, assistant professor of organizational behavior at Stanford Graduate School of Business.[15]

These digital footprints are as valuable to marketers as the discovery in Tanzania of the largest group of fossilized human footprints is to archaeologists. Social media reveals who among us are the doers, thinkers, leaders, and followers. Although extroverts are more active on social media than introverts, social media tends to level the playing field.

Moods are contagious. Social media is proof. The viral spread of moods can work for or against us. A University of Michigan study on happiness found that extended use of Facebook increased depression rather than enhanced feelings of well-being. This isn't a surprise, as a study by the Pew Research Center released findings in January 2021 that 36 percent of US adults acknowledge that they "regularly" access Facebook for news—more than any other social media platform—even though users question the accuracy of the information presented.[16] As we advocate throughout this book, moderation is a key to living a healthy, happy life. That's also sound advice for social media consumption. We can mindfully benefit from social media by linking with people we know and care about. When we feel like we're emotionally drowning in the stormy sea of negativity and disinformation, we can throw ourselves a life raft—logging off.

"Routine social media use may compensate for diminishing face-to-face social interactions in people's busy lives," states research scientist Mesfin Awoke Bekalu, who conducted a Harvard School of Public Health study on the impact of social media on well-being. As long as we are mindful users, having a strong social network is associated with positive mental health. Bekalu's findings show that for many individuals, social media may provide "a platform that overcomes barriers of distance and time, allowing them to connect and reconnect with others and thereby expand and strengthen their in-person networks and interactions." The negative impact is especially concerning for young people who are at "increased risk of depression and anxiety symptoms," Bekalu says.[17]

Every time I'm electronically face-to-face with a friend or colleague on the other side of the earth, I'm awed that the best of technology has been placed in the service of our and our planet's well-being. This is definitely true in the healthcare industry, where robust interconnectivity, operating at breakneck speeds, can make the difference between life and death. The Internet of Things (IoT) devices are changing how we monitor our health. Devices transmit body data to our physicians, hear our bodies' subtle whisperings that we might be missing, and detect when our bodies haven't sounded the alarm but should. In fact, IoT has revolutionized medical treatment.

The beauty of social media is that, sometimes, we *can* go home again. Social media can be a roadmap that takes us back to people lost to us for years or decades. Along the way, we remember encounters with people who in some way influenced us. A gas station where we can refuel. A cafe where we breakfast on croissants. A sofa on which we comfortably share our compassion, empathy, and love. A workplace lunchroom where we're mindful not to contribute to the spread of misunderstanding and misinformation. A brain-like neural pathway to everywhere on which we tread lightly, mindful where and how we leave digital footprints, mindful that we don't walk it alone. Mindful to choose our path mates wisely.

As birds of a feather, we gravitate toward becoming one with the expanding flock, the murmuration of us who migrate with strong instincts toward home. Author Bernd Heinrich calls the homing instinct a "deep-in-the-bones pull toward a particular place." And it fits us as it does birds. The difference is that, for us, that place exists as a fantasy in our minds. It stems from our deeply rooted need to find resonance with the earth and its inhabitants that we perceive but are challenged to access. No doubt the magnetism we talk about is really a subconscious pull on the thinning human thread of our connection in a disconnected time.

For those of us whose nature it is to extend our hands, we should be able to do so fearlessly and without hesitation. Sometimes, there is no time to think before acting, especially when a life is at stake. We're not automatons. Our mindfulness can help us sort out needed information to override the bystander effect. Remember, we're hardwired to make sacrifices for others. Psychologists, philosophers, and scientists have helped us to understand that giving a metaphorical hand adds purpose and meaning to our lives.

Abigail Marsh is one of the world's leading researchers in what she calls "extraordinary altruists." Marsh assembled altruists—in this case, those who had donated kidneys to strangers—at her laboratory at Georgetown University. After psychological testing and brain imagery, the donors' profiles appeared pretty much the same as those of the non-donors. With one not-so-small exception. Donors' amygdalae—our "emotional radar," an almond-shaped cluster of nerves in the brain—was larger in those whose behaviors and beliefs categorized them as altruists. Marsh's research revealed that the altruists with large amygdalae were "supersensitive to fear or distress in another's face."[18]

I suspect that Marsh's study partially explains why there are some individuals in a crowd who extend a hand regardless of the rest of the group's bystander effect. I say thank heavens for those large amygdalae!

Practice

Progressive Muscle Relaxation

The more we're under stress, the more we tense our muscles. We're prepared for flight or fight. Increased tension becomes a self-fulfilling prophecy. Progressive muscle relaxation not only helps us relax muscles and reduce the harmful effects of stress. It also brings our awareness to parts of our body that are responding to stress, such as our neck, shoulders, back, legs, and feet. Progressive muscle relaxation also helps to calm our reactions to stress, such as rapid breathing, or too shallow breathing, rapid heartbeat, stomach distress, even nausea, and headache.

Allow yourself twenty minutes for this practice that I believe you'll love to use whenever the opportunity to reduce stress permits. In the beginning, choose a quiet place where you can lie down undisturbed. Eventually, you'll be able to do all or part of this practice sitting up at your workplace or wherever lying down isn't possible.

- Relax your entire body mindfully. Let yourself feel limp. Take a few slow, deep breaths. Imagine tension flowing out with each breath.

- Inhale and curl your toes, contracting the muscles of your feet. Hold that contraction briefly, then fully relax your feet as you exhale while continuing to imagine tension flowing out with your breath. Take more time to exhale slowly and relax the muscles in your feet than you took to inhale and contract them. Be aware of the sensations of contracting and relaxing the muscles. Repeat two or three times.

- Repeat this with each muscle group individually up your body. Contract the muscles of your lower legs, upper legs, buttocks, and abdomen, chest, back, shoulders, arms, and hands. For this practice, keep your attention below your collar bones so that you protect your jaw and teeth. Isolating each muscle group helps to get in the moment. If any muscle group seems particularly tense, repeat the contraction and relaxation in that area.

- Lie still for five minutes. Be aware of the experience of feeling truly relaxed in contrast to tensed. Continue to breathe slowly and deeply—full inhalations and exhalations. Feel tension flow out and away and relaxation become deeper and deeper with each breath. If you doze off, don't worry. Your body is telling you that you need more sleep.

- Count backwards from four to one when you're ready to get up. You may feel groggy at first. In a few minutes you'll feel awake and refreshed.

Practiced regularly, this exercise not only relaxes you, but it also trains your body to become aware of and mindfully reduce muscle tension. Use this technique daily, along with other stress-reduction techniques in these chapters. Quietly incorporate a mini-relaxation session on your neck and shoulders at your desk, at home, or at work.

Exercises

In your journal,

- ❧ List seven living people you would like to spend more time with. What attributes attract you to those people?
- ❧ List three historical figures or heroes you most admire. What attributes did these people have that you admire?
- ❧ My aha moment from this insight is

Inspiration

Give your hands to serve and your hearts to love.
—Mother Teresa

TEN

Let Go and Hold On

With everything that has happened to you,
you can either feel sorry for yourself or treat
what has happened as a gift. Everything is either
an opportunity to grow or an obstacle to
keep you from growing. You get to choose.
—Wayne Dyer

Insight 8:
Forgive and Release

I forgive myself and anyone who may have harmed me
or discouraged my self-esteem and personal potential.
I release into the past all shame and regret and only
bring into my future the insights they offered.

The He(art) and Science
Behind the Insight

Forgive Me

They may be the toughest two words we can say to someone. Yet, we have control over when we say them, to whom we say them, and how sincere we are when we do say them. When we genuinely seek forgiveness to repair damage we've done, we're taking responsibility for hurting someone. We feel at the mercy of another's absolution, not knowing if we'll receive it. The more insecure we are, the more we're likely to be in denial and avoid a confrontation that acknowledges our role in a broken personal or professional relationship, and the more likely we are to push blame for the damage onto someone or something else. We may be afraid to wake up, smell the coffee, and recognize our failure.

To me, there is a difference between apologizing to someone and asking for forgiveness. Saying I'm sorry—film titles aside—is important, but sometimes it's not enough. "I'm sorry I broke your favorite tea mug" isn't in the same league with "Forgive me for making you feel so unloved and unappreciated. I didn't mean to be so insensitive to your needs." We say to others all the time, "I accept your apology." We may hear "I truly forgive you" only once or twice in our lifetime.

There is no antidote to the discomfort we feel before attempting to rebuild a bridge. The best way to shore ourselves up is to take a deep breath, let humility flood in, and be aware and empathetic of another's pain. You may find it helpful to first write your forgiveness request so you can include the things that are important to say, being mindful of the tone of honesty and contriteness. Have no expectations about how your request will be received. Unless their faith requires it, the recipient is under no obligation to forgive you. And some acts are difficult to forgive. If that person refuses, be gentle. No need to say "I understand." Chances are you don't. Be mindful not to pour salt on a wound that is obviously in need of healing. You can acknowledge that you hoped the person would see that you're sincere and that wronging the person is painful to you. Demonstrate your trustworthiness and desire to never repeat the behavior. Then let it go. You did your best.

Forgive Others

For many of us, forgiving may be harder than asking for forgiveness. It isn't called a paradox for no reason. Modern-day "forgiveness trailblazer" Robert Enright staked his life's research on understanding the when, why, and how of forgiveness from a purely secular point of view. In 1994, the psychologist and professor of educational psychology at the University of Wisconsin-Madison, created the International Forgiveness Institute. Just as I've trained athletes and individuals who care about their physical health, Enright has been teaching "workouts" around the world to strengthen our forgiving heart muscle and make it "forgivingly fit."[1] Where to start? Slowly. First, commit to do no harm so we don't have to ask for forgiveness in the first place.

Saying "forgive me" is a huge step toward restoration of a relationship in which that potential exists. But what happens when we're on the other side of that request? Giving "absolution" to another is powerful medicine for us and them. Sometimes we need to jump through a lot of mental hoops before we can do that. The words don't just roll off our tongue. We become a not-so-impartial judge, jury, and victim witness. It may be natural to feel that the person doesn't deserve our forgiveness. How do we gather the strength to forgive those who have inflicted great pain and suffering, who are perpetrators against the integrity of ourselves, as we've seen survivor families of victims do? What can we learn from the victims' families of horrific mass violence? How do we find it in our hearts to acknowledge there is a greater judge than we?

After loving, I believe that forgiving is the second most important action insight in this book. Forgiveness recognizes the human frailty in all of us. The other keys to a mindful life lived to our fullest potential are loving ourselves and others and taking care of our bodies, minds, and spirits.

Bitterness and hatred cost us well-being. They tax our system with stress and wreak havoc on our health. Studies show that when forgiveness comes from our heart, we reap both physiological and psychological rewards. Forgiveness doesn't whitewash someone's guilt or condone an unthinkable act. We may forgive a lover, a friend, a family member, or a stranger. And the act of our forgiving doesn't mean we've chosen to continue a previous relationship where one once existed. We may even choose to sever ties with someone we've just forgiven. We have no need for that person in our lives once we have freed ourselves from the burden we carried.

Sometimes the emotional pain is so intense that forgiveness feels impossible. We may choose not to forgive. Enright makes clear that sometimes the aftermath of hard blows is a continual reminder of the initial hurt—physical or emotional, or both. His studies revealed a surprising phenomenon. Sometimes, those of us who are injured, whether we call ourselves victims or not, begin to shift "other" blame to self-blame and criticism. We wonder about our own failures and wrongdoings that might have triggered or exacerbated the original injustice. An event's trauma can permeate our lives and shroud the reasons worth living. Enright discovered—as did ancient philosophers—that forgiveness can give us back our lives. "Forgiveness works because it can reverse all the lies you might believe about yourself. You are not defeated by others' unjust actions." Studies show that "forgiveness can heal you and allow you to move on in life with great meaning and purpose."[2] Enright's work demonstrated cardiac patients benefited from the act of forgiving.

Forgive Yourself

What's the point? Isn't that just self-talk? Yes and no. That depends on its heart-centeredness and motivation. Remember that our self-talk becomes belief and false beliefs can lead to inappropriate and harmful behaviors. Emotional wounds aren't always inflicted by others. Self-forgiveness can reverse what Enright calls the big lie about oneself and rescue sinking self-esteem. Forgiving oneself can restore respect and self-appreciation. In regaining our sense of intrinsic value, we see others as ourselves—people who also have the right to be themselves, individuals worthy of achieving their highest potential.

Let's be clear. Offering forgiveness involves more than simply telling someone or yourself that they're forgiven. True forgiveness in its hugest, most sweeping sense is about bringing goodness and charity—which we know as love or the ancient Greek term "agape" in the form of mercy—

to a hard and hurtful event. As you've experienced, forgiveness doesn't happen at the snap of our fingers. It takes time to be able to separate the things people are capable of doing, which we can condemn, from their humanity—however hidden it may be. This difficult concept recognizes that all of us started life as a dividing cell. We may develop scientific theories about what went wrong and when that triggered the capability to commit horrific crimes. That's out of our purview. What is our task is to free ourselves from self-destructive thoughts, feelings, and behaviors that perpetuate ill health and distance us from our goal of well-being.

> If you must look back, do so forgivingly.
> If you must look forward, do so prayerfully.
> However, the wisest thing you can do
> is be present in the present . . . gratefully.
> —Maya Angelou

Beyond Forgetting

I didn't title this insight "forgive and forget" for very good reasons. The injunction to forget may sound biblical, but it isn't. As I became more adept at practicing mindfulness, I reviewed my early automatic responses to childhood trauma and questioned the effectiveness—at least for me— of this weathered maxim. I had forgiven, certainly and fully. But I hadn't forgotten. I think few of us are capable of forgetting the exceedingly painful events in our lives and, certainly, the God of scripture didn't ask that of us. Neither do psychologists.

My focus to achieve true mind-body-spirit healing and wellness was sharpened by the experiences, comments, and questions of my workshop and lecture participants. I shared with them what had been true for me. A healthier practice was "forgive and release." A strange and wonderful thing happens when we practice magnanimity of spirit and forgive, then release. In time, even sooner than we imagine, we begin to let "it" go. We stop dwelling on the transgressions. As we cease revisiting them and embedding them in our psyche as a representation of who we are, they begin to fade from awareness.

While we can intentionally push transgressions from active memory, this is seldom effective. More beneficial is to take control and not ruminate on them. We can change the channel or stop the spontaneous replays as they pop onto our screen of awareness. That's where mindfulness can provide relief. Without judgment, we can acknowledge a painful memory and re-focus our attention on something or someone else that brings us peace, joy, or happiness. We call these distractions. We do this successfully with our children. We redirect their energies. In chapter 12, we'll explore healthy distractions. One client describes how she acknowledges the ugly view out the window to her past, then closes the curtains patterned with butterflies that make her smile. We call that a positive distraction, and we'll explore those further in Insight 10.

Does that sound easier said than done? What happens when an old transgression triggers a fresh episode of anger? First, leave judgment at the portal of mindfulness. It's normal to feel angry. But it's difficult to impossible to feel anger and forgiveness simultaneously. Shifting our thoughts to forgiveness is a healthy digression. Another technique is to head off the anger enemy at the pass. When we're angry, we experience warning signs that our senses detect. Our heart rate increases, we breathe faster, our blood pressure spikes, our body tenses up. Simultaneously, anger triggers our body's release of the stress hormones adrenaline, noradrenaline, and cortisol.

When we're angry—either as a primary response or a secondary response to feelings like sadness or loneliness—we tend not to think or behave logically or beneficially to our health and well-being. Our emotions may spiral out of control. We see that in the life-and-death consequences of road rage. But we can acknowledge the anger and take control over it. When possible, distancing ourselves from the triggering event or the person who is out of control may be the best action. If we can't put time and space between us and the event, we can apply mindful awareness to harness helpful and healthy distractions to defuse the event's negative energy or effect. We can focus on solutions rather than on the problem. For our own safety, we need to assess whether this is the right time to intervene if someone is threatening violence to another person or property. Call for help if there is clear and present danger.

Self-Empowering Thoughts and Actions

When we're the ones experiencing anger, the severity of that emotion may or may not be warranted. Sometimes we feel like victims of an injustice or harm because we are. We can experience many forms of trauma from so many sources. Military combat. Natural disasters. Physical assault. Sexual assault. Child abuse. Transportation accidents. Torture. Ponzi schemes. Addiction. The clinical names for how we respond to these events on the short term and long term are Acute Distress Disorder and Post Traumatic Stress Disorder, which we know as PTSD. PTSD can result from myriad types of trauma. But not every victim of trauma develops PTSD. Three percent of people in the United States have been clinically diagnosed with PTSD.

Others may develop anxiety or mood disorders, or experience mild or severe depression, or a host of other symptoms that diminish our opportunity to experience well-being and optimal health. Counseling may be appropriate for many people, while others may benefit from learning techniques such as self-awareness, self-empowerment, and cognitive behavioral therapy (CBT) to change negative thinking and bring themselves into states of wholeness and happiness. As we've seen, forgiving has the potential to help many of us move on and retell our story not as a survivor but as a thriver. Forgiving snips the strings that make puppets of us through our victim stories.

Viennese neurologist and psychiatrist Viktor Frankl—whom we introduced earlier—had been sent to Theresienstadt concentration camp, where one in four people died or were murdered, including many members of his own family. In camp, Frankl recognized that "those who didn't lose their sense of purpose and meaning in life were able to survive much longer than those who had lost their way." Frankl's insight birthed his desire to study happiness and its relationship to self-control, self-awareness, and self-empowerment. He learned that "everything can be taken from a man but one thing: the last of human freedoms—to choose one's attitude in any given set of circumstances, to choose one's own way."[3]

The Ever-Present Past

The past embroidered the letter jackets of our blazing youth; the jackets' identity patches symbolized who we thought we were. Over time, for those of us who wore them, our letterman jackets, varsity sweaters, and team jerseys affirmed we were part of something bigger than ourselves—a group working together toward a common goal. Regardless of our gender, our shared identity transcended background, social class, age, and race. For a time, we had each other's backs. Some of us look back nostalgically at those moments of connection, along with the real or imagined memories associated with them. Our discolored and frayed garments and beliefs were twisted into the thread of continuity pulled from yesterday to today and into tomorrow.

The past is never gone and forgotten. Unless we have amnesia, it lives vividly at the cellular level in our remembered joys, laughter, trauma, and pain. Felipe de Brigard, Duke University professor of psychology and neuroscience, researches how memory and imagination intertwine. Since "you have to carry your past with you,"[4] if every time an old hurt resurfaced the pain was as intense as the original experience, we'd be walking zombies. Miraculously, our minds and bodies developed a coping mechanism known as fading affect bias. Memories of negative emotions fade more quickly than our recollections of positive experiences.

Wait a minute, you say. What about the severely traumatic experiences that haunt some of our memories, particularly the memories of those who have been diagnosed with PTSD? Studies show that our tendency toward what they call "retrieval-induced forgetting" means we more often than not resurrect positive memories. That's a natural self-preservation adaptation. Our perspective of painful remembrances passes through a filter researchers call our current lens.

Memory isn't a part of our mental makeup to help us keep from losing the car keys. Scientists tell us that our autobiographical memories perform an important function: mood repair—lifting us up. All of these adaptations intertwine to "create a coherent identity and a favorable sense of self over time." They also "regulate emotion in the present and enhance optimism about the future."[5] To imagine the future, "we have to look to the past," says Daniel Schacter, professor of psychology at Harvard University. The author of *The Seven Sins of Memory: How the Mind Forgets and Remembers*, Schacter believes that we fish in the pond of memories to hook validation of our motivation and resilience. In so doing, we foster hope for the future and the prospects of happiness.

Researchers Terence R. Mitchell and Leigh Thompson call our propensity to look at the past through rose-colored glasses "rosy retrospection."[6] We do that when the events that registered as happier carry more memory weight than those events we'd sooner forget but can't. For example, I'll never forget the trauma of my childhood. But my current filter gives me a rosier retrospection because I choose to see the hardest, most hurtful times as learning moments. They were the motivational spark to become someone my parents were not and to optimistically craft a successful future in which I not only looked for the silver linings frequently mentioned here but found them.

Rather than live in the past or dwell on old hurts, we can transform the past into a loom for weaving a happier present and future. We can intersect our lifelong warp yarn with a resilient weft. With that sturdy foundation, we can weave a magic carpet that transports us from birth to death. The bumps and lumps of life are still there, but we float over them with less struggle and pain. The motif of our magic carpet tells our story and depicts our memories, our history.

We so crave a history, "a cohesive narrative of our own existence,"[7] that we will subconsciously invent stories to fill in gaps and create an album to show us who we are. Psychologist Kimberley Wade, who researches memory and the law at the University of Warwick, explains that memories force us to face up to their presence as fact or fiction. Every time a thought comes to mind, we have to ask ourselves questions. "Have we experienced it [an event], imagined it, or have we talked about it with other people?"[8] Most often, we get the answer right.

The emotion attached to a memory has a lot to do with how embedded it will become. Julia Shaw of University College, London, discovered that study participants could be made to believe a false memory of committing a crime in their youth. The startling implications of memory distortion are that other people, "even strangers, can re-write our history." Others can elicit from us shame and guilt for fictional actions. As we now know, "the events, emotions, and experiences we remember from our early years can help to shape who we are as adults, determining our likes, dislikes, fears, and even our behavior."

This information is a clarion call for creating a future now, in the present. We don't need to stop being nostalgic for the rosy retrospection happenings of yesterday. We do need to start today to inject into each present moment those things that we'll consider memorable in our future. How? We turn on our awareness. I try not to turn mine off. I think of awareness more like a light dimmer, a rheostat that I can adjust at will: I can choose varying intensities of illumination. Amp up the power to see, hear, feel, touch, taste. Highlight small events in big ways. For example, I know people who don't celebrate birthdays, saying that "they're just like any other day." No, they're not. Birthdays mark the most momentous day of your life! Do something to celebrate the gift of life. Plant a tree on the lower forty. Teach a daughter or grandson to flyfish. Meditate on a walk while focusing on life-sustaining breath. When we let life's rough gems—the unrecognized treasures that come to us all—slip by uncut, we miss the sparkling brilliance that is their potential.

That's a Shame

Our story evolves until we close our eyes for the last time. Whenever we return to a page we've already written, we revisit as a very different person than when we wrote it. We're beginning to understand why science calls us unreliable narrators of our life's story. We may think of amendments or clarifications to our recollections. New information or an intervening event may change our interpretation of a past occurrence. How can we test the validity of a memory? Look and ask for proof and verification from photographs, videos, scrapbooks, and adults whose stories we can compare with our own. Ironically, "fuzzy fragments" can be more reliable than the vivid movie-reel recollections.

Please don't discard the warm, soothing memories in your collection just because you suspect that they might be the product of that late-night sorbet and old home movies. The brain's precious tall tales and shared experiences—embellished or enhanced—are invaluable. They can act like a "social glue," says Brock Kirwan of Brigham Young University in Provo, Utah. As we implied with the letterman jackets, sweaters, and jerseys, shared experiences and stories cement group identity and create cohesion.

Mindfully conduct the orchestra of your reminiscences, but listen to the musicians' improv. Harmonize mind, body, and spirit by choosing to listen to a new symphony of your own composition.

If our interpretation of the past isn't congruent with reality, we could be holding on to shame and guilt needlessly. As a child, I could easily have slipped into carrying around both emotions: guilt over being a burden to my stepfather and family, and shame over having a family that I perceived was different from that of my friends. Neither held me back. At ten, I was fortunate to have had an adult take an interest in me and become the first of many mentors. That interest affected my self-esteem and helped me develop a healthy self-worth.

Shame and guilt aren't the same. Shame is bad for your health. That's a primary concern for Annette Kämmerer, a psychologist and professor emerita at the Institute of Psychology at Heidelberg University in Germany. People who feel shame are at a higher risk for depression and anxiety disorders.[9] It swoops over us when we're at our most vulnerable and can send us into a downward spiral of low self-esteem and loss of self-worth.

This powerful, toxic emotion can get in the way of our healing from trauma. We feel embarrassed, even humiliated. We feel deeply flawed. The chasm between who we think we are and who we wish we were widens. The self-perpetuating, debilitating, and isolating nature of this emotion can keep you cornered in a dark place. Turn on the light of self-compassion, kindness, forgiveness of self and others, and love. Seek help and practice calming techniques and healthy distractions like those presented in Insight 10.

Guilt—as contrasted to shame—arises from our reflection on and evaluation of a personal or social inappropriate behavior. We feel bad that we hurt someone, but our faux pas doesn't shatter our self-esteem, self-worth, or intrinsic value. The focus is on the act, not us. Guilt can be a strong motivation for change.

Change of Heart

In *Change Your Thoughts, Change Your Life: Living the Wisdom of the Tao*, Wayne Dyer offers strategies for self-empowerment and breaking the stranglehold of our past's painful emotions. Forgiveness is always on the list. Another is how to use our awareness to detect when something triggers a toxic emotion. At that point, simply acknowledge the emotion without attaching meaning to it or focusing attention on it. Breathe. Release. Let it slip away.

There are many good reasons to release hurts rather than forget them. We've touched on this earlier, but it's worth remembering. If we're open to the lessons, the past has something to teach us, and some of those lessons can literally keep us alive. Journaling is a good and safe way to acknowledge feelings and what triggered them. Write them down, then turn the page.

We've heard the cliché, "let anger fester, and it eats us up." Practice forgiveness for your health, just as you exercise and eat balanced, nutritious meals. Forgive others for perceived and real transgressions. Forgive yourself. When you're having trouble forgiving, remember this, says psychologist Kurt Smith, "Forgiveness is not a justice issue; it's a heart issue."[10]

Moving on may mean there is no reconciliation between us and the transgressor. Perhaps the only connection was our being affected by the transgressor's actions. We forgive and go on our way. The opposite can also be true. We've probably all experienced how forgiving someone close to us can deepen our relationship. The person who needs our forgiveness becomes aware that we've drawn a line in the sand. We haven't glossed over the hurt. Rather, we've been forthright about it and offered reconciliation, along with the understanding that the behavior isn't repeated. We expect better. By forgiving, we raise the bar.

I've learned from personal experience that when our wounds are fresh, our trauma unspeakable, our point of view arises from the root of pain. Forgiveness may not culminate in a single moment but gradually pave an undulating, though fresh, path on a journey of liberation and the discovery of new meaning, purpose, and joy. We've heard "to forgive is divine." As we mentioned earlier, while there is no civil imperative to forgive, for many of us, our faith commands it. Forgiveness is a choice—a messy one when those we consider forgiving are often those who have no intention of making things right. Once we step over the threshold of offering or receiving forgiveness, there's no going back. We are changed. And change is never easy.

"The weak can never forgive. Forgiveness is the attribute of the strong," said Mahatma Gandhi. You have the strength to forgive and release. Let go of resentments. Do not permit hurtful memories to become thorns that continue to burrow into your side. Let the healing begin.

Practice

Sound Meditation

Sound's healing power has been known to the world's earliest peoples. Its evolutionary sophistication over the millennia has brought us both timeless music to soothe our souls and a resurgence of interest in ancient "sound baths." Many studies on the physical and mental-health benefits of sound have been conducted over recent decades. University of California researchers were particularly interested in the benefits of sound meditation using Tibetan (or Himalayan) singing bowls—metal or crystal—to deepen relaxation, clear the mind, improve mood, reduce tension, promote a sense of well-being, defuse anger, reverse fatigue, lower anxiety, lessen depression, and even mitigate pain. More than silence alone, the tones emitted by the singing bowls lowered blood pressure and heart rate. They published their findings in the September 2016 issue of the *Journal of Evidence-Based Complementary and Alternative Medicine*.

Gongs, bells, string instruments, drums, and our voices are also used during sound meditation. Even the hearing impaired can benefit from the experience of sound through its vibration and frequency.

- Be aware of and stay with the sound's tone and vibration from its inception until it fades.
- Observe the sensations in your body without thinking about or judging them.
- Repeat the sound and let yourself naturally fall into synchrony with it.

"Ah" and "Om," often spelled "Aum," are important vocalizations for awareness-based sound meditation. It's been said that Om is the foundational sound of the universe.

Try using Ah to express the joy of rebirth that we feel at rising in the morning. Baskaran Pillai, PhD, contemporary master of the South Indian Tamil Siddha tradition, founder of the Pillai Center for Mind-

Science, and author of *Life-Changing Sounds: Tools from the Other Side*, shared the empowering, manifestation Ah sound with Wayne Dyer.

Om (Aum) is the sound of gratitude, and is appropriate for the evening. Om is a Sanskrit word—a sacred syllable—meaning "everything, the whole of," as the Latin *omne* in omnipresence and omnipotence. Chanted as a mantra since ancient times, Om has been described as the first vibration from the beginning of time. Yet, we see its definition also incorporates the present and future. Its vibrational frequency is thought to deactivate the right part of the amygdala associated with negative emotions.

You'll find demonstrations for using these sounds on my website and simple instructions below.

- Find a calm space. In a relaxed, cross-legged position on the floor with back erect or sitting in a chair, close your eyes.
- On the out breath, with the mouth, mindfully begin the chant, or draw out, the "a" sound of Ah or Om (Aum) through a slow exhalation. As you begin to form the "m," your mouth will be closed.
- Be aware of the vibration in your larynx. Chanting the Om (Aum) sound engages the body from the abdomen to the brain.
- Relax, then take a slow, deep inhalation.
- Repeat. As you practice, work up to nine times.
- At the end of your cycle, relax and breathe normally, focusing on your breath.

Exercises

In your journal,

- ❧ What regrets are you now ready to let go?
- ❧ Who do you wish you could forgive but haven't quite managed to do so yet? What's stopping you?
- ❧ Who do you wish would forgive you?
- ❧ How do you feel when you've let someone know that you've forgiven them?
- ❧ My aha moment from this insight is

Inspiration

Forgiveness and reconciliation are not just ethereal,
spiritual, otherworldly activities. . . . They are realpolitik, because
in a very real sense, without forgiveness, there is no future.
—Desmond Tutu

AWARENESS III

Being Present for the World

ELEVEN

Advance Your Joy and Purpose

When your why is big enough,
you will find your how.
—Leslie "Les" Calvin Brown

Insight 9:
See with 3D Vision

I embrace lifelong learning and continue to grow my knowledge of the world and the people in it, which enables my ability to Discover, Develop, and Disperse my joy and purpose.

The He(art) and Science Behind the Insight

Lessons from My Shoeshine-Boy Days

"They grow up so fast. It seems like yesterday they were small," we who are parents say about our children. In reality, modern humans are the slowest to reach the maturity finish line. Scientists such as Jean-Jacques Hublin, director at the Max Planck Institute for Evolutionary Anthropology in Leipzig, Germany, say that's a consequence "directly related to the emergence of human social and cultural complexity . . . long maturation of the brain and an extended education period." In fact, modern humans' biological strategy of "live slow and grow old" successfully replaced the "live fast and die young" of previous species.[1] Live slow and grow old have profound importance for us today.

Author Aldous Huxley, a friend of literary and Hollywood luminaries, was described as a man who meditated on and put under a microscope "the central problems of modern" humans. "The secret of genius," Huxley wrote, "is to carry the spirit of the child into old age."[2] Most of us tend to agree. Oh were that always so.

In 1960, at MIT, where he was visiting professor of Humanities, Huxley presented a series of lectures he titled—borrowing from Hamlet—"What a Piece of Work Is a Man."[3] The times were not yet ripe for sensitivity readings and inclusive language. But we remember the phrase and honor the thinker for his marriage of science and Eastern religion, which spawned his embrace of "the nonverbal world of culturally uncontaminated consciousness. We must learn how to be mentally silent; we must cultivate the art of pure receptivity. The universe in which a human being lives can be transfigured into a new creation. We have only to cut a hole in the fence and look around us with what the philosopher, Plotinus, describes as 'that other kind of seeing, which everyone has but few make use of.'"

Children poke holes in fences to peer through and perceive the world through the filters of their unbounded imaginations. If I tell you that childhood thinking differs from adult thinking, you'd probably smile at the naivete of my comment! We expect our thinking to mature along with our years, and yet ask friends and family how old they feel inside. That is, except for hoping to be a bit wiser, do their thoughts and emotions "feel" different than when they were ten, twenty, or thirty years younger? Maybe you say to yourself and others, "I feel young at heart."

Our long childhood still holds mysteries that are sure to reveal patterns of living for us well into our so-called golden years. Life gives you that zingy sensation, and you get up in the morning feeling like there are places to go and things to do. Is youth just a state of mind?

In many people, there's a correlation between feeling young and better overall health—getting and staying healthier, finds Ronald Siegel, assistant professor of psychology at Harvard Medical School.[4] That feeling has a physiological basis, as researcher Jeanyung Chey of Seoul National University in Korea discovered. Researchers found that study participants who felt mentally sprightly had more brain gray matter in the areas associated with language, speech, and sound. As a result, they tended to lead more stimulating lives.[5] But which direction does the cause-and-effect relationship go is still being debated. Do we lead more stimulating lives because we're mentally equipped to handle the challenges, or do the activities and exposure to experiences increase our mental capacity? What's up with our brain development?

In his book *Why Youth Is Not Wasted on the Young: Immaturity in Human Development*, evolutionary developmental psychologist David F. Bjorklund proposes that our long childhood—among the longest in the animal kingdom—is an adaptation that helped make our species successful. The precise physical mechanisms at work are complex and still up for debate among developmental psychologists. Many caution, however, that it's unwise to artificially prolong childhood, with the exception of nurturing the positive traits of curiosity and playfulness, as Huxley would have it.

There's another childhood trait that can be advantageous to carry into adulthood. Children tend to overestimate their capabilities. They maintain youthful motivation in the face of failure, pursuing a coveted goal more than many adults who slip into an "I can't" defeatist attitude. How many times I heard my daughter, Makenna, say, "Daddy, I can't" when she faced the terror of crossing the monkey bars for the first time. Yet she never gave up. The words weren't fences. They had holes in which she peered into the beyond.

Bjorklund cautions that we'd be wise not to rush development by pushing children into experiences before they're cognitively ready, believing early exposure and conditioning give them an edge over late bloomers.

Humans are definitely late bloomers. Neuroscientists are still theorizing if the fact that our large brains' huge energy consumption contributes to slower growth. Still, situations beyond their control catapult some children into adult worlds for which nature hadn't intended them and for which they're not prepared. Some of these not-yet-adults survive by sheer determination and a will, but often at great psychological and physical cost.

Neuroimaging gives us insights into how positive and negative early experiences affect brain development. A child's brain develops "from the bottom up."[6] In other words, the brain prioritizes which functions the body needs to survive and automatically focuses on keeping the heart and lungs doing their jobs. Life comes first. Escape being dinner before considering what's for dinner. Only when the brain has rescued us from a potentially unhappy ending can it take on peripheral tasks, or so-called sophisticated functions, such as complex thinking and judgments that may be required to make critical decisions.

At the age of two, a child's brain already has created approximately 100 trillion synapses—the teeny gaps between neurons across which electrical impulses pass. That's many more than any of us will ever need. What happens to all of those synapses? They succumb to a kind of use them or lose them fate. Which synapses are pruned depends on experiences that strengthen them or cause them to be discarded[7] like those skis that we bought, sat in the closet, and we finally donated to Goodwill.

Teenagers lose about half of their original staggering number of synapses. Those left will serve them from then on. That's a difficult image to conceive. So is learning that by age three a child's brain has reached 90 percent of its adult size. Amazingly, emotions, language, and abstract thought form rapidly in the first three years. But the brain's development happens in fits and starts. In the process, healthy experiences and good nutrition are critical. Unfortunately, the real world robs many children of one or both: nurturing and positive stimulation. Young brains adapt to hostile or toxic environments, but not in positive ways. Many of us have had to recover from or are still overcoming childhoods fraught with trauma or that were devoid of positive stimuli and life-enhancing experiences.

Psychologists and neuroscientists are helping us to understand the potential benefits to children of early intervention to provide the nurturance and stimulus that foster healthy brain development. I'll never forget the great blessings that were the adults who took an interest in a young, naïve, shoeshine boy from a dysfunctional family. They made me feel that who I was and what I wanted out of life mattered, and they provided valuable follow-through when I needed it.

So many of us have suffered childhood traumas or stresses or feel like we raised ourselves in dysfunctional surroundings. We've had to learn and, perhaps, continue learning healthy responses to whatever life dishes out. The takeaway here is that we're not alone. To echo Insight 7, life is gentler and kinder when we offer and accept a hand every day.

Becoming an Expert and Consultant

What is our human potential? "You are like a supercomputer, but you haven't found a keyboard yet," says Sadhguru. To the Indian yogi and author, "we are the first generation on the planet for whom our survival is organized better than ever before." A little tongue in cheek, I think that means there's never a better time to unlock our highest potential. First, we must shake off what Sadhguru calls "the nonsense that's happening within" us. I said it to my daughter, Makenna, and Sadhguru imparts the same wisdom your mind and body already know: "I can tell you a thousand times to give up your fear. If your chemical soup is blissful, there's not even an idea of fear in your mind."

In our youth, our world view was shaped by our limited understanding of both the meaning of our experiences and environment we shared with others. We either connect with the growing world or we're alienated from it out of circumstance or fear.

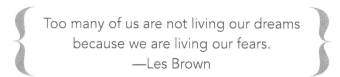

{ Too many of us are not living our dreams
because we are living our fears.
—Les Brown }

The funny thing about fear is that we tend to cling to it. Strange that it's hard to let go. You might wonder what this chapter about lifelong learning has to do with dreams and fears. As it turns out, plenty.

It's taken hitting a lot of potholes to discover that I learn more when the road is bumpy than when it's smooth. I pay more attention. I'm not on cruise control. When I'm focused, valuable experiences translate into information, which settles somewhere in my brain as knowledge. If I'm fortunate, that knowledge gives me a perspective that serves me for life.

As you see, knowledge and wisdom aren't the same thing. A cool thing about knowledge is that as we absorb it, it displaces fear—fear that holds us hostage. We've all heard of the School of Hard Knocks. Many of us are graduates. We may recall collision courses with reality that left us reeling with dizzying and indelible impressions that taught us volumes about ourselves and imparted a good deal of wisdom about life.

Throughout these pages, I've encouraged gathering knowledge of self and others, gently, purposefully, through awareness and mindfulness meditation. Doing our mental and spiritual practices and exercises, we uncover the real desires of the soul that have lain hidden beneath the social constructs of success and the commercialization of happiness. We can let ourselves feel true happiness that resides within despite the abrasions of daily life.

Ray Dalio knows firsthand that "You don't achieve happiness by getting rid of your problems. You achieve it by learning from them." Called the king of lifelong learning, Dalio was named one of *Time* magazine's 100 Most Influential People. Oh, yes, and he's also the founder, co-chairman, and co-CIO of Bridgewater, the world's largest hedge fund, and author of the bestseller *Principles: Life and Work*. Other than investments, his passions are ocean exploration and conservation, which speaks volumes for his capacity for empathy and stewardship. Dalio is also an interventionist in the sense that he puts his money and energy where his goals are. One of which is helping underprivileged kids get through high school and acquire jobs. Another is putting a fire under people to take his *Principles* recommendations seriously, whatever their walk of life. An advocate for the power of dreaming, he walks his talk.

Here are Dalio's recommendations. Foremost, you must think for yourself—rather than having someone think for you. Figure out what it is that you want for yourself and out of life. Discover what is true for you. Learn what you need to do to achieve what you want in light of what is true for you. Without knowing yourself and your truth, your success may be up a creek without a paddle.

In the process of building success—whatever that means to you—Dalio offers a little warning. Leave humility in the dust. "As you are young, it is important to realize that your success comes from knowing how to deal with your not knowing more than it comes from anything you know."

I tend to see life in 3D—perceiving it beyond the dimensions of height, length, and width. My "3D vision" is not only a play on words but also a pneumonic for Discover, Develop, and Disperse, which I'll cover shortly. Like Dalio's principles, they're a call to action. We don't know what's true for us until we examine our values, thoughts, and beliefs. And success will often elude us until these are in alignment. Misalignment can be a powerful motivation for change. We know something's not right, and we can't fix it until we learn what's broken. Learning, whether we're an individual or an organization, is a critical adaptation for survival.

When we're pushed beyond our comfort zone, we have three choices: remain stuck, retreat, or advance. If we increase our self-awareness, we can recognize and acknowledge without judgment what we know and don't know and need to know to advance. Dalio asks: "Are you willing to embrace 'not knowing'? Are you self-aware and are you on a journey to become wiser through self-reflection and being comfortable being uncomfortable?" When we can find joy and purpose in self-discovery and other-discovery, we have acquired a boatload of wisdom.

In spite of the dysfunction at home, at ten, when I painted *Shoeshine Preservation Expert and Consultant* on the side of my shoeshine box, I was a starry-eyed, full-of-promise-and-anticipation kid.

Good Enough Is Often Good Enough

"Perfect is the enemy of good," wrote Voltaire. He may not have given much thought to the negative health and wellness issues associated with striving for perfectionism, of which stress and anxiety are just two.

Perfectionists, meet the Principle of Good Enough (POGE). We might tend to shy away from our heart surgeon who says, "I'm not the greatest, but I'm good enough." When it comes to time-oriented services and products, perfection may not be practical or necessary. When is good enough . . . well . . . enough?

Our society emphasizes high achievement, but it's a worrisome goal to physicians Savithiri Ratnapalan and Helen Batty, who study the negative mental and physical effects of striving for personal or professional perfection. In their paper "To Be Good Enough,"[8] the researchers discuss the emotional and physiological penalties of missing one's own brass ring. POGE takes the real world into account and accepts that perfection may be the road less traveled for a reason. "The paradigm is one of improving while doing, learning from failure, coping with complexity, and adjusting to human foible."

Letting go of perfectionism is not in the same ballpark with accepting mediocrity. Mediocrity has no heart and soul behind the behavior or product. Plato acknowledged that his uncompromising perfectionism could exist only in thought, not in the physical world.

POGE suggests that we need to identify the point past which investing more resources will not improve or change the outcome in any meaningful way. Establishing that invisible point, or standard, that's good, but not perfect, depends on the individual, the circumstances, and the probability or improbability of achieving the original goal. Producing low-quality or mediocre work is not good enough. There is always a cost to striving for perfection. We need to weigh the benefits. It's important to understand that not every goal needs to be achieved. Just because it's not possible for us to climb Kilimanjaro doesn't mean we don't benefit from cross-country training and getting our bodies in good-enough condition.

Do you feel that you need to be exceptional or extraordinary in everything you do or touch to meet your own or someone else's expectations? Does perfectionism define who you are? If so, you're in for a lot of heartache. Certainly, there are times and places when nothing but our best will do—and we expect that of our heart or brain surgeons. The other side of the coin needs to come with a warning: beware of complacency and its attitude that almost good enough is enough. Learn to discriminate.

More Is . . . More

More is better. We seem to have a built-in app for that leaning. An algorithm, as professor of psychology Glenn Geher at State University of New York (SUNY) New Paltz calls it.[9] We're programmed to believe that if a little is good, a lot is great. Obviously, we know that's not the case when it comes to consumption of controlled substances, less-than-nutritious food, medicine, or risky behavior. We'd be better off functioning in the Goldilocks Zone. That's not the obsessive-compulsive or indulgent zone. It's the common-sense place where we're mindful of extremes and favor the "just right." There is such a place at home, at work, on the team, on the golf course. Again, our innate ability to be discerning stems from our mindful awareness of the situation and all the variables associated with it.

Earlier, we discussed optimal engagement in an activity. When we follow our bliss, we lose track of time and are happily involved in a project. Feeling "a little nervous, a little excited" is an indication that we've reached a sweet spot, explains Geher. "Optimal levels of adrenaline and cortisol boost your concentration and performance; these hormones protect your body, in direct opposition to an excess of those substances hurting it." We call that positive, optimal state being "in the flow." Search your memory for those times when you've felt in the flow.

As Geher and others who work with people whose thoughts, beliefs, or behaviors are obsessive or excessive see it, unhealthy states are often induced by our myopic media-creates-the-message mindset. We fixate on social sound bites that try to convince us that bigger is better and more is more. Art Markman, a professor of psychology at the University of Texas, Austin, also ponders our propensity to go to extremes and, subsequently, develop habits or addictions that are difficult to get under control. For example, Markman notes that "No particular cigarette is the one that kills a person; it's the accumulation of toxins over time that creates the negative health consequences." Contrast the bombardment of enticements to overindulge with the media's mixed messages, such as the maxim "you can never be too rich or too thin." The best practice? Practice mindful awareness of your body, mind, and spirit to make informed choices that foster well-being.

Can one be too cheerful, too generous, too empathetic, too self-confident, too much of a risk-taker? If you expect me to say "depends," we're on the same wavelength, and you're in your own good mindfulness company.

Dazzling Failure before Blazing Success

The world history of luminaries is crowded with those who failed and failed again. When we fall flat on our faces, we have three options: stay there and wallow in self-pity; get up, give up, and fall backward; or get up, persevere, and move forward to the best of our ability. No one who was ever anyone—at least whose name we'd recognize—was satisfied with either of the first two options. Perhaps you recall the *nana korobi ya oki* phrase from Insight 2: fall seven times, get up eight. It bears repeating.

John C. Maxwell, author of *Failing Forward: Turning Mistakes into Stepping Stones for Success*, recounts stories of real people—achievers who "seem to leave 'average in the dust.'"[10] Our rough dirt roads are often unmarked and aren't easy on the traveler. Between 1881 and 1890, Dutch post-impressionist artist Vincent van Gogh painted almost nine hundred works.[11] According to history and his own letters, he failed as an art dealer, flunked his entrance exam to theology school, and was fired by the church after an ill-fated attempt at missionary work. His fragile and deteriorating physical and mental health and his discouragement of having sold only one painting had not crushed his passion for art. A few sentences in one of van Gogh's letters to his brother Theo reveals his determination and motivation to give "my canvases my undivided attention. I am trying to do as well as certain painters whom I have greatly loved and admired. . . ."[12]

Albert Einstein's unremarkable academic beginning belied the brilliance that lay hidden beneath boredom and lack of parental support. His father died believing his son had not a shred of potential in him. That deep disappointment broke young Einstein's heart. He bounced from job to job and was finally hired as patent clerk. The mathematical stimulation of the work awoke the sleeping genius. Einstein's gift cost him his marriage and his role as a father and head of his household. It gave the world the theory of relativity and much more.

Winning often follows a lot of losing. As proof, Maxwell recounts Michael Jeffrey Jordan's journey. The greatest basketball player of all time missed twelve thousand shots and lost nearly four hundred games. Achieving his goal was no slam dunk.

Successful people are often eager to share the lessons of their cuts, scrapes, crashes, and burns. Walt Disney, J. K. Rowling, Oprah Winfrey, Stephen Spielberg, Dr. Seuss (Theodore Seuss Geisel), Sir Isaac Newton, Charles Darwin, Thomas Edison, Fred Astaire, and Winston Churchill are among a roster of many who failed forward and never stopped learning about themselves and the world around them. They found their gifts and soldiered on with them through dream-eating jungles, slaying the dragons that torment even the resilient. Stories abound of people wildly successful in one field or endeavor who stumbled into their niche by accident while lost on the wrong trail. Reminder: not every goal needs to be achieved. But many goals need to be reassessed.

> The difference between average people and achieving people is their perception of and response to failure. They learn from mistakes in their judgment and behavior.
> —John C. Maxwell

What do failure and success have to do with lifelong learning? Everything. If we train only for success, we can be crushed by failure. We've closed the book on and our eyes to a world of alternatives and the salvation of serendipity. From this book's first page, we've been training for your success by giving you the tools to be resilient in the face of challenges. The Twelve Insights invite you to take the perspective of an optimistic realist. They remind you to walk the walk mindful, self-aware (knowing your strengths), confident, compassionate, and humble. They encourage body-mind-spirit integration and empower you to get up eight times after falling seven.

We reach a point in our growth when our emotional intelligence and experience enable us to stop blaming others for our so-called failures and look at our goals with fresh insight. We acquire the wherewithal—information and skills—to non-judgmentally evaluate the thoughts, beliefs, and actions that didn't serve us. And we learn how to be stronger than fear. Sound familiar? If so, welcome to the club. We're all learning from our mistakes, not wailing and wallowing in a morass of tears and regrets. The world only needs so many Michael Jordans and J. K. Rowlings. It needs you.

3D Vision in the Perpetual Age of Self-Discovery

Discover

From first breath to last, our life is an exploration in self-discovery. All of the insights so far have emphasized self-knowing, self-acceptance, self-appreciation, self-respect, self-development, self-fulfillment, self-empowerment, and self-love. And the point of our growth and evolution? Self-actualization.

There's a paradox in accepting oneself and simultaneously improving upon or developing oneself. You see the little twist: these two actions are symbiotic. Self-acceptance doesn't require us to feel the current situation is the best one. We can acknowledge there is something we can change and honor that our higher self knows what's best for our well-being. Certainly, being self-condemnatory and judgmental are negative and defeatist attitudes that have no place in our quest for body-mind-spirit wellness. As we've practiced mindful meditation and become increasingly aware of ourselves, others, and the world around us, we've been discovering the many priceless gifts that we are and that we offer. Some of these gifts—perhaps discovered during aha moments—may become synonymous with our purpose. Or our gifts may complement our purpose and enrich our joy and the balance and harmony we learn is possible through mindful awareness.

The more we grasp about how we learn—specifically, the act of self-discovery—the better we understand that this optimistically realist behavior may be our subconscious default. If we were to stop the inflow that is self-discovery, our pool of self-and-other-wisdom would stagnate, and our mind and spirit would dry up. This life force is our vitality.

As with most thoughts, beliefs, or actions, we can achieve a happy medium, that balance place between self-absorption and healthy self-focus and self-care.

> Happiness is like a butterfly;
> the more you chase it, the more it will elude you,
> but if you turn your attention to other things,
> it will come and sit softly on your shoulder.
> —Henry David Thoreau

That we must be proactive about achieving happiness is fallacious thinking. We don't always have to take this or that course or perform at peak levels in everything we do. This mindset leads us into the trap of believing that only *when* we have achieved a goal, changed a behavior, or dropped the desired number of pounds, *then* we will be happy.

The *when-then* motivation for happiness is self-defeating and implies right out of the gate that we're not acceptable now, just the way we are. Nathaniel Branden, pioneer in the study of who we judge ourselves to be, reminds us that our self-concept becomes our destiny. A negative concept of who we are can become a road map to a destination we may have no conscious intention to reach.

The best-selling author of *Honoring the Self: Self-Esteem and Personal Transformation*, Branden has seen the handwriting on the wall: "the reputation you have with yourself—your self-esteem—is the single most important factor for a fulfilling life." In fact, so critical is self-esteem to our success as healthy individuals that Branden calls self-esteem the immune system of consciousness. We are not talking about conceit, narcissism, or self-aggrandizement. We are talking about unbiased, non-judgmental assessments of the person we present to ourselves and others. It's time for the big reveal of the magnificent creations we've been since before our moment of introduction to this world.

Discovering within ourselves values and virtues on which to develop healthy self-esteem is a fundamental human need, Branden reveals. "Its impact requires neither our understanding nor our consent. It works its way within us with or without our knowledge." We are free to become mindfully aware "of the dynamics of self-esteem or remain unconscious of them, but in the latter case, we remain a mystery to ourselves and endure the consequences."[13]

How do we gauge healthy self-esteem? By discovering our gifts and seeing them as strengths. Putting those strengths—talents, skills, and positive personality traits—to use in meaningful ways enables us to lead purposeful lives as contributing members of our human family.

What are our personal strengths that we take for granted every day? In the practice section at the end of this chapter, you're invited to list as many strengths as you can think of. If you say, "I don't know what my strengths are," then you may find one or more of the following self-evaluation assessments tests insightful.

The Myers-Briggs Type Indicator uncovers our motivations and the things that drive us. HR professionals use this test to determine if the personalities, motivations, and values of potential hires align with their company's culture. The results are revealing to individuals as well. Here are a handful of other reliable assessments: California Psychological Inventory (CPI), Minnesota Multiphasic Personality Inventory (MMPI), Caliper Profile, DISC Assessment, Gallup StrengthsFinder, and 16pf Questionnaire (16 Personality Factors). Harvard Professional Development picked three favorite free online emotional intelligence assessments and one fee-based test to "help you discover ways to increase your capacity for self-awareness, empathy, and emotional regulation."[14] Its picks are *Psychology Today*, Mind Tools, Institute for Health and Human Potential, and Talent Smart. You'll find links to these and other helpful sources on my website.

Outside assessments can be fairly accurate. So, too, can be our unvarnished inner assessments through mindful meditation. Awareness of our feelings in present-moment experiences are also revealing. Discover the source behind those feelings. What motivates you to get up in the morning? What warms your heart, puts a smile on your face, makes you laugh, or cry tears of joy? What new passion lets you immerse yourself to the point of losing track of time? What embers from an old passion can you rekindle? What stories can old photo albums trigger and family members tell?

It's a cliché, but knowledge *is* power. About self and the world. The more we learn, the more flexible we are in our ability to make choices and change courses when necessary. We can envision more options and test them in the fields of our mind before exercising them in the field of life. Lifelong learning fires our imaginations, heightens our creativity, and blazes the trail for us to make connections between seemingly unrelated things. Learning—whether through formal education or experience—raises our self-esteem and equips us to seize opportunities. It not only contributes to making us wiser, but knowledge also makes us more interesting. Less judgmental. More valuable. Better prepared to achieve our fullest potential. Better problem solvers. Better leaders. If we're followers, are we aware that we're a follower by choice rather than by default? Knowledge of self and the world encourages us to bridge cultural gaps, peel back the façade that artificially separates us, and open doors slammed shut by prejudice.

When we're truly open, we have the potential to discover the wellspring of joy that can deepen our body, mind, and spirit connection. Chances are good that's when we'll find our strengths and gifts, which aren't necessarily one and the same. Their discovery can be through deliberate exploration, or it can be serendipitous. Great secrets, wisdom, and truths are often revealed during meditation, in silence, as we listen. To what? To ourselves. To others. To the lessons echoing from the universe.

Develop

When we find tangible things or activities that bring us joy, we can't put them down. We're driven to learn more about them and develop them further. Perhaps they're enjoyable pastimes, hobbies, or recreational activities. For example, as I've indicated, I play golf. This recreation gives me an opportunity to exercise in nature, practice mindful meditation on the course, and spend valuable time with friends.

Consider the intangible assets that bring us joy—innate skills such as the ability to write poetry, paint, or sculpt. Perhaps we're natural speakers or storytellers or actors or performing arts directors. Perhaps we're such good listeners that we've gravitated toward a profession—such as therapist, psychologist, or financial advisor—that can help others.

We understand that recognizing and acknowledging our strengths builds self-esteem. As we gently and lovingly accept ourselves for who we are and where we are—whether we ever win an Olympic gold medal or Nobel Prize—we remain intrinsically motivated, not driven by social or external pressure. We focus on and work toward our goals and dreams with verve, perseverance, and moxie.

Self-acceptance is a bigger blanket than feeling good about a single attribute. It's a realistic appreciation for the whole enchilada. As we strive for a unified self, we can mobilize strengths to bolster or change a weakness. Intuitively, we know what nourishes our self-esteem. When we raise our self-esteem, our entire immune system gets a boost more powerful than a week of green smoothies. A fun and healthy way to assure body and mind harmony is to get up early and dive into a new passion that excites, enlivens, and energizes us.

Set expectations aside. Practice patience. Our work today is a foundation that may not be visible tomorrow. Remember that we humans have a long childhood for a reason. When we're consciously lifelong learners, there is more than brain and body growth at stake. To reach our fullest potential takes decades or even a lifetime. Abraham Maslow's five-tier model of human needs demonstrates that we are naturally motivated by our unique desire for personal growth and discovery beyond the basic requirements to sustain life. That state is called self-actualization. Self-actualized people derive meaning and purpose in an enrichment state of perpetual "becoming." Our journey of growth is one of continual arriving at an ever-extended destination. Our odyssey involves trial, much error, and a lifetime of searching for and walking paths paved with our core values.

Maslow obsessed over what makes people happy and gives their lives meaning. What role did their having "full use and exploitation of talents, capabilities, potentialities" play? Simply, he concluded, whatever a person can be, a person must be that. We notice immediately that all fifteen of the characteristics Maslow attributed to self-actualized people are grounded in self-awareness. How do we know others and the world if we do not know ourselves? Self-actualized people

- practice self-acceptance and have an accurate perception of reality,
- respond with empathy and focus on problem-solving,
- act with spontaneity based on their accurate self- and world-views,

- ❧ visualize new perspectives that can be the foundation for creative solutions, and
- ❧ feel intense emotions of joy, wonder, and awe, and achieve peak experiences.

Maslow's theory wasn't without its detractors. Critics still contend that not every self-actualized person rises through the hierarchy as Maslow structured it. A few pundits disclaim the existence of a hierarchy. Period. All the saber rattling doesn't diminish the integrity of research on the correlation between self-actualization (finding one's highest purpose, fulfillment, and meaning) and happiness. For Plato, like his teacher, Socrates, personal growth is the font of happiness. "So happiness, it turns out, doesn't just feel good—it precedes, relates to, and leads to success in life," finds Sonja Lyubomirsky, the author of *The Myths of Happiness* and researcher with colleagues who studied the long-term effects on happiness of expressing optimism and gratitude.

There's something wildly seductive about the prospect of "unbridled happiness." For eons, we have failed to describe happiness, capture it, tether it to us. Poets and scholars have hemmed and hawed, puzzled and pined over defining happiness and joy. Are these two sometimes synonymous, sometimes different? Is happiness fleeting, joy abiding? Or is it the other way around? Is happiness transient like an afternoon in a field of butterflies, the cooing of a content baby, a race to the finish line, an ocean breeze blowing through the open window? Does joy undergird our days, our gratitude for life and health, the grounding of our faith, the assurance of sunrises, our spirit traveling among the stars?

J. D. Salinger, in his novel *Catcher in the Rye*, wrote, "The fact is always obvious much too late, but the most singular difference between happiness and joy is that happiness is a solid and joy a liquid."

What matters, it seems, is that to live joyfully—"the basis of the quality of life"—we must "not to make misery out of everything," counsels speaker and author Sadhguru. The litmus test of the rightness of our thinking and actions? "If you know how not to make misery out of everything that you do, whatever you are doing is the right thing." Our first task is to work toward being a blissful human being.[15]

Among my childhood revelations, one stands out: the discovery that if I want to experience happiness, I must *be* happy.

> Sometimes your joy is the source of your smile,
> but sometimes your smile can be the source of your joy.
> —Thich Nhat Hanh

"Happiness is what you think, what you say, and what you do when you are in harmony," said Gandhi. Vietnamese Zen monk, global spiritual leader, and peace activist Thich Nhat Hanh beautifully captures the never-ending flow, or yin and yang, within us that occurs when the aspects of ourselves are in harmony.

What could be better than experiencing joy?

Disperse

Giving it away. That's what we do when we live purposefully as blissful human beings. To Confucius, happiness is a self-fulfilling prophecy. We embrace and cherish it, and as we would do with a captive bird, we open our hands and let it fly. It is not gone. At one and the same time, it remains within our hearts and is free to return to visit again and again. Our joy is the bird's joy.

We've learned that learning something new boosts happiness—we can let ourselves be free to exude the joy of discovery. And just as we can learn about ourselves and others and the wonderful strangeness and strange wonderfulness of the world, we can *learn* to be happy.

It takes practice to become aware of our innermost and outermost environments: our thoughts, feelings, sensations; our compassion for and kindness toward others. It takes even more practice to be mindful on a moment-by-moment basis and live, as Lao Tzu would have it, at greatest peace in the present.

How do we disperse the joy that arises from our discoveries and living life to the fullest if we don't engage with the world? The question piqued the interest of David Rock, co-founder of the NeuroLeadership Institute. Rock needed to take the definition of engagement to another level beyond getting out there and interacting with others. He determined that engagement is a state of being in which one is "willing to do difficult things, to take risks, to think deeply about issues and develop new solutions."[16] What stops us from engaging fully and frequently? Our primitive emotion: fear. Our fear of meeting strangers ranks right up there with speaking before a crowd. So how do we break through that built-in, powerful preservation instinct? After all, "the fearful are caught as often as the bold," Helen Keller maintains.

What are the consequences of engaging? No giant hole in the earth will open and swallow us up when we meet someone new and ask, "How are you?" No fire-breathing dragon will swoop down and carry us off if we respond to that same question with "I'm great, couldn't be better, and you?" What's stopping us from sharing something upbeat and positive that's good medicine, even for people you may never see again? How would the world be different if we greeted the person next to us at the crosswalk light with a sunny smile and "Have a great day"? What if among our purposes in life is sharing the overflow of joy we feel when we're mindfully grateful?

"If you find some happiness inside yourself, you'll start finding it in a lot of other places, too," says Gladiola Montana, a pseudonym intended to represent all the strong and savvy ranch women in the West. Unlike Cinderella's glass slipper, this author's boot of wisdom fits all.

Awaken to the odyssey that is life and, fully aware, discover the people, places, and things that stir your awareness of joy. Develop your natural and learned strengths through gratitude, practice, and perseverance. Throw open your arms and heart and disperse your joy. The miracle of radiant happiness and enduring joy is that they are self-perpetuating. The more we spread them around, the fuller become our hearts and minds, the more enriched are our lives. When we give ourselves room to grow into our role as fully dimensional, 3D humans, we find ourselves with ever more to give. In sharing joy and practicing kindness, we create the potential to change someone's life. We're given that life-changing power when we become a mentor. We may never know how many lives we touch.

Practice

Apply 3D Vision

Be aware of or seek opportunities to use your 3D vision to "Discover" something new, "Develop" yourself and others, and "Disperse" your joy through living your purpose.

When the opportunity is right, in a warm, non-threatening way, ask a few people you don't know, or know only a little, questions that encourage them to talk about themselves. Test the water to be sure you're not closing in on someone who might feel nervous about your approach. Smile and see what response you get. Engage naturally. This could be at a professional meeting, a child's sporting event, or a luncheon for newcomers. Pay attention and discover something about the person that you can comment on. Really listen. If the timing permits, find common ground on which to build a potential foundation for a new relationship. If building a new friendship isn't in the cards, then savor the short-term contact as a rewarding experience for both of you. What did you learn?

Purposefully and mindfully learn something new each day this week. Jot down aha moments and insights. How does this new information affect you and, perhaps, others with whom you're in contact? What changed?

Did you disperse your joy and happiness? What responses did you notice? Were you able to share what you learned with anyone? What changed as a result of that shared knowledge? How did it help you in your relationship with others?

Exercises

In your journal,

- ❧ List seven things you'd like to know more about. They can be an entire field of knowledge, individual topics, or insights into yourself and others.
- ❧ List seven things or experiences that bring you joy, times when bliss is palpable.
- ❧ What is your purpose? In your description, try to avoid using any clichés to talk about what you feel and insights you've gained. Think of specific purposes unique to you and your gifts. If you're not sure of your purpose, don't chastise or judge yourself. Let that evolve.
- ❧ My aha moment from this insight is

Inspiration

Happiness is the consequence of personal effort.
You fight for it, strive for it, insist upon it, and sometimes
even travel around the world looking for it. You have
to participate relentlessly in the manifestations of your
own blessings. And once you have achieved a state of happiness,
you must never become lax about maintaining it. You must
make a mighty effort to keep swimming upward
into that happiness forever, to stay afloat on top of it.
—Elizabeth Gilbert, *Eat, Pray, Love*

TWELVE

Start with a Fresh Slate

When we are paying attention to our lives,
we'll recognize those defining moments. The challenge
for so many of us is that we are so deep into daily
distractions and 'being busy, busy' that we miss out
on those moments and opportunities that—
if jumped on—would get our careers and
personal lives to a whole new level of wow.
—Robin S. Sharma

Insight 10: Breathe Life

I pursue healthy distractions and engagements
that balance my stress and fortify my well-being.
Creating time and space for myself refreshes my spirit
and rejuvenates my body. I breathe for life.

The He(art) and Science Behind the Insight

When Distractions Are Good

Healthy distractions: the phrase sounds like an oxymoron. We know that not giving our full attention under many circumstances can have serious consequences. So can distracting ourselves from mental or physical pain with harmful substances or risky behavior. Healthy distractions are mindful, conscious decisions to take the nearby exit off the interstate when we see a wreck up ahead. As soon as we see the flashing red and blue lights of a situation or an emotion, we can rapidly process the information and make a conscious choice to bypass our undesirable and habitual responses. Awareness that we're about to become involved in an emotional or physical pileup enables us to assess healthier alternatives and take a safe off ramp.

Avoidance can be a wise decision. Choosing to detour doesn't deny the existence of negative situations. Our self-awareness simply acknowledges that when we go down certain roads, we're apt to encounter them. The goal of distraction is to mindfully pass through, over, or around whatever is our personal chaos with the least impact on our well-being. Healthy distractions are valuable coping skills that need to be in everyone's resiliency tool kit.

In fact, distraction is one of three types of coping strategies, and the one I work with most in my presentations and workshops. The others are soothing—internal and external—and balancing. Although we can mobilize any of these skills on our behalf as we practice mindful awareness, I've found that engaging in a healthy distraction first often negates the need for the other two coping mechanisms. Soothing refers to comforting ourselves when we've collided head on with an experience that knocks us for a loop or off our mental feet. Self-soothing techniques promote relaxation, like a warm bath soaks away tension and stress. Balancing requires our discernment and ability to take control and prioritize demands on us. When the going gets tough, the tough open their resiliency tool kit and make clear-headed choices grounded in mindful awareness of the issues involved.

Like shifting gears, healthy distractions demand our full attention to assure we're going the right direction at the right time. In other words, discernment enables us to distract ourselves appropriately. When we're at a dead stop on the freeway and tempers are as hot as the asphalt and we need to be awake and alert to potential dangers, that's not the time and place for the same stress-reducing CD that lulls us to sleep.

Ancient Greeks and Romans believed that music penetrated the body and produced equilibrium between the body and mind. By the eighteenth century, the magical effect of music to produce different states of mind and behavior became clearer. Neuroimaging technology demonstrates how different music genres work differently on the four major lobes of our brain and body chemistry to relieve stress, brighten our day, aid concentration, induce sleep, or pump us up for action. Music triggers the same neural processes as the feelings of euphoria we often derive from food, sex, and drugs.

Studies also show that listening to music as a distraction can increase beneficial immune cells that bolster our immune system. I bring brass Himalayan singing bowls to my presentations to reduce anxiety and promote relaxation. Scientific studies show that the vibrations—not the sound—from singing bowls can positively affect brain waves and listening. If you're pregnant or have epilepsy or other medical conditions, consult your physician about the potential effects of the vibrational levels before participating in a sound therapy session using singing bowls.

Because our bodies tend to synchronize our breath and pulse rate with the tempo of music, post-operative recovery and healing have been shown to be more rapid in patients who receive appropriate music therapy. Think rap music and hip-hop will rattle your brain negatively? Studies at Cambridge University and elsewhere reveal some surprising results. When lyrics aren't aggressive, but positive—such as rising-from-the ashes themes—hip-hop appears to benefit those with depression or low self-esteem.

Neuroscientist David Lewis-Hodgson of the UK's Mindlab International at the University of Sussex studied the effects of music on indigenous cultures and recommends doing what these people do to enhance well-being and improve health. Brain images show that music stimulates regions of the brain associated with emotions and the production of the feel-good chemical dopamine.

"Music has charms to sooth a savage breast," wrote seventeenth-century poet William Congreve." Neuroscientists have proven Congreve correct. A report published by the University of Sussex confirmed certain genres of music can lower heart rate, slow breathing, and decrease levels of the stress hormone cortisol in the blood. Other researchers have observed music's effect on speeding recovery after surgery and reducing anxiety and depression.[1]

Alarmed by a study conducted by Harvard and Stanford that concluded job stress is responsible for more health issues that cause more deaths than diabetes, influenza, and Alzheimer's, sound therapists collaborated with Marconi Union to produce the soundtrack "Weightless." Biometric feedback demonstrated that its "carefully arranged harmonies, rhythms, and bass lines help slow a listener's heart rate, reduce blood pressure, and lower levels of the stress hormone cortisol" more efficiently than a massage, walking, and more than a dozen other relaxation tracks. But driving isn't the time to let "Weightless" distract you, as the soundtrack can also induce sleep.

Are You a Daydream Believer?

According to research, smart people are. Feel your blood pressure rising on the job or is your mind spinning with frustration? Take a deep breath and exhale slowly. If it's safe to do so, imagine yourself a happy child flying a kite. Unless it's storming and you've got a key attached to the end of the string, mentally follow the kite up and up, drifting and darting freely into the immense blue sky.

A neurological study more than a dozen years ago told us that half of our thoughts are daydreams. So why not daydream mindfully rather than haphazardly? Give yourself permission to re-energize. Gaze out the window at the intensity of the blue sky or at those powerful, burgeoning thunderheads. Under appropriate circumstances, daydreaming can be a healthy distraction that gives our bodies and minds a few moments to relax and slip into something more comfortable, ushering in a problem-solving mode that has been shown to increase our productivity and creativity.

Psychology professor Eric Schumacher of the Georgia Institute of Technology co-authored a study that found a "significant positive correlations between trait mind wandering and fluid intelligence and creativity."[2] The translation? Smart people daydream. There was a notoriously playful daydreamer who gave us the special theory of relativity. When he took leave of his blackboard for moments to ponder, Albert Einstein's insights into humanity were as earth-shaking as his physics equations. "I am enough of an artist to draw freely upon my imagination," he said in 1929. "Imagination is more important than knowledge. Knowledge is limited. Imagination encircles the world." In essence, the identity "I" that feels trapped in a dilemma is permitted to step aside and allow the effortless flow of life and experience from the universe to rush in.

"The more advanced and pervasive technology becomes, the more important humans are to the equation. Organizations need to develop workers' human capabilities—curiosity, imagination, creativity, empathy, and courage. Collectively, these enduring human capabilities are like superpowers," writes Brenna Sniderman, executive director of the Deloitte Center for Integrated Research about its vision for an ideal corporate culture. "Organizations can draw on these powers to accomplish far more—to jump higher, run faster, see farther, maybe even challenge the laws of the universe."

You, too, can take short forays to faraway places where imagination reigns when doing so doesn't put you or your job in danger. For example, if you operate heavy machinery or work on an assembly line, obviously daydreaming should wait for your lunch break. Like all the recommendations for mindful living, moderation is key.

Our minds are mavericks, free-spirited mustangs galloping off into the sunset or splashing along surf's edge. Harnessing our thoughts isn't much easier than taming feral horses. Both require patient conditioning, habituation, love, and appreciation of their high-spiritedness. We need to build in and allow for distraction times to run free and daydream, and for the three Rs: rest, recovery, and rejuvenation. Daydreaming as visualization helps us achieve our goals by creating future scenarios. We run the video of potentialities in our head and plot scenes that might work or probably won't. Incubators—that's the term neurologists and psychologists use when our brains are on daydreaming steroids.

The late godfather of research on daydreaming, Jerome L. Singer, professor emeritus of psychology at Yale School of Medicine,[3] explored the "positive, creative, and productive aspects of daydreaming"[4] and gave it a thumb's up. His lifelong fascination with the scope and depth of our vivid

inner life and imaginal processes led to insights into the pragmatic benefits of our plunges into fantasy worlds, adults' "childlike spirit and sense
of wonder." Singer and his wife, Dorothy Singer, consulted to the pro-
ducers of influential children's shows such as *Mister Rogers' Neighborhood*.
It would seem that we'd outgrow our need for "pretend play," but, thank-
fully, we do not.

It's recess time. When you hear, "Let's go play," get up, pocket your
cares, and get ready to release your body's feel-good chemical, endorphins. Play for the sake of play. Play rejuvenates us, unleashes joy, contributes to our well-being. The more we get our bodies moving, the more
stressful situations and thoughts dissolve, and we have free rein to express
joy unabashedly. When we remain playful throughout our lives, we take
things less seriously, learn more, keep our brains sharp, stay connected
with others, and stave off depression. For a few pleasurable moments,
we're taken out of time. Experiences of happiness shared with family and
friends strengthen our bonds and release tension that might have negatively charged the atmosphere that so often fuels family feuds.

Join in the play by acting. Get involved in a theater troupe and improve your overall sense of well-being and confidence with drama or
comedy. Getting lost in your character is a perfect distraction. Perhaps
I should say it's fun escapism. Just imagine a world of audiences without
performing artists of all kinds. Acting offers the intellectual challenge of
learning scripts and focuses the creative mind on precise interaction with
others. The excitement elevates mood, dilutes social anxiety, and teaches
to express our thoughts and feelings with greater clarity. Above all, actors
must be present in the moment and hone their listening skills rather than
be self-absorbed.

There are as many healthy distractions to unhealthy situations as there
are people who need to temporarily or permanently disconnect from
them. Explore what works for you. For starters, get involved in something that interests and absorbs you. Give something you love doing your
full attention. Turn a passion into service. Teach children at your local
elementary school how to restore a forest with biodegradable, plantable
tree pots and monitor their growth—the kids' and the saplings'. Winston
Churchill opened the door to a world of healthy distractions when he
said, "We make a living by what we get, and we make a life by what we

give." Give a hand and heart to a nearby homeless shelter. "Volunteering is fun and fulfilling, and helping others is a key to happiness," says the Gospel Rescue Mission in Tucson, Arizona. "We will work with you to match your gifts and talents with our needs, or you can choose your area of service." Be a mentor.

> A mentor is someone who allows you
> to see the hope inside yourself
> —Oprah Winfrey

The weightier the outside world that's yoked to our psyches—news of floods, earthquakes, climate change, politics, terrorism, epidemics—the greater our need to lighten the inner. Perhaps more important than what we do is why we do it. Stacking wood with music streaming through our earbuds or painting the fence on a perfect day can be healthy distractions if we do them consciously, joyfully, and feeling the pleasant anticipation of jobs well done. We can reorganize our book shelves according to topics if we find the task interesting and enlightening. Maybe you'll find books you purchased and never read. Or discover a yellowed letter from your grandfather in a long-closed book.

> The work you do while you procrastinate
> is probably the work you should be doing
> for the rest of your life.
> —Jessica Hische

A healthy distraction isn't procrastination. It isn't taking up a task that doesn't involve you mentally, but leaves your brain free to mull over and over the thoughts and feelings you're consciously making an effort to forget or set aside. The needle can get stuck in the old record groove no matter what you're doing if your heart's not in it. You'll only hear repetitive, discordant notes when what your soul craves is a melody. Tackling a project over which you have control is empowering and dismisses the often-pervasive feeling that you have none.

Healthy distractions aren't antithetical to mindful awareness. *Au contraire*. It takes awareness of our minds and bodies to recognize when we're on a collision course with escalating emotions or are teetering on physical collapse if we don't temporarily disengage from our current course. Note that I didn't say that the situations are the cause of our need for distractions. Our perceptions of and responses to them are. The situation that seemingly causes our productivity railcars to jump track today might not emotionally derail our train tomorrow when we're refreshed, stronger, and used mindful awareness to sort out best choices.

Choosing healthy distractions requires a different mindset and results in a different outcome than procrastination. Purposeful distractions give you breathing space. Chances are that when you return to the problem-solving mode, you're less attached to the outcome or the process. Sometimes, issues solve themselves when left alone. "When you don't force yourself upon life, you discover that you *are* life. We align with our innate trust when we are not forcing and instead allow life to take place."[5]

A distraction is taking the scenic route for inspiration instead of going through the construction zone during rush hour. As we noted earlier, no one says you have to face down the two-hour, bumper-to-bumper gridlock with grit when you've got access to the off ramp just ahead. No need to feel guilty for choosing an alternate route when your avenue is clogged and depressing.

Then I Don't Feel So Bad

Richard Rogers and Oscar Hammerstein's 1959 showtune "My Favorite Things" for *The Sound of Music* resonates with us even today. Like a sprite, Julie Andrews whisks away the pain of life's owies with a reminder of the many favorite things that make our world right again.

My favorite thing is nature. We have plenty of it in the desert Southwest. Some say that in Arizona, we have two seasons. Hot and less hot. The fascinating truth is that we have five in the Sonoran Desert of southern Arizona: winter with temperatures that can plummet well below freezing and surprise snows; spring with its perfect skies and equally perfect temperatures; dry summer with highs that can sizzle asphalt; wet summer made dynamic by soakings from its monsoons; and fall.

Phoenix, in central Arizona, is the largest city in the Sonoran Desert, shared by the US and Mexico. In a valley surrounded on all sides by mountains, in the summer, Phoenix sizzles. I'm a frequent presenter for judicial and government organizations and companies' employees. On one breath-stealing July day, I made a conscious decision to override instinct and take a slow, mindful, four-block walk to the venue where I would be presenting. I'd already dealt with the interstate from Tucson and inner-city traffic. My goal was to stand before my audience refreshed, to come from a better mental place than with senses that had been assaulted by hot asphalt, cement, glass, and steel. I recalled Zen master and poet Thich Nhat Hanh's teaching on the tradition of walking mindfully, as on rice paper, lightly, leaving no trace, yet fully alive. "Every step touches the wonders of life. Every step brings healing. Every step brings peace and joy because every step is a miracle."[6]

As I headed onto the tree-lined streets, my focus was on how many birds I could spot. My mind took an immediate negative turn—no birds are going to brave this scorching afternoon. I let go of the thought, tuned out the heat, and tuned into the birdsong symphony. To my surprise, I became aware of hundreds of birds. Two iridescent ravens gurgled and shared a hotdog bun. A Northern Mockingbird ran through long, lyrical phrases from its extensive repertoire. The "tough as nails" Pyrrhuloxia, relative of Northern Cardinals, identified itself with its clear whistle. I arrived at the presentation feeling revitalized rather than roasted, focused rather than frazzled. I, especially, must practice what I preach, I told my listeners. What's your attention focused on? Think about your "favorite things" multiple times a day. I do.

I revealed earlier that one of my passions—a healthy distraction—is gardening. Here are a few others. I love musical instruments and have great fun playing a tongue drum, African drum, and a love tuner (a type of whistle) that is a favorite tool of Deepak Chopra's. I also have Himalayan singing bowls of various sizes. All of these produce vibrational energy, and I think of them as tuning forks for body, mind, and spirit. A natural distraction is enjoying the company of animals. Our pets are usually eager to reciprocate, especially when we have the most on our plates. Perhaps they sense there's no better time than when we're stressed to the max. I have two dogs, and we pet parents know the power of unconditional love on a day-to-day basis. But the easiest and hardest healthy distraction is connecting with people.

> We human beings are social beings. We come
> into the world as the result of others' actions.
> We survive here in dependence on others.
> Whether we like it or not, there is hardly a moment
> of our lives when we do not benefit from
> others' activities. For this reason, it is hardly
> surprising that most of our happiness arises
> in the context of our relationships with others.
> —Dalai Lama XIV

In seminars and lectures, I often refer to one of the world's longest longitudinal studies. For more than eighty years, Harvard University's Grant and Glueck Study has been collecting data on adult development "to identify the psychosocial predictors of healthy aging" and the effect on health and happiness of the quality of our relationships.[7] The Grant Study was composed of 268 Harvard graduates from the classes of 1939 to 1944. The Glueck Study worked with 456 young men, many from Boston's inner-city troubled and disadvantaged neighborhoods—tenements without hot and cold running water.[8] The comparative studies were designed to discover if and how much "psychosocial variables and biological processes from earlier in life predict health and well-being in late life (eighties and nineties), what aspects of childhood and adult experience predict the quality of intimate relationships in late life, and how late-life marriage is linked with health and well-being."

Wisdom as Old as the Hills

After decades and decades of interviews, blood tests, brain scans (once they became available), and follow up, the "clearest message," said Harvard study director Robert Waldinger, "is this: Good relationships keep us happier and healthier. Period." "This is wisdom that's as old as the hills."[9] Like much in life, it's quality over quantity.

The biggest predictor of our life's overall happiness and fulfillment—drum roll, please—is one simple word that represents the most complex and least-understood concept in the world: love. But there's a caveat that the study unearthed. It isn't enough to simply love. The other element in the happiness equation, says Harvard psychiatrist and former study director George E. Vaillant, "is finding a way of coping with life that does not push love away."[10] When we find ourselves pushing away those we care most about, it's time to evaluate the coping mechanisms that aren't working and that promulgate untrue beliefs that lead to unhealthy behaviors.

We've learned that having good genes is a great boost to health, but being joyful is better. We live longer, happier lives with someone—or more than one someone—by our side and on our side. "Tending to your relationships is a form of self-care, too," Waldinger said of the study's revelations. "The people who were the most satisfied in their relationships at age fifty were the healthiest at age eighty."[11] But loneliness kills. "Living in the midst of good, warm relationships is protective."[12]

I'm very fortunate—a word that has far more significance to me than lucky. I have lots of great people in my life. I love a good number of them, and I feel a good number of them truly love me. I know that's a key contributor to my sense of purpose, meaning, fulfillment, empowerment, self-esteem, happiness, and joy.

Still, some people who are drowning in misery say they "just don't get it." But that's the point. We give it before we get it. (Remember "disperse"?) And we keep on giving love and spreading joy even to those from whom we may never get it. Sadhguru had it right: we mustn't make a misery out of everything.

Giving—time, energy, knowledge, empathy, talents, love—is one of our most tried and true healthy distractions and avenues for living happily, with joy. When we give our time, we give something we can never get back. Please don't misinterpret my point. We, too, need to receive. That's what relationships are about, as we discussed in Insight 7: balance, being there for someone and trusting someone is there for us. It's acceptable and advisable to reach out when we need a hand, not only when we offer one. It's like a supplement with few side effects.

As we're seeing, healthy distractions aren't cures for situations that will, ultimately, need to be addressed. When we buy time to take a breath, pause for a creative moment, stretch our bodies, patience, and coping mechanisms, we need to fit our distraction to the occasion. We don't have to take a trip to Yosemite with the family for a week to cool off from the boss's

Friday afternoon meltdown. A short-term refresher—a Saturday softball game with friends—may be a big hit. Sometimes, distractions need to be longer term. We can also think of those that can be done easily, with little effort, and others that take a great deal more planning and energy output to pull off. In the end, we come back stronger—that's our intent—to solve a problem, find a solution, fix something broken, or just take a break.

The common denominator for all these distractions is that they immerse us in the moment. Our now action may temporarily evade another for which we're not physically or mentally prepared, but we're in the present and gaining insights through mindful awareness of how we feel, think, and act. On our website, we'll explore many more ideas for healthy distractions, such as delving further into the fine art of doing nothing mindfully, which is different than our do-nothing meditation.

Dolce Far Niente

My father-in-law practiced meditation to his last breath at age ninety-five. It was just one of the many things he did to stay fit. I admired him greatly. He had thrived as a physician helping others get well and stay well. It was a thread among many that bound us. I vividly recall one afternoon when I went to his house for a visit. He was eighty-five. On his desk lay a hefty copy of *The Ham Radio Prep Technician Class License Manual*.

"What's that for?" I asked, wondering about a new hobby when I saw no radio.

"To prep for the exam—just the first of three levels for now," he replied. "I don't know if I'll ever use a ham radio. But I want to study for the test. Keeps my mind active."

It did, and this Renaissance man who acted in the local theater, played guitar, sang, and passed the exam, of course. For him, the quality of life hinged on being intimately connected to it. As the Harvard study proved, connection is not simply the opera's overture, the beginning of our road to finding other beyond self. It's also the acts, arias, and recitatives—the enduring and meaningful relationships that run in and through the opera of our lives.

Practicing this technique or that to achieve relaxation and to distract ourselves from the daily grind is good, of course. We also need to learn *dolce far niente*. "Sweet idleness." The delight of doing nothing and doing it well, as Elizabeth Gilbert teaches us in *Eat, Pray, Love*. That's a solitary act, even if we're in a crowd. A less-than-stellar childhood taught me to be at ease in my own company. It didn't come naturally. It was a learned skill. Being alone with one's thoughts can rattle rather than relax many people, according to a recent study at Penn State University. It seems counter-intuitive, but some people who are naturally anxious get stressed out by being shown how to relax. In fact, some of us find it so unnerving that we would rather zap ourselves with an electric shock than be alone with our thoughts for as few as fifteen minutes, finds a 2014 study by the University of Virginia.[13]

While that seems bizarre, I've found that many people struggle with voids in their time when there's seemingly nothing to do but think about how they feel about that void. They'll tell you it can feel pretty uncomfortable. So, what do we do? Put something in place of the void. We can use strategies to mindfully plant positive and pleasant thoughts in the fertile soil of our mental garden. Then see what happens. We don't have to fill every moment meeting objectives toward fulfilling goals. We can push the pause button on our neural blender and stop pureeing every thought until their original forms are unrecognizable, believing that and behaving as if nothing that isn't goal-oriented is worthwhile.

For heaven's sake, we can take pleasure in doing something for no sake at all, much less heaven's. In fact, we take the joy out of gazing at clouds if we do so only analytically or in search of metaphors for our 7 p.m. panel discussion. When we stop placing expectations or parameters on our yet-experienced experiences, we can let them play out without our intervention. Like my 118-degree walk in Phoenix, encountering birds, I went out with no agenda—except, perhaps, to engage in a healthy distraction in nature with no agenda.

Daniel Kahneman, the Nobelist introduced earlier, in his book *Thinking, Fast and Slow*, mines the pitfalls and power of the two ways our brain processes thought. System 1, fast thinking, is automatic, intuitive, and emotional. System 2, slow thinking, is deliberate, analytical, and requires conscious attention.

One of the wonders of System 1 is its ability to feed creative insights to System 2. This often happens precisely when System 2 is taking a rest. Kahneman calls it "lazy" to let down your System 2, but our interviews even with scientists suggest that it is "very hard" to sustain long sequences of abstract thought. Not only that, instead of being lazy, it may sometimes be genius. Many famous anecdotes exist about the benefits of incubation, or time away from a task, for coming up with creative insights to a problem. In recent years, scientific findings support the importance of letting the mind incubate.[14]

Executive and life coach Nivedita Das Narayan, Mumbai, India, who has worked in the corporate world, shares my sentiments and the value I place on healthy distractions. In her article "Be your spontaneous best," she writes, "We give definitions, we create hashtags, we assign taglines, we create theories, and yet life gets ahead of us! We pretend we know, we argue, and explain. We forget to remain curious; we forget to be surprised like we did as children."[15]

Curiosity is an essential trait of a good leader, an enthusiastic and engaged employee, a sculptor, a painter, and a wellness consultant and presenter like me. What better distraction when we can't escape to parts unknown than to give ourselves permission to fall down a rabbit hole of rabbit holes in the delicious sense made by a Pulitzer Prize-winning *The New Yorker* author who fearlessly let herself become interested in something to the point of distraction.[16] In the process, we're likely to stumble into happiness.

In Insight 11, we'll go down the rabbit hole of healthy distractions and alternatives to food and drink cravings, particularly carbohydrates, fats, and alcohol. Before we do, let's clear up a misconception. Think a nightcap will soften the edges of a tough day? Think again. Alcohol isn't a distraction; it's a depressant. Alcohol may help you fall asleep faster, but there's a good chance you'll find yourself waking up and counting sheep the rest of the night. Alcohol notoriously reduces rapid eye movement (REM) sleep and the deep sleep your body needs to restore itself. You wake up feeling exhausted. Instead, try a bedtime smoothie, turmeric milk, tart cherry juice loaded with sleep-friendly melatonin and the amino acid tryptophan, or a host of healthy "nightcaps" that your body will love and your brain will appreciate.

Trust your instincts. Intuitively, you know what fortifies your well-being. Take the time to fall down a rabbit hole of your own choosing and refresh your spirit.

Practice

Self-Guided Meditation for Relaxation and Stress-Reduction

While there are many guided meditations available, it's helpful to teach yourself to find the sweet spot in your day and give yourself a mini vacation without an external stimulus. That way, you can practice self-guided mediation anywhere that it's practical and safe to do so. Self-guided meditation offers many benefits. Use it to nurture your self-esteem, expand your self-love, express self-compassion, diminish or wash away physical or emotional pain, strengthen your immune system, ride life's roller coaster, and much more. Let's start by igniting the power of your imagination to relax and refresh.

- ❧ Find a comfortable position sitting or lying down.
- ❧ Close your eyes and keep them closed.
- ❧ Take a few relaxing breaths. You can breathe in through your nose and exhale through your mouth. Throughout this practice, take gentle "even breaths." Inhale for six seconds; exhale for six seconds.
- ❧ Choose a favorite place in the world to be, even if you've never been there.
- ❧ Begin to "see" this special place. Visualize your surroundings in three dimensions, the colors, the textures, your movement in these spaces. Be there.
- ❧ Hear the sounds.
- ❧ Feel the warmth, coolness, breeze, water washing against you.
- ❧ Check in with how you feel. Comfortable? Relaxed? Safe? Happy? Mellow? Overflowing with love? Light? Calm? Peaceful? Bask as long as you like.
- ❧ Breathe in the pleasant fragrances: sweet, flowery, spicy, woodsy, pungent, lemony, fruity, and so on. Remember them. You can bring them back to mind any time, any place.

❧ Slowly, maintaining your even breathing, begin to leave your special place. Know that you can return whenever you wish and experience the specialness of your real or imaginary place. Hold your feelings of warmth, contentment, subtle joy. Over the count of three, bring your awareness back to your breath, back to the present moment.

Exercises

In your journal,

- List seven healthy distractions or engagements agreeable to your tastes and interests.
- List seven new experiences that you'd be willing to try as a distraction. What might you learn from them?
- How do healthy distractions help you break old habits that you want to leave behind?
- My aha moment from this insight is

Inspiration

I often talk about how we consciously "distract" ourselves
in healthy ways when we do so with intention.
Doing this allows us to interrupt the negative, unconscious,
and habitual patterns of our minds and our culture that often
get in the way of us experiencing the peace, joy, and
abundance that is naturally and authentically
around us and within us all the time.
—Mike Robbins

THIRTEEN

Nourish Your Natural Self

Health is the natural order of things, a positive attribute to which men [people] are entitled if they govern their lives wisely. The most important function of medicine is to discover and teach the natural laws which will ensure a healthy mind in a healthy body.
—René Dubos

Insight 11: Ground Yourself in Nature

I recognize that Nature is my nature. I choose to nourish my body with naturally wholesome foods and activities and connect with the earth and all life that grounds me.

The He(art) and Science Behind the Insight

What Is Natural for You?

Friends and seminar participants have heard my long-time mantra: "Strength, energy, and vitality!" These three words put a positive spin on the declaration *veni, vidi, vinci*, "I came, I saw, I conquered." I came to an awareness that I had the power to make healthy choices. I saw the benefits of living a healthy lifestyle naturally. In the process, I conquered my cravings with little effort by substituting delicious, healthy alternatives, including activities that connect me with nature. The responses that I've received from people who have enhanced their strength, energy, and vitality by putting these insights into practice have been immensely gratifying.

The Twelve Insights focus on highly effective strategies to achieve and enhance body-mind-spirit well-being with emphasis on these positive habits:

- Developing healthy, supportive relationships
- Finding purpose and meaning in our lives
- Discovering joy in small things
- Expressing gratitude for the many things we take for granted
- Growing throughout our lives by remaining inquisitive and curious
- Believing in ourselves
- Honoring and loving the gift that is our body
- Acting compassionately and empathetically toward ourselves and others
- Eating the highest-quality natural foods
- Getting sufficient restful sleep
- Building strong bodies and minds through regular exercise
- Becoming more intimately connected with nature

What is natural to us? Just because we have never done something before doesn't mean it can't become natural to us. There is a first time for everything. Walking and talking have become natural to us. Reaching out and hugging people dear to us feels natural. Expressing our feelings is natural to some of us and not others. That may be a quality that needs to be learned. We also use the term to describe an inborn trait, e.g., saying "she's a natural basketball player."

We achieve a state of well-being—accompanied by its undercurrent of joy and peace—through the lifelong process of discovering what is natural for us. Let's be clear. Doing something one way for seemingly ages that has become a habit doesn't mean it's natural or good for us. When something derails our goal to lead a healthy, happy lifestyle, we can take these three positive steps to get back on track:

- Determine if the choice or activity feels natural to us, not to our brother or best friend, but to us, or we won't follow through. That doesn't mean we can't or shouldn't stretch ourselves, expand our horizons, or feel motivated to step outside of the box or our comfort zone. It does mean that we'll know when something is right and can accept when something isn't. Let it go.

- Find pleasure in what we do or choose. Yes, we need to be open to serendipity, and we can learn to like things that are new and different, in much the same way that beginning runners eventually reach that place where they feel their inner and outer best when they're on the move. As we've consistently emphasized, we need to love what we do and be passionate about it. We can have fun and be passionate about preparing meals that are wholesome, appealing, and delicious.

- Connect with nature every day, in some way, somewhere. Our minimum daily requirement is seventeen minutes. That's about two hours a week.[1] Walk, jog, run, peddle, garden, whatever outdoor exercise feels natural to you, give it the opportunity to nourish your mind and spirit while strengthening your body. You don't need to drive out of the city to be surrounded by nature. Consider my mindfulness walk in Phoenix before a presentation. I stepped outside the world of asphalt, steel, and glass and entered the natural world of trees, bees, blooming shrubs, and hundreds of birds that might have gone unnoticed. The walk rejuvenated me. We'll come back to our need for nature nourishment shortly.

253

Before we leave this section, I'd like to share my thoughts about the word "diet." Diet is the sum of the food or habitual nourishment that we consume. Let's not think of diet as a dirty word that reminds us of frustrating ups and downs on the scale of weight goals unmet. When we talk about diet, we're referring to the sum total of the foods recommended to amplify our body's own natural healing capabilities and function at its best.

Eating to Live or Living to Eat?

"Sorry, there's no magic bullet," says Morgan Spurlock, the documentarist of the film *Super Size Me* and *Super Size Me 2: Holy Chicken*, when it comes to the relationship between large portions in the American diet and the fast-food industry. "You gotta eat healthy and live healthy to be healthy and look healthy. End of story."

Actually, Spurlock's prescription is the beginning. While we're becoming more food wise in these supercharged stressful times, we are also becoming increasingly prone to food addictions. We long for a reprieve from stress, and our brain can give that to us. Our brain's pleasure centers light up like holiday trees when we expose them to highly palatable salt, sugar, and fat.

As we'll explore further, those pleasure centers in the brain are the same ones triggered by cocaine and heroin. Is it any wonder that the pleasure and reward chemicals released by compulsive eating or overeating can be so powerful that they keep us from feeling satisfied and full? These chemicals effectively counteract our self-control. And the consequences of losing control—living to eat rather than eating to live—can become an unhealthy cycle that feels impossible to break. But there is hope.

Ask the world-famous Mayo Clinic. Physicians at the Mayo and other medical practice and research institutions recommend adding a little DASH to your eating habits. No, not the mix of seasonings in a jar. DASH is an acronym for Dietary Approaches to Stop Hypertension. And, you've guessed it: studies back up the blood-pressure-reducing properties of the recommended foods that are lower in sodium, added sugars, and saturated fat.[2]

Later in this chapter, we'll look at some of my favorite healthy diets, such as the Japanese, Mediterranean, and DASH. Each has its unique approach to the components of a well-balanced diet: proteins, carbohydrates, fats, vitamins and minerals, and water. But first, let's look at the highly studied, complex psychological and physiological behaviors called addiction to foods (eating) and then to other substances.

How Sweet It Is

We love the sweet life. People have treasured honey's golden goodness for more than eight thousand years. One of a handful of sweetener alternatives to refined cane or beet sugar, honey offers protective antioxidants that turn off damaging free radicals in our bodies. Honey has been touted for its phytonutrients, which studies show help to reduce the risk of heart attacks, high blood pressure, strokes, and some types of cancer. There is increasing evidence that these compounds also reduce low-density lipoprotein (LDL) cholesterol, triglycerides, and inflammation while raising our healthy high-density lipoprotein (HDL) cholesterol.[3]

Science has yet to support local raw honey's reputation for alleviating seasonal allergies. As some people may be sensitive or allergic to raw honey, we need to be aware of our body's response to it. Raw honey should never be given to infants under the age of one. Should you choose to enjoy this sweetener in moderation, purchase all-natural, raw honey from a trusted local producer. Primarily the sugars fructose, glucose, maltose, and sucrose, honey contains about 64 calories per tablespoon. A little goes a long way.

Agave nectar—concentrated "honey" water from blue agave plants—has become a popular sweetener for vegans who don't eat honey. Although its flavor is more neutral than honey, agave nectar has about the same number of calories. It's one and a half times sweeter than sugar and can be used in recipes calling for refined sugar. According to the American Diabetes Association, agave nectar—like any sweetener—should be consumed in limited amounts. Our bodies process sweeteners that we think of as natural—honey, agave nectar, coconut or date sugars, molasses, and maple syrup, for example—as sugar, explains Colleen Tewksbury, senior research investigator at the Perelman School of Medicine at the University of Pennsylvania.[4]

So, if our body treats one sugar pretty much like another, why snack on grapes, apples, pears, blueberries, blackberries, or raspberries, instead? Because, says Tewksbury, the fiber, nutrients, and antioxidants in many fruits—particularly in berries—offer big health bonuses over refined sugar with empty calories. For starters, fruit helps aid in digestion, increases the feeling of fullness, helps prevent sugar spikes by regulating blood sugar levels, and provides energy over a longer period.

Salt of the Earth

Have you ever licked the coarse crystals off a pretzel before taking a bite, or sprinkled salt on watermelon or a lemon? Most of us love that salty, zingy tingle, and many of us consume way too much salt. There are reasons. First, our bodies and brains require sodium for healthy functioning. Second, that flavor we have come to expect is highly addictive. Only in the last decade have researchers identified the mysterious and illusive taste receptors for both low concentrations of sodium—salt—and high concentrations. That makes sense, since too much salt is unpleasant and unpalatable.

You may have heard the idiom "worth one's salt." The phrase dates to Roman antiquity and refers to the high value placed on salt. As part of their wages, Roman soldiers received a measure of the crystalline mineral. We recognize the idiom as an affirmation that one measures up and commands respect for a job well done.

Salty is one of the five tastes we're able to detect. The others are sweet, bitter, sour, and umami. Whether the crystals in your grinder are pink, gray, black, white, Himalayan, Celtic, sea, or rock, salt is salt. The minerals touted in exotic salts are trace amounts, so don't be fooled by thinking you're getting more of those trace minerals by increasing the shakes on your food.

Like water, salt is essential to life. Salt is made up of sodium and chloride. Chloride ions comprise important electrolytes necessary for proper nerve and muscle function and regulate our blood pH. Salt regulates the way the body retains fluids and, therefore, plays a role in the volume of blood coursing through our bodies, affecting our blood pressure, and so much more.

The very complex and delicate dance between sodium and our cell and organ function is a feat of choreography. So why does salt get such a bad rap? A little makes our foods taste so much better, but a lot contributes to heart disease, hypertension, stroke, and osteoporosis. Our bodies' responses to salt—such as high blood pressure—depend a lot on our age, weight, gender, race or ethnicity, and certain medical conditions.

According to the American Heart Association (AHA), our bodies require a minimum of 500 mg. daily of this vital nutrient for proper cell and organ function. Over the eons, however, we have driven our sodium cravings to more than four times that of our Paleolithic ancestors. The AHA urges a happier, healthier medium: from our current 3,300 mg. per day to less than 1,500 mg. Not only was the intake of pre-agricultural humans low in sodium but it was also high in critical potassium-rich plants.

One of the seven essential macrominerals, potassium regulates sodium's negative effect on fluid balance and blood pressure, and it relaxes the walls of blood vessels. The correct potassium levels for you keep heart, kidneys, muscles, and nerves working well. Studies show that it may also increase bone mineral density. Science tells us that the optimal balance is about three times as much potassium as sodium from our diet. Although the National Institutes of Health (NIH) lists the average adequate intake levels of potassium for healthy children and adults, scientists have yet to establish a Recommended Daily Allowance (RDA). The NIH has dedicated one web page on potassium information for consumers and another for professionals, which includes a table listing the potassium content of selected foods.[5]

If you believe you're not getting adequate potassium from the foods you consume, talk to your primary care provider before taking supplements. Blood tests will reveal your potassium levels. A too-high potassium level—called hyperkalemia—can be life-threatening. Symptoms of high potassium include nausea, tingling or unusual sensations, feeling tired or weak, abnormal heartbeat, chest pains, and shortness of breath. Potassium and sodium are yin yang to our healthy eating practice.

We developed our taste for salt in infancy. Research shows that early exposure appears to define our preference for salt as an adult and subsequent future risk of high blood pressure and heart disease. Like many of the behaviors and habits we've discussed, more isn't better. Yet, not everyone who uses salt liberally experiences a rise in blood pressure. Still, achieving a moderate-to-low, healthy salt intake is within our control. A good first step is to root out where excess sodium lurks.

> Came from a plant? Eat it.
> Was made in a plant? Don't.
> —Michael Pollan[6]

The Centers for Disease Control (CDC) tells us that we're not necessarily shaking and grinding too much of this ancient flavor-enhancer on our home-cooked meals. In the US, the high-sodium culprits—accounting for more than 70 percent of our sodium consumption—are processed foods as well as forays to our favorite dining spots. The US Food and Drug Administration (FDA) defines "processed foods" as any food "other than a raw agricultural commodity." That still covers a lot of territory, as we know many fruits, vegetables, nuts, seeds, and grains are processed before they reach our kitchens. To narrow our search for salt, the FDA processing umbrella includes canning, cooking and steaming, freezing, dehydration, or milling prior to market distribution. In other words, if the food isn't in its natural, raw form, it's been processed in some way. The preservation process often involves sodium or other additives.

Just because the label says "all natural" or "whole grain" doesn't mean the food is in its natural form. Sobering is that "about eighty percent of the food on the shelves of supermarkets today didn't exist one hundred years ago," says nutritional specialist Larry McCleary, MD.

Look for minimally processed foods, such as flash-frozen vegetables, which are usually low in sodium and often have none added. It may seem strange, but taste alone won't necessarily reveal if a processed food contains sodium, much less an overload. That's because there are at least a dozen sodium-containing chemicals that are typically added to our foods, particularly to cured and canned meats or lunch meats, cheeses, and a boatload of grab-and-go snacks. Sodium nitrate, sodium nitrite, sodium sulfite, baking soda, baking powder, and sodium alginate are just a handful of many. To make it even more difficult to gauge salt levels when you're dining out is that sneaky sodium is often masked by other flavor enhancers. Some seasonings, sugar, and acidic enhancers can offset the salty taste.

What's a conscientious, mindful eater who strives to maintain healthy heart and kidneys do about hidden sodium? Read labels. But you already do that, right? Be aware that even when the label states "low sodium," that amount may be greater than is good for you. Plus, the terms are confusing. You'll see salt-free, or sodium-free; very low sodium; low sodium; reduced sodium; light sodium; and no salt added, also called unsalted, but the latter simply indicates that no additional salt was added during processing.

From the beginning of the *Twelve Insights for Mindful Living*, you've heard me promote the emotional and physical health benefits of exercise. After a high-intensity workout of longer than an hour, you may need to replenish lost electrolytes—salts—with sports drinks to rebalance the fluid and pH levels in your muscles, nerves, and brain. You may want to dilute some sports drinks and beverages fifty-fifty with water to prevent a sour stomach. For workouts of shorter duration, you'll achieve sufficient hydration with pure water. Steer clear of beverages sweetened with sugar.

Be mindful that packaged foods even hyped as "healthy" usually contain sodium in any of its many forms. Eat fresh. That means being mindful of the foods your children consume, too. What quick, packaged cheese, meat, and cracker snacks get tossed in their lunch boxes? What are they eating at school? What are you grabbing at work from the vending machine as a quick pick-me-up?

At home, rachet-up the flavor of your favorite recipes by increasing the herbs and adding a squeeze of lemon juice or a half-teaspoon of lemon zest. Other steps in the sodium-lowering direction include cutting back on convenience and fast foods like pizza, tacos, burgers, and fries. After a long day at work, especially when we've been up since five, it's tempting to stop on the way home for prepared, ready-to-eat foods that we can put right on the table. But let's look at the labels. One original Kentucky Fried chicken breast contains a ship-sinking 1,190 mg. of sodium. A Popeye's chicken breast loads its eaters with 1,330 mg. of sodium. A McDonald's Bacon Smokehouse Artisan Grilled Chicken sandwich packs a whopping 1,940 mg of sodium, which is 81 percent of our RDA, according to a

2019 article in *Forbes*, citing a study by Boston University. And fast-food chains are increasing salt content in their recipes to keep us addicted.

The study compared 1986 sodium content in entrees at 36 percent of our RDA to today's and found that chains have added 50 percent more salt. Few of us believe fast food is healthy. But convenience often outweighs our better judgment.

Many packaged snacks are sodium heavy-hitters. Instead, choose unsalted nuts and seeds. Can't imagine popcorn on movie night at home without the added salt? Sprinkle on other seasonings such as chili or curry powders, oregano (a little goes a long way), cocoa powder, cinnamon, or tabasco for a kick. Craving salt? You may be dehydrated or have a sodium imbalance. Talk to your physician about the optimal daily sodium intake for you.

Comfort in Healthy Comfort Food

Who among us doesn't once in a while turn to food for comfort? It's such a cliché that we even name certain dishes "comfort food." Scientifically, these are called hyperpalatable foods, and they hyper-stimulate a number of our senses, particularly taste, sight, and smell. Hyperpalatable foods are saltier, fattier, gooier, sweeter, and richer than is good for us. The most addictive combination? Sugar and fat.

Don't eat anything your great-grandmother wouldn't recognize as food.
—Michael Pollan

When the chips are down, we almost automatically set aside mindfulness and turn to comfort food. In fact, many of us instinctively turn to food before we rely on natural stress-reduction techniques such as short-term, beneficial daydreaming that we talked about earlier, focusing on our breath, engaging in walking meditation along the river, or taking the dog for a quick jog. We've all experienced times when we've set awareness aside and indulged in whatever foods prompts the expression, "That hit the spot."

Unfortunately, that spot comes with a high price. Most of the foods we consume to self-medicate contribute to obesity and other diseases. Recent studies on the effects of stress on eating habits show that the connection between our emotional and physiological response varies widely. Subjects experienced as much as a 40 percent increase in calories consumed or a 40 percent decrease in calories. Roughly 20 percent of participants maintained their normal eating behaviors during periods of high stress.[7]

Researchers have long known that sweet and starchy comfort foods temporarily increase our body's production of the calming hormone serotonin. We know that when the body is in high alert, the adrenal glands produce the stress hormone cortisol, which regulates not only our body's use of carbohydrates, proteins, and fats but also affects mood. As we've learned, continual exposure to stress can derail normal cortisol production levels. Serotonin produced from consumption of carbohydrate-high foods makes us feel more in control, less depressed, anxious, and irritable.

Is healthy comfort food an oxymoron? Not if we prepare our meals mindfully. We can turn to many healthy foods such as salmon, turkey, pineapple, nuts, seeds, and more to boost serotonin production. And we can still enjoy those old-fashioned favorites by bulking them up with hearty, heart-healthy, and extra-fiber additions such as kidney or pinto beans, sweet potatoes, broccoli, kale, brown rice, and many other nutritious alternatives to wheat pasta, white potatoes, and dumplings. These healthy ingredients tend to make us feel satisfied with smaller portions. For recipes calling for rice, substitute ancient grains. Consider gluten-free, delicious teff, soup-worthy amaranth, or the nutritional powerhouse, millet. Quinoa—we love the tri-color variety—is exceptionally versatile.

To cut down on fat, instead of incorporating several cups of grated cheese into a dish, sprinkle a sharper cheese on top where its browned goodness tantalizes your senses first. Since it's beyond the scope of this book to go into the benefits of gluten-free foods and healthy fats, I recommend exploring the "Healthy Eating Plate" guide on the Harvard T. H. Chan School of Public Health website. Its guide is downloadable and available in twenty-five languages. The Mayo Clinic's website also offers valuable healthy eating and nutrition information.

Hey, Honey, What's for Dinner?

Probably no one asked this question before the Neolithic Revolution around 12,000 years ago. The period that coincided with global climate change and the end of the last ice age is also called the agricultural revolution. It was a pivotal time in our history. The domestication of plants and animals "forever changed how humans live, eat, and interact."[8] Hunter-gatherers who had foraged for food became farmers. Raising fields of wheat, barley, peas, lentils, and perhaps also flax, made it possible for elders and children to become involved in food production. Before then, only able-bodied members of the clan hunted together and brought home the woolly mammoth and rhinoceros. Gatherers harvested berries, nuts, seeds, and other edible plants.

"Harvest," the research project spearheaded by Amanda Henry, a paleobiologist and associate professor at Leiden University, Netherlands, confirms that early peoples' diets were plant-based.[9] Cereals and nutrient-rich tubers provided glucose for brain health and energy. To be edible, these foodstuffs required processing. Cooking converted the toxins of many tubers, and grinding grains into a groat or flour unlocked their bioavailability.

Henry's research shows that the average Paleolithic person who survived infancy lived to age fifty or sixty. These unexpected lifespans from Henry's and other studies suggest that Paleolithic people likely died "from a combination of infections, parasites, and physical trauma." Henry emphasized that the project's discovery that plants were king means that we've got the concept of today's Paleo Diet wrong. "A lot of Paleo diets talk about health, but by this they mean weight loss. And I can't think of a single human ancestor who wanted to lose weight."

So, what happened to human longevity when we became farmers? Worldwide research associates the agrarian lifestyle and animal-rearing with an increase in diseases that jumped from animals to humans. The twist is and the data shows that populations exploded when there was sufficient food. Adults died younger, but they had more babies. Studies conducted in the US in the 1970s revealed counterintuitively that agricultural populations "were experiencing significant increases in nutritional deficiencies and infectious diseases."[10]

A project called "Hidden Foods," which studies the predominantly plant-based diets of the late Paleolithic era, corrects our current misconceptions. Remains of grains, legumes, nuts, and seeds found in ten-thousand-year-old teeth tell their own story. "Our idea of a Paleo Diet as primarily based on protein intake is completely wrong," says Emanuela Cristiani, who is associate professor in prehistoric archaeology at Sapienza University of Rome and director of the Ancient Diet and Technology Department. "It's important to understand for real what the ancient Paleolithic diet was," Cristiani says. "It was a very balanced way of eating."[11]

Food as Medicine: Fueling a Healthy Lifestyle

Since my early days as a personal trainer and fitness consultant, I've advocated whole foods, regular physical activity, restorative sleep, and avoidance of toxic and addictive substances. Over these many years, I've guided hundreds of clients toward balanced diets and lifestyle changes to increase exercise, strengthen their core, and enhance mental alertness and emotional resilience. My immersion in the study of mindful awareness and the practice of mindful meditation enabled me to help others achieve greater mind-body-spirit wellness. Daily, we're increasing our knowledge and awareness of the power of food not only to heal but also to reverse chronic diseases such as heart disease, diabetes, and obesity.

> It is health that is real wealth,
> not pieces of gold and silver.
> —Mahatma Gandhi

Breakthrough multi-national scientific studies help us understand the complex relationship among nutrition, cardiovascular and metabolic diseases, and neurodegenerative disorders.[12] I'm heartened that Western medicine is increasingly connecting the dots between stress influences and food choices, as we've discussed earlier.[13] Scientists have seen—as have I—the cycle in which negative emotions and stress negatively affect the way our body metabolizes the unhealthy meals we've chosen. Unhealthy meals and poor nutrition lead to an unhealthy gut and chronic inflammation. Decades of research confirm the link between healthy dietary patterns and better cognitive health during aging. The World Health Organization's statistics indicate that in 2019 there were one billion people over the age of sixty. WHO predicts that by 2050, the elderly population will exceed two billion, particularly in developing countries.

In an unprecedented act of collaboration across multi-national organizations, the United Nations declared 2021–2030 the Decade of Healthy Aging. Asia and Europe claim the greatest number of individuals above the age of sixty-five. Japan leads the way with 28 percent of the population, followed by Italy with 23 percent. That's no surprise. Japan's exceptional longevity correlates to its low rate of obesity and fewer deaths from heart disease and cancers. Red meat isn't often on the table, but fish, plant foods, seaweed, soybeans, and green tea are. In the 1970s, Japanese eating habits changed dramatically. Salt intake decreased and longevity increased. The UN Food and Agriculture Organization (FAO) also points to another factor contributing to longer lifespans: fewer dairy products, sugar, artificial sweeteners, fruits, and potatoes on their tables than in other developed countries. As a consequence, the average Japanese consumes one thousand fewer calories per day than the average American.

The true Japanese diet with its low consumption of saturated fatty acids and high consumption of omega-3 fatty acids is among the healthiest. As we'll see, scientists are watching closely for a downward shift in longevity as Japanese tastes trend toward Western fast food with its high salt content, unhealthy fats, and high carbohydrates. For a time, Japan had one of the lowest incidences of cardiovascular diseases in the world. But Westernization is making a sweeping impact on health. Studies following Japanese people who have immigrated to the US and adopted our lifestyle show that their rate of heart disease quadrupled.[14]

Eating like the Mediterraneans Did

Popularity of the Mediterranean Diet began to spread around 1975. Several decades earlier, physicians and medical researchers compared the low incidence of heart disease and stroke in the countries that border the Mediterranean Sea—with their plant-based, traditional cuisine—to the higher rates of coronary disease in the US. The findings were startling. We truly are what we eat.

A 2017 genome study conducted at the University of California, Berkeley, published in *Molecular Biology and Evolution*, revealed that Europeans, particularly those living in the southern regions, had adapted many thousands of years ago to a decidedly plant-based diet, likely because early on they had settled into an agrarian lifestyle.[15] Other cultures, mostly those in northern regions of the world, developed biological systems that functioned on diets high in animal fats, such as those from ocean animals. This study helps to explain why the introduction of modern American foods is having such an impact on peoples whose bodies are primed to consume lots of vegetables, fruits, and whole grains.

The United Nation's FAO found that in recent decades Mediterranean people have increased their daily caloric intake by 30 percent.[16] In fact, a 2015 study showed that less than half of the thousands of people surveyed ate like their grandparents and great-grandparents. Worrisome to physicians is that obesity has skyrocketed among younger Italians and other Mediterranean peoples. Increasingly, people around the world are eating more like Americans: fattier fried foods along with unhealthy quantities of refined carbohydrates in larger portions.

These studies endorse the natural mind-body health and efficacy of the original Mediterranean Diet. The Mayo Clinic credits its focus on meals rich in vegetables, fruits, legumes, whole grains, nuts, seeds, and beneficial herbs and spices. Fish, seafood, poultry, and dairy are added in moderation. Red meat is on the menu infrequently, and desserts are less sugary and fatty. The primary source of added fat in the Mediterranean Diet is olive oil, a monounsaturated fat that has been shown to lower total cholesterol and low-density lipoprotein—or "bad"—cholesterol levels. Other sources of monounsaturated fats come from heart-healthy nuts such as almonds, walnuts, and pistachios—technically seeds—hazelnuts, chestnuts, and pine nuts. On the seedy side of the Mediterranean Diet, there are pumpkin, sunflower, and sesame seeds, which provide essential omega-6 fatty acids. But consume them in moderation.

Rich in omega-3 fatty acids that help fight inflammation and lower triglyceride levels and reduce the risk of stroke and heart failure are fatty fish, such as salmon, mackerel, herring, sardines, and albacore tuna.

Research shows that the health benefits of omega-3 also include lowering depression, and studies are increasingly finding positive protection for the brain. Omega-3 has been shown to reduce the symptoms of ADHD in some children. A breakthrough is that it also appears to slow cognitive decline in older adults, potentially protecting against the effects of Alzheimer's disease and dementia.

You'll find plenty of recipes online for authentic Mediterranean Diet dishes. How about wine? In moderation: two drinks or less per day for men, and one drink or less per day for women. We've read that low-to-moderate consumption of alcohol is associated with a reduced risk of heart disease. But the CDC and other research organizations recommend that if you don't drink, don't start. Believing that drinking is healthier than not drinking is not only fuzzy logic, it's dangerous. We've long known that excessive alcohol consumption poses dire health risks. Heavy drinking is responsible for high blood pressure; heart disease; stroke; liver disease; digestive problems; cancer of the breast, mouth, throat, and esophagus; weakening of the immune system; depression; anxiety; fetal alcohol spectrum disorders (FASD) in pregnant women; death; and more. Excessive drinking was responsible for one in ten deaths among working-age adults ages twenty to sixty-four.[17]

DASH to the Rescue

DASH stands for Dietary Approaches to Stop Hypertension. And it does this so effectively for so many people that it is now advocated as the first line of pharmacologic therapy in addition to changes in lifestyle. DASH got its start in 1992 when the NIH, part of the US Department of Health and Human Services and the umbrella medical research agency over twenty-seven institutes and centers, began in-depth exploration of interventions to reverse America's escalating rate of hypertension, or high blood pressure, and obesity.

Studies have shown that the DASH Diet—which is similar to the Mediterranean Diet—can lower blood pressure in as little as two weeks. It recommends five servings of vegetables per day and healthy carbohydrates from green leafy vegetables, whole grains, low-glycemic index fruit, and legumes and beans for their micronutrients and energy. Good fats, as in the Mediterranean Diet, provide essential fatty acids that help prevent inflammation. Since the DASH Diet nixes high sodium, processed and cured meats, which exacerbate hypertension and contain known carcinogens, are excluded from its menus.

The Mayo Clinic, among others, touts the DASH Diet for its inclusion of foods that are rich in potassium, magnesium, and calcium, nutrients known to help lower blood pressure, and their effectiveness in lowering LDL, blood glucose levels, and insulin resistance.[18] The list of health benefits stretches across myriad scientific studies. The bottom line is so impressive that I encourage you to talk to your doctor about the DASH Diet and see if it's right for you. Please remember, however, no eating plan is a magic bullet to achieving a healthy body and mind without your lifestyle-change commitment. If you smoke, stop. Say no to alcohol. Instead, exercise. Get out into nature and enjoy mindful walking meditation. If you want to be healthy and stay healthy, you've got to move. You're stepping in the right direction with good nutrition and exercise.

You might want to have a heart—a healthier, happier one, that is—and skip the deep-fried SlimFast bars, chicken-fried bacon, chocolate bacon on a stick, and the fried ice-cream cheeseburger. Being mindful of your middle equates to being kind to your heart. Whichever plan you and your doctor choose, you'll find that leaving the Standard American Diet (SAD) behind makes parting such sweet sorrow.

Fad Diets and Fasting

Every year, forty-five million Americans of all races and sizes start some sort of plan to lose weight or get healthier. That trend has burgeoned into a $71 billion a year industry. Topping the 2021 list of forty programs rated by *U.S. New and World Report* is the Mediterranean Diet, which in the past tied with the DASH Diet. Near the bottom: the paleo, ketogenic ("keto"), and Atkins diets. Rated number two is the Flexitarian Diet that's quasi-vegetarian with occasional consumption of meat. Others include the hybrid Mediterranean-DASH Intervention for Neurodegenerative Delay (MIND) Diet that claims to reduce the risk of Alzheimer's disease.

Beware of the potentially dangerous human chorionic gonadotropin (HCG) Diet. The FDA warns against purchasing HCG supplements or getting injections unless under medical supervision. The HCG hormone, produced during pregnancy, is not approved for over-the-counter use.

Of course, there are vegetarian and vegan diets for those who choose not to consume animal products. Fasting and intermittent fasting aren't safe for everyone, so consult your physician before launching into a stint without food. Consider, too, that for some people, fasting can trigger counterproductive overeating or binge eating.

Researchers estimate that 23.5 million Americans have some form of autoimmune disorder. Some special programs, such as the quality-over-quantity Anti-Inflammation Diet, were designed to alleviate some of these conditions that studies link to the Western diet.[19] The resulting long-term, or chronic, inflammation can wreak havoc on the body's immune system and potentially lead to diseases such as Crohn's, rheumatoid arthritis, and other autoimmune disorders.

Eating healthy means tailoring your nutritional plan to meet your body's unique needs. You'll find a lifetime of recipes on the Internet to make eating healing and wholesome foods fun and delicious. Love what you eat and you'll stick with your commitment to make a healthy lifestyle change. Dessert? How about a walk in the park? And for optimal body-mind-spirit health, suggests Andrew Weil, take a dog along.[20]

Trees: The Rx for What Ails Us

We are drawn to trees as we are to a breath of fresh air. Little wonder. Trees emit airborne chemicals called phytoncides, volatile organic compounds, or "essential oils," which protect trees from bacteria, fungi, and insects. And it turns out that those same phytoncides also protect us by increasing the number of our "killer cells," the white blood cells that boost our body's response to viruses and tumors. Although not all things that attack us are infectious, many of us spend an average of 93 percent of our time cooped up indoors. Science now understands why forests are good medicine for what ails us, mentally, as well as physically.

Native peoples knew this intuitively. The Cherokee people call trees the "Standing People." The Northwest Coastal Indian culture refers to itself as "People of the Cedar" and tucked pieces of this sacred tree in the medicine pouches they wore. When we're among stately trees, we respond emotionally. Some of us feel a sense of reverence as if walking into a cathedral. Trees are also good medicine for the earth, contributing to its biodiversity, and the quality of its water and air.

While phytoncides aren't an elixir for long human life, with nature's prescription for reducing stress and battling lifestyle-induced illnesses, a longer life is possible.

> I think that I cannot preserve my health and spirits unless I spend four hours a day at least—and it is commonly more than that—sauntering through the woods and over the hills and fields, absolutely free from all worldly engagements.
> —Henry David Thoreau

In Japan, a popular health pastime is "forest bathing." This sensory exercise of practicing mindfulness in nature by holding our attention to the present moment is a centuries-old, non-medical therapy to boost well-being. Forest bathing is gaining international attention and a medical following in the UK and US, thanks to Qing Li, MD and PhD immunologist at the Nippon Medical School in Tokyo. Li is the world's leading expert in the secret power of forests and author of *Forest Bathing*. Li believes that when he lunches under the canopy of leaves in the nearby park, he's tapping into nature's treatment for diseases of the mind and body.

Li and fellow scientists in the UK have determined that these close encounters of the nature kind trigger the body's immunological and healing mechanisms to counter severe and catastrophic illnesses, reduce depression, anxiety and stress, boost the immune system, lower blood pressure, and aid sleep. In the lab, Li has seen the potential for forest bathing to "build bodies that may be resistant to cancer development."[21]

No need to pare down to our birthday suits to derive the benefits of forest bathing. We do need to leave our smartphones and cameras behind.

Slowly, mindfully aware of the present moment, we consciously relax. As we're drifting through the forest, we're aware of sensations: touching the trees and overhanging branches, paying attention to the patterns of leaves and shadows, and breathing deeply. To deepen our sense of calm and contentment, we can stretch out on the forest floor, look up and experience the soothing blue sky and green above us.

Li is hopeful that forest bathing, and the three-day encounters called *shinrin-yoku*, developed in the 1980s, will catch on and offer people worldwide the opportunity to take their seventeen-minute dose of health and well-being naturally.

In the UK, Mathew White is the lead researcher for the University of Exeter Medical School's study on the health benefits of as little as two hours a week outdoors.[22] How we divvy up that time doesn't matter. Whether we fit in a weekend of car camping by the lake or an after-dinner stroll around the quiet, tree-lined streets of our neighborhood, all of us, including older adults with long-term health issues, improve our well-being. White's team, which worked with data from nearly twenty thousand participants, found that to derive the maximum benefits of connecting with nature, it wasn't necessary to spend additional hours. Where can you go and what can you do in your seventeen minutes per day?

Forests aren't required to have a dialogue with nature. I live in the Sonoran desert, lush with fragrant sage, mesquite, acacia, and creosote—the native plant that gifts us our heavenly "wet desert" smell when it rains—heady citrus blossoms, and jasmine. Wherever we are, we simply need to get out and get in touch. And, as did the poets through the ages, we can let nature have the last word.

Practice

Mindful Eating

Let's try the raisin mindfulness exercise of chapter one. We can choose any similar food that we're also familiar with—in either its fresh or liquid form—such as a prune, sundried tomato, or dried cranberry. We can even choose a small piece of dark chocolate, which started out as cocoa beans. The idea is that we mindfully explore our sources of nutrition using as many senses as possible before and when we place it into our mouth, slowly bite into it, sense the flavor explosion, and then make the choice to consume it.

Although the raisin exercise is a perfect introduction to mindful eating for a seminar or presentation, you're probably reading or listening to this alone. So, let's take this exercise to the next level. Whether we're ordering off a menu or preparing food at home, we can be aware of making healthy choices about the quality and quantity of our meals. We know which foods are good for us and which are indulgences.

When we avoid eating at our desk or in front of the TV, we give our health a head start. We make wise selections and appropriate portion sizes, and we give ourselves the opportunity to experience our meal rather than wolf it down. We don't have to sit at a table to reduce stress. If you wish to eat from a napkin in your lap as you sit under a shade tree, you've consciously chosen an environment to foster a sense of calm.

Before taking a mouthful of food, spend a moment expressing thankfulness—even silently—for whatever you're about to eat. Here are some things you can do for a happier and healthier eating experience:

- Be aware of the food on your plate. Put your senses into gear. Is each item presented pleasantly? Does it look appetizing? What colors do you see?
- Where were the various items grown or raised and by whom?
- Who harvested the fruits and vegetables? Who rushed them to your grocer's or farmer's market?

> If you chose a serving of protein from meat, fish, or poultry, where did it come from? Is the portion more than you need for this meal, and will some be left over for tomorrow's lunch? Make that decision in advance to eliminate the tendency to overeat.

> Does what's on your plate smell mouthwatering good? Does it taste as good as it smells? What flavors do you detect? Salty? Sweet? Sour? Bitter? Umami? Or a combination of these? What herbs and spices can you identify?

> What textures do you experience?

A great practice is to put your fork down between bites to keep from rushing. Chew slowly and deliberately, which aids digestion. Researchers at Kyushu University, Japan, found that subjects who chew slowly feel full faster, which contributes to lower body mass index. But more, the smaller the food particles, the more they are exposed to the digestive enzymes in saliva. This is called predigestion, and it helps increase nutrient uptake and reduces the workload on our stomach and small intestine.

Exercises

In your journal,

- List seven foods or beverages you regularly consume for which you'd like to make healthier choices.
- List seven activities that fortify your natural state of well-being.
- Describe what the outdoors and being in nature means to you? How do you feel after an outing? Does food taste differently when it's enjoyed outside?
- My aha moment from this insight is

Inspiration

Wellness is an active process of becoming aware of
and making choices toward a healthy and fulfilling life.
Wellness is more than being free from illness;
it is a dynamic process of change and growth. It is a state
of complete physical, mental, and social well-being
and not merely the absence of disease or infirmity.
—University of California, Davis

FOURTEEN
Exercise Kindness

Love is patient, love is kind. It does not envy,
it does not boast, it is not proud. It does not
dishonor others, it is not self-seeking, it is
not easily angered, it keeps no record of wrongs.
Love does not delight in evil but rejoices
with the truth. It always protects, always trusts,
always hopes, always perseveres. Love never fails.
—The Apostle Paul

Insight 12:
Live in Love

I live with the knowledge that Love is the
most powerful energy in the universe and that
in order to live in Love, I must first love myself.
With gratitude and joy, I live in Love.

The He(art) and Science
Behind the Insight

A Book of the Heart

In the introduction, I promised to share with you a few insights into the *Twelve Insights'* book cover: the choice of fractal hearts. The beauty and implications of fractals mesmerize for their self-similar, never-ending patterns. A mental journey deep into the geometry of a fractal is like exploring space. In 1975, mathematician Benoit Mandelbrot coined the term fractal from the Latin "fractus," meaning fractured, or broken. The author of *The Fractal Geometry of Nature*, Mandelbrot opened the mathematical, philosophical, and theoretical doors to fractal use in the arts and sciences. We see fractals in ice crystals, snowflake, trees, ferns, river networks, our neural networks, the capillaries of our lungs, and even the sound of our hearts.

"Our inner fractals can resonate with the outer fractals, and we can have a kind of continuity and a sense of wholeness with the environment," says Franco Orsucci, a scientist and professor at the University College London.[1] Orsucci and others are discovering the benefits of fractals to reduce physiological stress.[2] Their quality of infinite continuity represents the interconnectedness of all things. "We're in the universe at the very same time that the universe is in us, and that's absolutely profound," Santa Monica, California, psychologist Terry Marks-Tarlow, PhD, says about the emotional healing and metaphorical applications of fractals,[3] often referred to as the fingerprint of life. In fact, "our eyes have become fluent in the visual language of nature's fractals," which are deeply embedded in our psyche.[4]

For all these reasons, we chose fractal hearts to symbolize the true nature of this book, which is, above all else, a love story. It is the story of meeting ourselves where we are as who we are, mindfully recognizing the treasure that we are, fully aware that we are in the midst of infinite hearts in a universe made more expansive by our capacity to dream and to imagine. Our rocket to the moon is fueled by love.

We've written much in this book—yet have just touched the tip of the ancient scholarly and scientific iceberg—about the mindful exploration of self as we journey through self-compassion toward our destination of inclusive love, for others and for all of creation, in our cosmic neighborhood and beyond.

What do we mean by a book of the heart? The metaphors of an "inner book" and the "heart as book" were stitched together in ancient Egypt. To early Christians, the heart symbolized soul, consciousness, and place where memories were stored. At the Last Judgment, the book of our heart would be opened and our deeds and misdeeds read. For painters and poets of the Middle Ages, the heart and the book of our secrets, passions, emotional ruptures, and spiritual raptures were bound into a single metaphorical volume of mystery and magic. It is then that the heart shape we know so well became the ubiquitous symbol of love.

What difference does that make in our lives? I invite you to view the cover as a visual springboard to imagine fractal hearts unfolding forever. These simple metaphors will speak volumes to the wise heart. And lower our stress levels. We needn't be obsessed with the world's trials and tribulations. We can't heal the world. We can only heal ourselves. We can take time to mindfully appreciate beauty. My hope is that this short section has sharpened your life-enhancing awareness that fractals can be discovered everywhere in nature. We can see our bodies as trees, and our hearts and minds as one pulsing organism.

Cupid's Arrow

In our science class, we learned that quasars are the most powerful thing in the universe. As we grew older and wiser, we came to recognize and understand another potent power. This one emerges from within us and flows outward: Love. For as long as we've had the capacity to wonder at our magnificent feelings and the language to name them, we've proclaimed that love comes from the heart.

Today, scientists don't totally refute our primitive notion, as they've discovered how complex and inter-related are the networks that link our body and mind. We now know that emotions arise from our brain's limbic system. The limbic system, the area between the brain stem and the two hemispheres, includes our amazing amygdala, the emotional center that decodes our perception of fearful events, the pleasure-seeking hypothalamus, and the hippocampus—shaped, some say, like a little seahorse—that stashes memories for the long term. Some part of the limbic system is always busy with issues of judgment, logic, reasoning, and impulse-control.

"The silent, often subconscious conversation that is taking place inside us is one of the most vital communications we will ever find ourselves engaged in," says Michael Miller, MD. "It's the dialogue of emotion-based signals between our hearts and our brains."[5] Miller, a professor of cardiovascular medicine at the University of Maryland School of Medicine, serves on the American Heart Association Leadership Council for Lifestyle and Cardiometabolic Health. Based on his studies, Miller formulated a prescription for heart protection that releases endorphins for health and happiness. His methods help patients achieve the same benefits that I've witnessed in practitioners of mindful awareness who purposefully live, love, laugh, and are happy and, therefore, lead healthier lives. Miller also advocates heart-protective mindfulness meditation that releases serotonin for relaxation; music that stimulates the positive effects of dopamine; and massage or hugging, both of which boost production of oxytocin.

We know oxytocin as the "trust," "cuddle," and "love hormone." Secreted by the pea-sized pituitary gland at the base of the brain, oxytocin is associated with childbirth and breastfeeding babies, bonding mother and her newborn. Birth chemically transforms the brain and hardwires many women to see their babies as irresistible, which is vital to maternal nurturing. It's the hormone that melts our hearts when we get close to human babies, puppies, kittens, and many other cute baby animals.

Lab experiments show oxytocin also plays a role in muscle repair and aging and may be beneficial for bone health and combating obesity, therefore extending healthy life.[6] When the heart throbs at the sight of a soulmate, could science be far behind? Our new heartthrob increases our levels of dopamine, adrenaline, and norepinephrine. But the flipside of love, finds a Loyola University Health System's study, is that our serotonin levels drop, which prompts the observation "love is blind."[7] Love, as we're seeing, can be good for us or drive us to distraction. Yes, we willingly follow moonstruck and star-crossed lovers through the pages of novels and the volumes of history, even as we know there is so much more to the four-letter word than romance.

How Do I Love Thee?

Let me count the ways.[8] In 1826, at the age of twenty, Elizabeth Barrett Browning anonymously published her "slender volume"[9] of poetry titled *An Essay on Mind, with Other Poems*. Her brilliance and passion catapulted her to the rarified heights of literary genius. The publishing world and her devoted and famous poet husband, Robert Browning, marveled at her uncommon humility. So few would shun the limelight and be content with the shadow.

Humility, introduced in chapter 3, and the highest form of love are intimately entwined. "Humility liberates love, and love rushes across the opening that humility has provided," writes Robert C. Roberts, professor of ethics and emotion theory and scholar with the project "Happiness and the Meaning of Life" at the University of Chicago.[10] When we are so full of ourselves, there is no room in our hearts to love all with whom we share the world.

When I say, as I have, "I love you," how does that differ from what I feel when I say "I love working in the garden"? The ancient Greek philosophers sorted out this conundrum of "how do I love thee?" and came up with seven ways. While the following types are useful to our understanding of the complex relationship between mind and heart, our experiences and instincts tell us that love can be messy and magnificent, bewildering and breathtaking, entangling and empowering all at once. One type and phase ebbs and flows into another, as you'll see.

- Eros, the Greek god of erotic love, also represents romantic love, sensual or passionate love, and desire.

- Storge, a Greek word that means family love and the bonds among family members, is often associated with the sacrificing love of parents for their children. It's a feeling that arises naturally and can be very emotive.

- Philia, in Greek, is the affectionate, platonic, brotherly love we think of as friendship for those who share our values, friends who are as close to us as siblings.

- Agape, another Greek term for love, refers to love that is selfless, unconditional, universal, a love of humanity and a higher power, a love most easily expressed through meditation, nature, and spirituality.

- Ludus, in Latin, means game, or school (a school of playmates), and describes the playful, uncommitted, flirtatious love, the game is merely to have fun.

- Pragma, from the Greek term for a practical relationship, is an enduring love built on a foundation of mutual respect, commitment, and compromise, all of which may have weathered the storms of eros love.

- Philautia, the Greek word for self-love, implies self-confidence and self-esteem that make us feel worthy and having a sense of purpose. Because it was associated with being consumed with one's own happiness, philautia has been maligned as a moral flaw. But the wise Greeks understood the opposite of its unhealthy, narcissistic side, as the ability to have healthy self-compassion.

Only when we learn unconditional love for ourselves, classical philosophers believed, was true happiness possible. In chapters 2 through 6, we uncovered the truth of this ancient wisdom as we explored our occasionally precarious relationship with the person we should know best.

All relationships are complex jigsaw puzzles. We're so sure pieces must be missing. Sometimes we try to force one type of love-shaped piece into a niche for which it wasn't intended. When our expectations are dashed, we're likely to come away from the experience licking our wounds, but wiser. Through mindful awareness of self, others, and the world with which we continually interact, we better understand the nature of love and its tremendous power to transform.

Never underestimate the ripple effect of even one seemingly small act of kindness or take for granted others' outward expressions of their gratitude for lives well-lived. Auto dealer Jim Click Jr. came to Tucson in 1971. His attitude of gratitude never ceases to inspire me. He was inspired by his father and uncle. At an early age, Click learned to visualize success and achieve it. He quickly discovered that the horsepower behind vision is tenacity. I call his mettle resilience.

What heartens me most is that Mr. Click—as I and many others call him out of respect—knows that neither visualizing success and achieving it nor developing personal resilience are worth their salt without the heart to pay forward the fruits of our labors and the gifts given us. Jim and Vicki Click do just that. Over the decades, the Click Family Foundation has raised many millions of dollars to benefit more than three hundred sixty southern Arizona charitable organizations—from the zoo to Boys and Girls Clubs to a fund that promotes civility, respect, and understanding to curb school bullying and raise mental-health awareness. The couple's motto is simple yet its impact is far-reaching. "This community has been good to our family, and we're just trying to be good back."

Love Your Neighbor

Despite what Tina Turner says, love isn't a secondhand emotion. She belts out the plaintive question why we need a heart when it can be broken. There's an answer in scripture, John 17:21, "That they all be one." The Qur'an teaches to do good to parents, kinsfolk, orphans, those in need, neighbors who are near, neighbors who are strangers, the companion by your side, the wayfarer.[11]

I often hear people use the term "loved ones," perhaps without always thinking about its implication. I've certainly used it. Does it mean that there are those outside of our circle who are excluded from our love, those whom we would not embrace? With our ability to feel and express many types of love, why would we choose to exclude anyone, even those whom we need to forgive?

The world's major religions teach us to love our neighbors as ourselves. Our world is composed of neighbors. Who are they? The immigrants who risk death to give their children a better life; the homeless person whose bed is a tattered piece of cardboard; the person on the subway who has no destination; the widows with no clean water to give their babies; and those whose skins range the spectrum from the darkest to the lightest with all shades in between.

Real neighbors see need first and respond. For a decade, the US led the list of the world's most generous countries in donations. Something extraordinary happened in 2020. Irish donors responded with an outpouring of love when the Navajo and Hopi Families COVID-19 Relief Fund went viral in Ireland. The Irish were happy to reciprocate to Native Americans for their donations in 1847—despite living in hardship and poverty themselves—to help alleviate hunger during the Irish Potato Famine that began two years earlier. Before the Great Hunger, as it was also called, ended in 1852, around one million people had died of starvation. But many who lived will never forget their neighbors with whom they embraced across an ocean. Today, in Bailick Park, County Cork, Ireland, nine twenty-foot-high stainless steel eagle feathers, arranged in a circle to form a bowl, symbolize the gift of a bowl of food from the Choctaw People. The sculpture is titled "Kindred Spirits." It's a small world.

Queen of Hearts

Tragedy strikes almost all of us, sooner or later. For some people, trauma, loss, and grief seem to take up residency in their lives, creating situations that would buckle many of us. Her childhood lacerated, my sister Paula could have entered her adult years full of anger, feeling vulnerable, unsafe, anxious, helpless, depressed, and a whole range of toxic emotions capable of poisoning body, mind, and spirit. But she didn't. I loved Paula dearly, and her resilience will forever be an inspiration to me. Paula survived our oppressive and abusive stepfather only to slip into marriages that echoed her painful past. Betrayed and left to fend for herself and a child with autism, Paula called upon inner resources only her higher self could reach. The news came years into her remarriage. The diagnosis was breast cancer. Her husband said he was sorry about abandoning her when she needed him most, but his girlfriend was pregnant.

A mother of three herself, Paula faced death square on as she had faced so much suffering and adversity throughout her life. Then came one more blow. Her nineteen-year-old special-needs son discovered medications in their home that produced a fatal combination with those already in his system. Of all the burdens Paula carried, anger and hatred were not among them. Forgiveness was natural to her. So was a heart as big and full of love as any I have witnessed. Our mother asked me to offer the eulogy. Paula and my mother loved playing cards, so I dedicated my tribute to our "Queen of Hearts." It was fitting. Without reservation or concern for what it would cost her, Paula gave hers away, again and again, and yet had love to spare for whoever needed it. In the days following her death, my other two sisters were going through boxes at Paula's home. In the last box, they found a single deck of cards. The top card was face up: the Queen of Hearts. They understood. Paula was letting us know that her heart was now free to spread love throughout the universe. Love had never failed her. It will never fail us.

Smile and the World Smiles with You

"Cry and you cry alone," wrote Stanley Gordon West in his novel *Growing an Inch*. A smile can predict how long you live, according to a University of California at Berkeley thirty-year longitudinal study.[12]

Never doubt your power. We deliberately use our smiling power to affect others' moods, turn the tide on uncomfortable situations, and make ourselves feel better when we gape in the mirror. Just as there are many kinds of love, there are many kinds of smiles. We're so geared to this most basic and universal human expression that we do it before we're born. A Swedish study proved what we already know: smile at someone and it's a sure bet they can't help but smile back. It's "evolutionarily contagious."[13] Eons and Charles Darwin told us so. His Facial Feedback Response Theory is prescriptive: smile and you'll feel better. We've seen that our brains are wired to so many automatic responses that it shouldn't be surprising to learn that MRI imaging confirms that we get happy when we see others look happy. UK scientists discovered that just one smile outflanks the "mood boosting value" of chocolate—two thousand chocolate bars—and is sugar- and fat-free. Another smile-inducing benefit is that the expression reduces the stress hormones cortisol and adrenaline, among others.[14]

We smile for all kinds of reasons and under a range of situations: we're frightened, or worse, mortified, embarrassed, flirting, and even lying, to Shakespeare's characters' advantage. The more real we are, and the bigger our smile, the greater the impact. The "sweet emotions of the soul," French neurologist Guillaume-Benjamin-Amand Duchenne dubbed our genuine muscular response in 1862. The Duchenne smile remains a benchmark—or facial cue—that the "sweet emotion" is behind the enigmatic response. When the going gets tough, the tough smile. It makes us more appealing too.

What does it take to smile? Researchers don't really know, all memes aside. We're not even all equipped with the same number of facial muscles. Smile from your heart. It's good not only for your well-being but also for those who pick up on your good vibe.

Spread Joy

We've learned that there truly is a heart-brain connection, and information goes both directions. A healthy heart sends messages to the brain through four pathways: neurological, which we know as the nervous system; biochemical, the hormones that trigger responses; biophysical, as a pulse wave; and energetically, as an electromagnetic field.[15] The heart's beautifully rhythmic patterns influence the brain and body and affect our physical and mental health as well as how we perceive and react to the world around us.

> What we call emotional coherence—a harmonious state of sustained, self-modulated positive emotions—is a primary driver of the beneficial changes in physiological function that produces improved performance and overall well-being. The heart . . . acts effectively as the global conductor in the body's symphony. Positive emotions and attitudes have a number of objective, interrelated benefits for physiological, psychological, and social functioning.[16]

We probably knew that. But there's an extraordinary function of the heart that scientists are exploring—its role in memory. Perhaps the ancients weren't so far off. In his article published in the *Journal of Cardiovascular Development and Disease* titled "The Memory of the Heart," Italian cardiothoracic surgeon Marco Cirillo echoes my wonder. "The embryological development of the heart is one of the most fascinating phenomena in nature and so is its final structure and function. The memory is what remains forever, what stays during our life and is preserved in the next generations," he says. Cirillo's view is of an evolutionary scale. And the implications are revolutionary.

Other researchers, such as Mitchell Liester of the Department of Psychiatry at the University of Colorado School of Medicine, who has studied near-death experiences, are focused on the same-generation transfer of memory from organ donors to recipients. How do we explain personality changes following heart transplants? As we mentioned in a previous chapter, the shift in preferences, changes in emotions and temperament, identity alterations, and memories of events in the donor's life are thought to arise from the transfer of cellular memory.[17]

The technology to give life through heart and other organ transplantation takes on new meaning as we grapple with understanding what our lifeforce is and where it resides. These are complex medical, philosophical, and spiritual issues. For now, we are sure of at least a few key imperatives. For one, we need to stay heart healthy. Each of us has the responsibility to protect what cardiac surgeon Cirillo calls the "beating engine of our life . . . that can stand the heaviest proofs, bare the most difficult situations, and face the worst diseases." Scientists agree on the other issue. There needs to be more research to help us better define life and death. Beyond these, it's important that we mindfully and accurately recall the defining moments of our lives. Then we need to use our awareness to see the ways that these moments shaped who we are and what we believe. After all we've been through, what makes life meaningful?

"If the unexamined life was not worth living, was the unlived life worth examining?" asked neurosurgical resident Paul Kalanithi in his book *When Breath Becomes Air*, written before his young life was cut short by cancer. He had looked to medicine for what he called "a different sort of sublime" and answers to "what makes life meaningful." In pursuing his career, he had postponed learning to live. Finally, it boiled down to this: What does one do with a day? One precious day. What would you do with one day?

Day after day, year after year, meaning and purpose eluded my young mother. It was absent from the bottle of alcohol where she sought it. It was buried beneath her black and blue soul that she covered up. It was as vaporous as broken promises. It was my hard-learned lesson that a son can't bear his mother's yoke. No one else could.

When I was eleven, I heard about Alcoholics Anonymous. I don't know where. "Please go," I said. I didn't beg. Like a crocus pushing through the snow, my mother responded to hope. The transformation was steady and welcome. Her world expanded. New AA members who struggled, slipped, and fell became her purpose, her meaning. Support is high on the list of what makes AA work, confirmed a study lead by John F. Kelly, associate professor in the Harvard Medical School of Psychiatry and associate director of the Massachusetts General Hospital Center for Addiction Medicine.[18] Mother didn't impose it. It was her gift.

In her third year with AA, my sober mother had blossomed and became the support for a young woman in a toxic, codependent marriage. Her husband was an enabler whose violence plunged her into a deep, depressive abyss. As long as his wife remained addicted, he controlled their maladaptive situation. When this woman faced a critical emergency at his hands, my mother went into action and swept me in with it. I was so proud that she saved this woman's life. The love I always had for her swelled. Deep respect began to wash over old wounds. Throughout the coming years, she sheltered many people trapped in addiction from the physical and emotional dangers she knew they faced. As she took power over her own addiction, she brought others along. I've marveled, seeing joy restored to the lives of those who were drowning in hopelessness. Or perhaps the people Mom helped were experiencing joy for the first time in their lives. I do know that joy and happiness, like smiles, are contagious.

Our hearts and minds are miraculous guardians of our sanity and health. Happiness, we know, is contagious, but sadness is not. It takes a village of happy souls to keep the energy going around and around, found a twenty-year longitudinal study by Harvard Medical School in cooperation with the University of California, San Diego. Five thousand participants proved the power of love. A little happiness goes a long way and amps up our tendency to pass it along. The chain reaction touches people we don't even know, two or three degrees removed from us. Extraordinarily, the effect can last up to a year, says study co-authors Nicholas Christakis and James Fowler.[19] But sadness? Not so much. In fact, while we're there for those who could use a shoulder, what tears fall there stay there. We get our electricity from our village. Reduce that to the family level, and the effect is still supercharged. The old adage, "a happy wife, a happy life," gets an update for the twenty-first century: A happy partner ups our happiness meter by 8 percent.[20]

Here's the good news for those who are content without commitment. Researchers who conducted a Michigan State University longitudinal study on relationships and happiness arrived at the same conclusion that you've learned through all the Twelve Insights: happiness is a mindset, not a light switch. "If you can find happiness and fulfillment as a single person, you'll likely hold onto that happiness—whether there's a ring on your finger or not,"[21] says team lead Mariah Purol.

What's the recipe for a happy life? Let bygones be bygones. You can't change the past. I included Insight 8, "Forgive and Release," for that very reason. The burden of resentment becomes heavier and heavier over time. Set it down. Walk away. Don't look back. We are all creatures who are flawed, just in different ways. We are no more perfect than the familial and social fabric that wove our personalities and judgments about ourselves and others. Let's flip "love your neighbor as yourself" to "love yourself *and* your neighbor." Be a part of the joy that radiates from your village. As for that imperfect partner you hoped was your soul mate, let's pull out all our awareness stops. When was the last time we saw the beauty in their faces and hearts or even in their seemingly bumbling effort to do something that they think makes us happy?

"People think a soul mate is your perfect fit, and that's what everyone wants," writes Elizabeth Gilbert in her book *Eat, Pray, Love*. "But a true soul mate is a mirror, the person who shows you everything that is holding you back, the person who brings you to your own attention so you can change your life." Not someone else's life. Your life. Our own.

The Incredible Lightness of Choice

Years ago, during a seminar, Wayne Dyer, internationally acclaimed self-help author, told one of his many juicy parables—a truly Dyer lesson on life. What would come out of an orange if he squeezed it, Dyer asked his audience. "Orange juice," of course, was the response. The dialogue went something like this: Why not apple, grape, or pineapple juice? Because what's in an orange is orange juice.

"What comes out when life squeezes you? When someone hurts or offends you?" Dyer pressed. After a moment of silence, he explained. If what comes out is negative stuff, like anger, hatred, fear, and hostility, "it's because that's what's inside. And what's inside is up to you, it's your choice. When someone puts the pressure on you and out of you comes anything other than love, it's because that's what you've allowed to be inside."

Zig Ziglar was famous for motivational one-liners that fans called "Ziglar Gold." Those of us who face audiences have learned that when we use zingers, the message nuggets linger longer in participants' minds than do boring explanations. A glazed-over expression tells me that someone's off in their own world and not here now. But back to finding love by being love. Ziglar had put the phrase "looking in all the wrong places" in the right words: "If you go looking for a friend, you're going to find they're very scarce. If you go out to be a friend, you'll find them everywhere."[22]

Happiness: the Scientifically Unwieldy Notion

At the beginning of this book, I revealed that I'm an optimist. I look for silver linings in everything. I also said and believe that if there were only one insight, it would be that we should love freely, unconditionally, with our whole hearts and minds. Counting the ways—as did poet Elizabeth Barrett Browning—has been quite a journey. We've known intellectually that love isn't contained by borders, boundaries, or boxes. It is within us. It surrounds us. It wells up from us, through us, despite us. Our health, happiness, and well-being emerge from it. Our well-being is the world's well-being.

On our journey, we've explored awareness of self in the context of oneness with all that we are, can be, and will be. We've expanded that to include our connectedness to all people and all things. It's easy to feel content and loving when we're vigorous, strong, and life is good. We know that bodily health is important to happiness, yet we also know that our world is full of people whose bodies are bent, broken, and battered, whose physical forms are stiff, paralyzed, immovable. Yet, among them are souls full of joy and radiant happiness. What do they know that we don't? I hope that this book has helped you discover those answers for yourself.

An epiphany years ago changed my life and my mission. I realized that there was more to health and happiness than being in peak condition and living without disease or discomfort. I learned that our bodies can be confined, motionless. But if our minds are active and healthy, we can imagine our Strength, Energy, and Vitality and use our virtues to contribute to the good of all. Our hearts can sing with joy even when our lips are silent. Beautiful souls remind me of Anne Frank's profound words: "A person who is happy will make others happy; a person who has courage and faith will never die in misery."

"Happiness is a scientifically unwieldy notion," concedes positive psychologist Martin Seligman. From the realm of all possibilities, he deduced that there are basically three lifestyles for us to explore: the pleasant life, the engaged life, and the meaningful life, each with its unique experiences, as he describes them in his 2002 book, *Authentic Happiness*. But, it is neither Seligman's nor my intent to imply that happiness is a destination. Throughout the *Twelve Insights for Mindful Living*, I've declared that happiness is the first step of our journey, the last, and all those in between. We understand, as did Viktor Frankl, that joy could never be an end to itself. It is an important byproduct of finding meaning in life. As we take care of ourselves, we can derive much happiness from contributing to the care and happiness of others.

This twelfth insight—to love—conceptually revisits the most important mile markers along our mindfulness journey, places where we stopped to smell the jasmine or summit a peak in the cloud forest to get a clear view of the territory ahead. When we live mindfully in the present, we see, hear, smell, touch, taste, and perceive reality positively. We're charged by the Highest Power in the Universe: Love. I hope you've felt that in this book. We put our hearts into it.

Practice

Gratitude Observation

We've been taught to express gratitude to others when they've done something nice for us. Sometimes, we express gratitude to someone for no reason except that we're grateful for who they are and that they're a part of our lives. Sometimes, we may think we don't say thank-you enough, or express our appreciation genuinely and with warmth and sincerity. Throughout the year, you probably write many thank-you cards to old friends, new friends, near strangers, and family. I do, and I'd love to do it more. Bets are that you've never written one that begins, "Dearest Self."

In this practice, you're going to explore one of the three aspects of your Self, your being—spirit, mind, or body—and focus on gratitude. Which would you like to choose? Another session, explore a different aspect of the Self that is you. Eventually, complete all three.

- Select a calm, quiet place to perform this practice.
- Take a comfortable position sitting or lying down.
- Close your eyes and keep them closed.
- Take a few relaxing breaths. You can breathe in through your nose and exhale through your mouth.
- Identify the aspect of yourself that is your focus. Is it your body? Your mind? Your spirit—however you conceive of it? Visually conceive that aspect of yourself as though it were a friend seated beside you.
- Engaging full awareness, identify the best qualities, strengths, skills, of that part of your Self and the contributions they bring to the whole of you.
- Feel gratitude for those gifts.
- Feel gratitude for your ability to imagine your fullest potential and growth in that aspect. What does that fullest potential look like?

- ❧ Let the gratitude warm you as though you had stepped into the sunshine on an icy day.
- ❧ Breathe naturally and bring yourself back to awareness of the present.
- ❧ Give gratitude for your ability and opportunity to perform this practice.

Exercises

In your journal,

- ❧ List seven people to whom you can show more love. Include yourself if you wish.
- ❧ List seven situations that you can change by changing your attitude.
- ❧ List seven people and seven things you are most grateful to have in your life right now.
- ❧ List as many occurrences as you wish that happened today for which you're grateful.
- ❧ My aha moment from this insight is

Inspiration

Do not forget your purpose or destiny as God's creature.
What you are in his sight is what you are and nothing more.
Remember that when you leave this earth, you can take nothing
that you have received . . . but only what you have given;
a full heart enriched by honest service, love, sacrifice, and courage.
—St. Francis of Assisi

The Twelve Insights™

Insight 1
Accept the Miracle of You

I accept that I am the ultimate miraculous creation
of the Highest Power in the universe: Love. There is nothing as
incredible as the human being, spirit, mind, and body.

Insight 2
Imagine the "I'm Possible"

I know all things are possible through my Creator, the Highest Power
in the universe. I realize my potential through thought, belief, and
action.

Insight 3
Check in With Myself

I maintain awareness of my thoughts, beliefs, and actions
by being mindful and living in the present while always
projecting my highest and healthiest future.

Insight 4
Leverage the Power of Optimism

I choose to be an optimist, knowing that
my thoughts and words will come to be. I expect to discover gifts
of joy within my body, mind, and spirit.

Insight 5
Walk My Talk

I align my behaviors with my beliefs to maintain permanent and positive motivation. Feeling confident about my security, survival, and recognition advances my health and harmony.

Insight 6
Accept Responsibility

I am responsible for my lifestyle and self-care. I will live long and strong by being proactive about my preventative exams and age-appropriate health screenings, and I will respond to any signs or symptoms that are not natural for me.

Insight 7
Offer and Accept a Hand

I connect and surround myself with like-minded people for support and to be supportive. I find purpose and joy through helping others. I take someone's hand every day and caringly offer a hand to those in need.

Insight 8
Forgive and Release

I forgive myself and anyone who may have harmed me or discouraged my self-esteem and personal potential. I release into the past all shame and regret and only bring into my future the insights they offered.

Insight 9
See With 3D Vision

I embrace lifelong learning and continue to grow my knowledge
of the world and the people in it, which enables my ability
to Discover, Develop, and Disperse my joy and purpose.

Insight 10
Breathe Life

I pursue healthy distractions and engagements that balance
my stress and fortify my well-being. Creating time and space for myself
refreshes my spirit and rejuvenates my body. I breathe for life.

Insight 11
Ground Yourself in Nature

I recognize that Nature is my nature. I choose to nourish my body
with naturally wholesome foods and activities and connect
with the earth and all life that grounds me.

Insight 12
Live in Love

I live with the knowledge that Love is the most powerful energy
in the universe and that in order to live in Love,
I must first love myself. With gratitude and joy, I live in Love.

Notes

Introduction

1 Steven Pinker, "Daniel Kahneman Changed the Way We Think About Thinking. But What Do Other Thinkers Think of Him?" *The Guardian*, February 16, 2014, https://www.theguardian.com/science/2014/feb/16/daniel-kahneman-thinking-fast-and-slow-tributes.

2 Bodhipaksa, "We Are What We Think," *Tricycle*, Fall 2014, https://tricycle.org/magazine/we-are-what-we-think/.

3 Deepak Chopra, *Golf for Enlightenment: The Seven Lessons for the Game of Life* (New York: Harmony Books, 2003), 23.

4 Bob Harig, "Can Phil Mickelson Win Some More and Other Big Lessons Learned at the PGA Championship?" ESPN, May 24, 2021, https://www.espn.com/golf/story/_/id/31503531/can-phil-mickelson-win-some-more-other-big-lessons-learned-pga-championship.

5 Deepak Chopra, "Present-Moment Awareness: A Better Way to Stay in Control," *Chopra*, September 15, 2017, https://chopra.com/articles/present-moment-awareness-a-better-way-to-stay-in-control.

6 Ronald D. Siegal, "Positive Psychology: Harnessing the Power of Happiness, Mindfulness, and Inner Strength," *Harvard Medical School Special Health Report* Book 4 (Boston: Harvard Health Publications, May 8, 2014), Kindle.

7 "Religious Composition by Country 2010–2050," Pew Research Center, April 2, 2014, https://www.pewforum.org/2015/04/02/religious-projection-table/2010/number/all/.

8 Jason G. Goldman, "Creativity: The Weird and Wonderful Art of Animals," *Uniquely Human: Animal*, BBC, July 23, 2014, https://www.bbc.com/future/article/20140723-are-we-the-only-creative-species.

9 Nathan H. Lents, "Why Do Humans Make Art?" *Psychology Today*, September 5, 2017, https://www.psychologytoday.com/us/blog/beastly-behavior/201709/why-do-humans-make-art.

10 Andrew J. Elliot, "Color and Psychological Functioning: A Review of Theoretical and Empirical Work," *Frontiers in Psychology*, April 2, 2015, https://doi.org/10.3389/fpsyg.2015.00368.

11 Debra L. Kalmanowitz and Rainbow T. H. Ho, "Art Therapy and Mindfulness with Survivors of Political Violence: A Qualitative Study," *Psychological Trauma: Theory, Research, Practice, and Policy* 9, no. 1 (2017): 107–113, https://doi.org/10.1037/tra0000174.

12 "#14DaySELChallenge: Art Activities for Mindfulness and Well-Being," Mahatma Gandhi Institute of Education for Peace and Sustainable Development, UNESCO, https://mgiep.unesco.org/article/14dayselchallenge-art-activities-for-mindfulness-and-well-being. See also David Gelles, "How to Be Mindful When Making Art," *New York Times*, September 27, 2017, https://www.nytimes.com/2017/09/27/well/mind/how-to-be-mindful-when-making-art.html.

13 "Goals," accessed May 21, 2021, http://psychology.iresearchnet.com/social-psychology/control/goals/.

14 "Goals," accessed May 21, 2021.

15 Ram Dass, *Be Here Now* (New York: Crown Publishing Group, 1978).

16 Amy Gallo, "What to Do When You're Feeling Distracted at Work," *Harvard Business Review*, December 20, 2017, https://hbr.org/2017/12/what-to-do-when-youre-feeling-distracted-at-work.

17 Amy Gallo, "Turning Stress into an Asset," *Harvard Business Review*, June 28, 2011, 2017, https://hbr.org/2011/06/turning-stress-into-an-asset.

18 Eckhart Tolle, *The Power of Now: A Guide to Spiritual Enlightenment* (Novato, CA: New World Library, 2004), Kindle.

19 Andrew Newberg and Mark Robert Waldman, *Words Can Change Your Brain: 12 Conversation Strategies to Build Trust, Resolve Conflict, and Increase Intimacy* (New York: A Plume Book, the Penguin Group, 2012), Kindle.

One

1 Sonja Lyubomirsky, *The Myths of Happiness: What Should Make You Happy but Doesn't, What Shouldn't Make You Happy but Does* (New York: Penguin, 2014), Kindle.

2 Carol Graham, *Happiness Around the World: The Paradox of Happy Peasants and Miserable Millionaires* (New York: Oxford University Press, 2009), 10.

3 Todd B. Kashdan, "The Problem with Happiness: Can Trying to Be Happy Interfere with Creating Happiness?" *Psychology Today*, September 29, 2010, https://www.psychologytoday.com/us/blog/curious/201009/the-problem-happiness.

4 Marcus Aurelius, *Meditations: A New Translation*, trans. Gregory Hays (New York: Modern Library, 2021), Kindle.

5 Ecclesiastes 3:4, *New International Version*, https://www.biblegateway.com/passage/?search=Ecclesiastes%203%3A4&version=NIV.

6 Aristotle, "1098a18," *Nicomachean Ethics Book 1*, Loeb Classical Library, https://doi:org10.4159/DLCL.aristotle-nicomachean_ethics.1926/pb_LCL073.33.xml.

7 K. Abdul Gafoor, "Considerations in Measurements of Awareness" (India, Kerala: National Level Seminar on Emerging Trends in Education, University of Calicut, November 12, 2012), 2, https://files. eric.ed.gov/fulltext/ED545374.pdf.

8 Robert Van Gulick, "Consciousness," *The Stanford Encyclopedia of Philosophy* (Spring 2018 Edition), ed. Edward N. Zalta, https://plato. stanford.edu/archives/spr2018/entries/consciousness/.

9 Kira M. Newman, "What Mindfulness Is Missing," *Greater Good Magazine: Science-Based Insights for a Meaningful Life*, June 9, 2016, https://greatergood.berkeley.edu/article/item/what_mindfulness_is_ missing.

10 Robert Booth, "Master of Mindfulness, Jon Kabat-Zinn: 'People Are Losing Their Minds. That Is What We Need to Wake Up To.'" *The Guardian*, October 22, 2017, https://www.theguardian.com/ lifeandstyle/2017/oct/22/mindfulness-jon-kabat-zinn-depression-trump-grenfell.

11 Robert Booth, "Master of Mindfulness."

12 Robert Booth, "Master of Mindfulness."

13 "What to Do When You Get Lost," *Backpacker Travel* (2020), https://www.backpackertravel.org/backpacker-101/things-go-wrong/ getting-lost/.

14 Adele M. Hayes and Greg Feldman, "Clarifying the Construct of Mindfulness in the Context of Emotion Regulation and the Process of Change in Therapy," *Clinical Psychology: Science and Practice 11*, no. 3 (May 11, 2006): 255–262, https://doi.org/10.1093/clipsy.bph080.

15 Jon Kabat-Zinn, "An Outpatient Program in Behavioral Medicine for Chronic Pain Patients Based on the Practice of Mindfulness Meditation: Theoretical Considerations and Preliminary Results,"

General Hospital Psychiatry 4, no. 1 (April 1982): 33-47, https://doi. org/10.1016/0163-8343(82)90026-3.

16 Akira Kasamatsu and Tomio Hirai, "An Electroencephalographic Study on the Zen Meditation (Zazen)," *Psychiatry and Clinical Neurosciences* 20, no. 4 (December 1966): 315-36, https://doi. org/10.1111/j.1440-1819.1966.tb02646.x

17 Debra A. Gusnard, Erbil Akbudak, Gordon L. Shulman, and Marcus E. Raichle, "Medial Prefrontal Cortex and Self-Referential Mental Activity: Relation to a Default Mode of Brain Function," *Proceedings of the National Academy of Sciences of the United States of America* 98, no. 7 (March 27, 2001): 4259–64, https://doi:org.10.1073/pnas.071043098. See also Richard J. Davidson and Antoine Lutz, "Buddha's Brain: Neuroplasticity and Meditation." *IEEE Signal Processing Magazine* 25, no. 1 (January 16, 2008): 176–174, https://doi.org/10.1109/ msp.2008.4431873.

18 Lee Smolin, "Resetting the Theory of Time," interview by Ira Flatow, *Science Friday*, NPR, May 17, 2013, audio, 21:02, https://www.npr. org/2013/05/17/184775924/resetting-the-theory-of-time.

19 Maria Popova, "How to Find Your Bliss: Joseph Campbell on What It Takes to Have a Fulfilling Life," *Brainpickings* (September 04, 2015), https://www.brainpickings.org/2015/04/09/find-your-bliss-joseph-campbell-power-of-myth/.

Two

1 Sadhguru (Jaggi Vasudev), interview by Evan Carmichael, "One Habit That You Need to Change Now!" *Evan Carmichael*, May 18, 2018, video, 53:28, https://youtu.be/xRKlPqVxFgI.

2 James Franklin Crow, "Unequal by Nature, a Geneticist's Perspective on Human Differences," *Daedalus*, Winter 2002, https://www.amacad.

org/publication/unequal-nature-geneticists-perspective-human-differences.

3 Robert Steven Kaplan, "Reaching Your Potential," *Harvard Business Review*, Analytic Services, July-August 2008, https://hbr.org/2008/07/reaching-your-potential.

4 Dina Gachman, "Aisha Tyler on 'Self-Inflicted Wounds,' Career, and the Power of Mistakes," *Forbes*, July 8, 2013, https://www.forbes.com/sites/dinagachman/2013/07/08/aisha-tyler-on-self-inflicted-wounds-career-and-the-power-of-mistakes/?sh=71aae93c7a2c.

5 Deepak Chopra, "The Importance of Being Aware," *Medium*, September 9, 2019, https://deepakchopra.medium.com/the-importance-of-being-aware-3308e2918020.

6 Anonymous.

7 David Cuschieri, online quote, accessed July 7, 2021, https://www.goodreads.com/author/quotes/5807635.David_Cuschieri.

8 Maggie Schauer and Thomas Elbert, "Dissociation Following Traumatic Stress," *Journal of Psychology* 218, no. 2, (2010): 109-127. Also online, February 26, 2015, https://doi.org/10.1027/0044-3409/a000018.

9 Joseph Campbell, interviewed by Bill Moyer, "Follow Your Bliss," *The Power of Myth*, Episode 4, Joseph Campbell Foundation, video of 1987 interview posted July 22, 2020, audio, 4:49, https://youtu.be/s28rwnz18j4.

10 Ron Chepesiuk, "Decibel Hell: The Effects of Living in a Noisy World," *Environmental Health Perspectives* 113, no. 1 (January 2005): A34-A41, https://doi.org/10.1289/ehp.113-a34.

11 Adam Brady, "Six Steps to Master Living in the Moment," *Chopra*, August 7, 2019, https://chopra.com/articles/6-steps-to-master-living-in-the-moment.

12 Shian-Ling Keng, Moria J. Smoski, and Clive J. Robins, "Effects of Mindfulness on Psychological Health: A Review of Empirical Studies," *Clinical Psychology Review* 31, no. 6 (May 13, 2011): 1041-56, https://www.ncbi.nlm.nih.gov/pmc/articles/PMC3679190/ and https://doi.org/10.1016/j.cpr.2011.04.006.

13 John Roach, "Fear of Snakes, Spiders, Rooted in Evolution, Study Finds," *National Geographic*, October 3, 2001, https://www.nationalgeographic.com/science/article/fear-evolution-spiders-science.

14 Joseph Lewis Henderson and Maud Oakes, *The Wisdom of the Serpent: The Myths of Death, Rebirth, and Resurrection* (Princeton: Princeton University Press: 1963, 1990), Kindle.

Three

1 Suzy Kassem, "Part Sun and Part Moon," *Rise Up and Salute the Sun: The Writings of Suzy Kassem*, http://suzykassem.com/bknd/.

2 Adam Frank, "Roll Over Copernicus! Turns Out We Are the Center of the Universe," *Cosmos and Culture*, NPR, March 1, 2011, https://www.npr.org/sections/13.7/2011/03/02/134137113/roll-over-copernicus-it-turns-out-we-are-the-center-of-the-universe.

3 Sandra M. Faber, https://carnegiescience.edu/trustee/sandra-m-faber and https://scientificwomen.net/women/faber-sandra-35.

4 Tom Yulsman, "Yes, You Are the Center of the Universe (in One Sense . . .)," *Discover*, December 31, 2014, https://www.discovermagazine.com/the-sciences/yes-you-are-the-center-of-the-universe-in-one-sense.

5 Kerry Lotzof, "Are We Really Made of Stardust?" National History

Museum, accessed May 13, 2021, https://www.nhm.ac.uk/discover/are-we-really-made-of-stardust.html.

6 Adam Frank, "Roll Over Copernicus!"

7 Forrest Church, "Forrest Church Interview," interview by Bob Abernathy, *Religion and Ethics Newsweekly*, PBS, February 27, 2009, https://www.pbs.org/wnet/religionandethics/2009/02/27/february-27-2009-forrest-church-interview/860/.

8 Adam Bulley, Jonathan Redshaw, and Thomas Suddendorf, "The Future-Directed Functions of the Imagination: From Prediction to Metaforesight," in the *Cambridge Handbook of the Imagination*, ed. Anna Abraham (United Kingdom: Cambridge University Press, 2020), 425.

9 Bulley, Redshaw, and Suddendorf, "The Future-Directed Functions of the Imagination."

10 Daniel C. Dennett, *Darwin's Dangerous Idea: Evolution and the Meanings of Life* (New York: Simon and Schuster), 339.

11 Dennett, Daniel C. "From Typo to Thinko: When Evolution Graduated to Semantic Norms." *Evolution and Culture*, eds. Stephen C. Levinson and Pierre Jaisson (Cambridge, MA: MIT Press, 2006), 135.

12 Katie Hunt, "When Did Humans Start Wearing Clothes? Discovery in a Moroccan Cave Sheds Some Light." CNN, September 16, 2021, https://www.cnn.com/2021/09/16/africa/clothing-bone-tools-morocco-scn/index.html.

13 Jeanne Carstensen, "Dress for Evolutionary Success. What Makes Us Quintessentially Human? Fashion," *Nautilus*, September 10, 2018, https://medium.com/s/nautilus-special/dress-for-evolutionary-success-489b4bcb6b88.

14 Börje Ekstig, "Complexity, Natural Selection, and the Evolution of Life and Humans," Foundations of Science 20, no. 2 (May 3, 2014): 175-187, https://doi.org/10.1007/s10699-014-9358-y.

15 Sadhguru (Jaggi Vasudev), "Were You Really Created by God?" Sadhguru, December 25, 2017, video, 11:53, https://youtu.be/diJrraOLF5k.e.

16 Alan Watts, "Essential Lectures 12: 'Conversations with Myself': Mount Tamalpais, 1971," transcript, https://www.organism.earth/library/document/essential-lectures-12.

17 "Culture plate," British Society for Immunology, accessed May 25, 2021, https://www.immunology.org/culture-plate-1887.

18 Anil Seth, "Your Brain Hallucinates Your Conscious Reality," TED, July 18, 2017, audio, 17:00, https://youtu.be/lyu7v7nWzfo.

19 Seth, "Your Brain Hallucinates."

20 Brian Resnick, "'Reality' Is Constructed By Our Brain. Here's What That Means and Why It Matters," Vox, June 22, 2020, https://www.vox.com/science-and-health/20978285/optical-illusion-science-humility-reality-polarization.

21 Michael C. Corballis, The Wandering Mind: What the Brain Does When You're Not Looking, (Chicago: University of Chicago Press, 2015), 84.

Four

1 Daniel T. Gilbert, "Prisoners of Now," award acceptance video, 40:26, August 12, 2019, https://youtu.be/4GkgHhja6RA.

2 Daniel T. Gilbert, Stumbling on Happiness (New York: Vintage Books, 2005).

3 Brie Gertler, "Self-Knowledge," *The Stanford Encyclopedia of Philosophy*, Spring 2020, ed. Edward N. Zalta, https://plato.stanford.edu/archives/spr2020/entries/self-knowledge.

4 Roger Lowenstein, "How Winston Churchill Failed Up," *The Wall Street Journal*, September 16, 2016, https://www.wsj.com/articles/how-winston-churchill-failed-up-1474050039.

5 Laura Yan, "The Smallest Computer in the World Fits on a Grain of Rice," *Popular Mechanics*, June 30, 2018, https://www.popularmechanics.com/technology/a22007431/smallest-computer-world-smaller-than-grain-rice/.

6 S. O'Dea, "Share of Smartphone Users That Use an Apple iPhone in the United States from 2014 to 2021," *Statista*, March 31, 2021, https://www.statista.com/statistics/236550/percentage-of-us-population-that-own-a-iphone-smartphone/.

7 Tibi Puiu,"Your Smartphone Is Millions of Times More Powerful Than the Apollo 11 Guidance Computers," *ZMe Science*, May 13, 2021, https://www.zmescience.com/science/news-science/smartphone-power-compared-to-apollo-432/.

8 Joab Rosenberg, "Only Humans, Not Computers, Can Learn or Predict," *TechCrunch*, May 5, 2016, https://techcrunch.com/2016/05/05/only-humans-not-computers-can-learn-or-predict/.

9 Claudia Bloeser and Titus Stahl, "Hope," *The Stanford Encyclopedia of Philosophy*, Spring 2017, ed. Edward N. Zalta, https://plato.stanford.edu/archives/spr2017/entries/hope/.

10 James B. Glattfelder, "The Consciousness of Reality," in *Information—Consciousness—Reality*, The Frontiers Collection (Springer, April 11, 2019), 515–95, https://doi.org/10.1007/978-3-030-03633-1_14.

11 Cate Montana, "The Illusion of Reality: The Scientific Proof That Everything Is Energy and Reality Isn't Real," Conscious Lifestyle Magazine, accessed July 27, 2021, https://www.consciouslifestylemag.com/everything-is-energy-illusion-reality/. See also http://www.esalq.usp.br/lepse/imgs/conteudo_thumb/The-Illusion-of-Reality---The-Scientific-Proof-That-Everything-is-Energy-and-Reality-Isnt-Real.pdf.

Five

1 "Human Genome Variation," National Human Genome Research Institute, April 6, 2018, https://www.genome.gov/dna-day/15-ways/human-genomic-variation. See also Nina Jablonski, "The Biology of Skin Color," HHMI Biointeractive video, 18:57, July 20, 2015, https://youtu.be/hFw8mMzH5YA.

2 Robin McKie, "Why Do Identical Twins End Up Having Such Different Lives?" *The Guardian*, June 1, 2013, https://www.theguardian.com/science/2013/jun/02/twins-identical-genes-different-health-study.

3 Lawrence C. Brody, "ACGT," National Human Genome Research Institute, audio, 0:45, accessed July 23, 2021, https://www.genome.gov/genetics-glossary/acgt.

4 Daphna Oyserman, Kristen Elmore, and George Smith, "Self, Self-Concept, and Identity," in the *Handbook of Self and Identity*, Second Edition (New York: The Guilford Press), 69-104.

5 David B, King et al., "Remembering Genocide: The Effects of Early Life Trauma on Reminiscence Functions Among Israeli Holocaust Survivors," *Traumatology* 21, no. 3 (2015): 145.

6 "Introduction: The Human Essence," *The Oxford Handbook of the Human Essence*, Ed. Martijn van Zomeren and John F. Dovidio (Oxford: Oxford University Press, 2018), 3.

7 Gareth Cook, "Does Consciousness Pervade the Universe?" *Scientific American*, January 14, 2020, https://www.scientificamerican.com/article/does-consciousness-pervade-the-universe/.

8 Patrizio Paoletti and Tal Dotan Ben-Soussan, "Reflections on Inner and Outer Silence and Consciousness without Contents, According to the Sphere Model of Consciousness," Research Institute for Neuroscience, Education and Didactics, *Frontiers in Psychology* 12, August 2020, https://doi.org/10.3389/fpsyg.2020.01807.

9 Ken McLeod, "Something from Nothing," *Tricycle*, Winter 2010, https://tricycle.org/magazine/something-nothing/.

10 Scott Mautz, "Harvard Study: 47 Percent of the Time You're Doing This One (Fixable) Thing That Kills Your Happiness," *Inc.*, May 13, 2019, https://www.inc.com/scott-mautz/harvard-study-47-percent-of-time-youre-doing-this-1-fixable-thing-that-kills-your-happiness.html.

11 Daniel Goleman, "Holocaust Survivors Had the Skills to Prosper," *New York Times*, Oct. 6, 1992, https://www.nytimes.com/1992/10/06/science/holocaust-survivors-had-skills-to-prosper.html.

12 Mark Oliver, "The Four Intelligences," accessed June 6, 2021, https://www.marktwoconsulting.com/talent/the-four-intelligence.

13 Anne Craig, "Discovery of 'Thought Worms' Opens Window to the Mind," July 13, 2020, *Queens University Gazette*, https://www.queensu.ca/gazette/stories/discovery-thought-worms-opens-window-mind.

14 Caroline Williams, "Different Meditative Types Train Distinct Parts of Your Brain," *New Scientist*, October 4, 2017, https://www.newscientist.com/article/2149489-different-meditation-types-train-distinct-parts-of-your-brain/.

15 Tom Ireland, "What Does Mindfulness Meditation Do to Your Brain?" June 12, 2014, Scientific American, https://blogs.

scientificamerican.com/guest-blog/what-does-mindfulness-meditation-do-to-your-brain/.

16 Deepak Chopra, "A Surprising Answer to 'Who Am I?'" June 12, 2017, The Chopra Foundation, https://choprafoundation.org/articles/a-surprising-answer-to-who-am-i/.

Six

1 "Kahlil Gibran Biography," July 1, 2020, https://www.biography.com/writer/khalil-gibran.

2 Tali Sharot, *The Optimism Bias: A Tour of the Irrationally Positive Brain* (New York: Vintage Books, 2012), xii.

3 Martin E. P. Seligman, *Learned Optimism: How to Change Your Mind and Your Life* (New York: Vintage Books, 2006), iii.

4 Reham Al Taher, "The Five Founding Fathers and History of Positive Psychology," Positive Psychology, July 5, 2021, https://positivepsychology.com/founding-fathers/.

5 Christopher Peterson and Lisa M. Bossio, *Health and Optimism* (New York: Free Press, 1991).

6 Martin Seligman, *Authentic Happiness: Using the New Positive Psychology to Realize Your Potential for Lasting Fulfillment* (New York: Free Press, 2002), 14–249.

7 Seligman, *Authentic Happiness*, 10.

8 Lewina O. Lee et al., "Optimism Is Associated with Exceptional Longevity in Two Epidemiologic Cohorts of Men and Women," *Proceedings of the National Academy of Sciences* 116, no. 37 (August 26, 2019): 18357-62; https://doi.org/10.1073/pnas.1900712116.

9 Andrew Bisharat, "Why Are So Many BASE Jumpers Dying?" *National Geographic*, August 30, 2016, https://www.nationalgeographic.com/adventure/article/why-are-so-many-base-jumpers-dying.

10 Joanna Schaffhausen, "The Pleasure Principle: Connections Between Reward and Learning," *Brain Connection*, August 1, 2020, https://brainconnection.brainhq.com/2020/08/01/the-pleasure-principle-connections-between-reward-and-learning/.

11 Yangmei Luo et al., "Well-being and Anticipation for Future Positive Events: Evidences from an fMRI Study," *Frontiers in Psychology* 8 (January 9, 2018): 2199, https://doi.org/10.3389/fpsyg.2017.02199.

12 Neil Farber, "The Truth About the Law of Attraction: It Doesn't Exist," *Psychology Today*, September 18, 2016, https://www.psychologytoday.com/us/blog/the-blame-game/201609/the-truth-about-the-law-attraction.

13 Bodhipaksa, "We Are What We Think," *Tricycle,* Fall, 2014, https://tricycle.org/magazine/we-are-what-we-think/.

14 Chloe Fox, "Tom Hiddleston, Interview: from Thor to a Sell-out Coriolanus," *The Daily Telegraph*, January 14, 2014. https://www.telegraph.co.uk/culture/theatre/10561842/Tom-Hiddleston-interview-from-Thor-to-a-sell-out-Coriolanus.html.

Seven

1 Beata Sounders, "The Vital Importance and Benefits of Motivation," *Positive Psychology*, March 22, 2021, https://positivepsychology.com/benefits-motivation/.

2 Rebecca Knight, "How to Overcome Burnout and Stay Motivated," *Harvard Business Review*, April 2, 2015, https://hbr.org/2015/04/how-to-overcome-burnout-and-stay-motivated.

3 Sounders. "The Vital Importance."

4 Deepak Chopra, "Turning Vulnerability into Personal Security," June 14, 2021, Linkedin, https://www.linkedin.com/pulse/turning-vulnerability-personal-security-deepak-chopra-md-official-.

5 Chopra. "Turning Vulnerability."

6 Oprah Winfrey, "Deepak Chopra: Spiritual Solutions," Oprah's SuperSoul Conversations, July 29, 2020, audio, 1:07, https://www.happyscribe.com/public/oprah-s-supersoul-conversations/deepak-chopra-spiritual-solutions.

7 Omar Itani, "You Are What You Think: How Your Thoughts Create Your Reality," Omar Itani, https://www.omaritani.com/blog/what-you-think.

8 Jennice Vilhauer, "How Your Thinking Creates Your Reality," *Psychology Today*, September 27, 2020, https://www.psychologytoday.com/us/blog/living-forward/202009/how-your-thinking-creates-your-reality.

9 Liat Levontin and Anat Bardi, "Using Personal Values to Understand the Motivational Basis of Amity Goal Orientation," *Frontiers in Psychology*, January 9, 2019, https://doi.org/10.3389/fpsyg.2018.02736.

10 Eckhart Tolle, "Realizing the 'Deep I,'" Eckhart Tolle, accessed July 29, 2021, https://eckharttolle.com/realizing-the-deep-i/.

11 Sara Brown, "MIT Sloan Research About Social Media, Misinformation, and Elections," MIT Sloan School of Management, October 5, 2020, https://mitsloan.mit.edu/ideas-made-to-matter/mit-sloan-research-about-social-media-misinformation-and-elections.

Eight

1 Harry Woods, "When the Red, Red Robin Comes Bob, Bob Bobbin' Along," on the album "It's a Good Day," 1949, https://www.songfacts.com/lyrics/al-jolson/when-the-red-red-robin-comes-bob-bob-bobbin-along.

2 Patch Adams, "Patch Adams Speaks," https://www.patchadams.org/patch-adams-speaks/.

3 Judith A. Whitworth et al., "Cardiovascular Consequences of Cortisol Excess," *Vascular Health and Risk Management* 1, no. 4 (2005): 291-99, https://doi:10.2147/vhrm.2005.1.4.291.

4 Juliette Kando Fi Chor, "Second Brain Found in the Heart and Gut Neurons," July 25, 2021, https://owlcation.com/stem/your-second-brain-is-in-your-heart.

5 Kando Fi Chor, "Second Brain."

6 Carl Zimmer, "How Many Cells Are in Your Body?" *National Geographic*, October 23, 2013, https://www.nationalgeographic.com/science/article/how-many-cells-are-in-your-body.

7 Zimmer, "How Many Cells?"

8 Dean Ornish, "Changing Your Lifestyle Can Change Your Genes," *Newsweek*, June 16, 2008, https://www.newsweek.com/changing-your-lifestyle-can-change-your-genes-91323.

9 Divya Goyal, "World's Oldest Marathoner Fauja Singh Now a Superhero in a Children's Book," September 23, 2020, https://indianexpress.com/article/india/worlds-oldest-marathoner-fauja-singh-now-a-superhero-in-a-childrens-book-6607040/.

10 Andrea Marz, "Fracturing, Learning to Listen to the Nuances That Lie Beneath the Surface of My Skin," *The Mindful Word*, July 15, 2021, https://www.themindfulword.org/2021/fracturing-surgery/.

11 "Female life expectancy," World Health Organization (WHO), https://www.who.int/gho/women_and_health/mortality/life_expectancy_text/en/.

12 Elizabeth Arias and Jiaquan Xu, "United States Life Tables, 2018," National Vital Statistics Reports 69, no. 12, 2018, Center for Disease Control (CDC), https://www.cdc.gov/nchs/data/nvsr/nvsr69/nvsr69-12-508.pdf. See also, Max Roser, Esteban Ortiz-Ospina, and Hannah Ritchie, "Life Expectancy," last revised October 2019, *Our World in Data*, https://ourworldindata.org/life-expectancy.

13 "Life Expectancy 2015," an interactive line chart, Our World in Data, accessed July 24, 2021, https://ourworldindata.org/grapher/life-expectancy?time=1800..2015&country=Africa~Asia~Europe~Latin+America+and+the+Caribbean~Northern+America~OWID_WRL~Americas~Oceania.

14 Ingrid Waldron and Susan Johnston, "Why Do Women Live Longer Than Men?" *Behavioral Medicine: Journal of Human Stress* 2, no. 2 (July 9, 2010), https://doi.org/10.1080/0097840X.1976.9936063.

15 Esteban Ortiz-Ospina and Diana Beltekian, "Why Do Women Live Longer Than Men?" Our World in Data. August 14, 2018, https://ourworldindata.org/why-do-women-live-longer-than-men. See also, Eileen Crimmins et al., "Differences Between Men and Women in Mortality and the Health Dimensions of the Morbidity Process," *Clinical Chemistry* 65, no. 1 (2019): 135-45, https://doi:10.1373/clinchem.2018.288332.

16 "Women's Blood Vessels Age Faster than Men's." *ScienceDaily*, January 15, 2020, www.sciencedaily.com/releases/2020/01/200115191534.htm.

17 Ortiz-Ospina and Beltekian, "Why Women Live Longer."

18 Maarten Wensink, "The Real Reason Women Live Longer Than Men." *The Conversation*, January 21, 2020, https://theconversation.com/the-real-reason-women-live-longer-than-men-new-study-130142.

19 Kelly P. Cosgrove et al., "Sex Differences in the Brain's Dopamine Signature of Cigarette Smoking," *The Journal of Neuroscience* 34, no. 50 (2014):16851–55, https://doi:10.1523/JNEUROSCI.3661-14.2014.

20 Bahar Gholiour, "Men Take More 'Idiotic Risks,' Study Finds," *Live Science*, December 11, 2014, https://www.livescience.com/49101-darwin-awards-are-men-idiots.html.

21 Eladio J. Márquez et al., "Sexual-dimorphism in Human Immune System Aging," *Nature Communications* 11, article 751 (February 6, 2020), https://doi.org/10.1038/s41467-020-14396-9.

22 Katharine Esty, *Eightysomethings: A Practical Guide to Letting Go, Aging Well, and Finding Unexpected Happiness* (New York: Skyhorse, 2019).

23 "Why Do Women Live Longer than Men? It's More Complicated than You Think," Daily Briefing, Advisory Board, July 22, 2020, republished July 19, 2021, https://www.advisory.com/en/daily-briefing/2020/07/22/longevity.

24 "Mars vs. Venus, the Gender Gap in Health," *Harvard Health Publishing*, Harvard Medical School, August 26, 2019, https://www.health.harvard.edu/newsletter_article/mars-vs-venus-the-gender-gap-in-health.

Nine

1 Judith Hall and Mark Leary, "The U.S. Has an Empathy Deficit," *American Scientific*, September 17, 2020, https://www.scientificamerican.com/article/the-us-has-an-empathy-deficit/.

2 Benjamin Chacon, "The Best Instagram Caption Length in 2021," *Later.com*, November 12, 2020, https://later.com/blog/instagram-caption-length/.

3 Stephen L. Carter, "Civility Has Its Nose Buried in a Smartphone," Bloomberg View, *Chicago Tribune*, February 23, 2017, https://www.chicagotribune.com/opinion/commentary/ct-political-discourse-civility-phones-20170223-story.html.

4 Hall and Leary, "Empathy Deficit."

5 Michael Pittaro, "Social Media and the Bystander Effect," *Psychology Today*, September 19, 2019, https://www.psychologytoday.com/us/blog/the-crime-and-justice-doctor/201909/social-media-and-the-bystander-effect.

6 Pittaro, "Bystander Effect." See also Margarita Svetlova et al., "Toddlers' Prosocial Behavior: from Instrumental to Empathic to Altruistic Helping," *Child Development* 81, no. 6 (2010): 1814-27, https://doi:10.1111/j.1467-8624.2010.01512.x and Adam Gorlick, "For Kids, Altruism Comes Naturally, Psychologist Says," *Stanford News*, November 5, 2008, https://news.stanford.edu/news/2008/november5/tanner-110508.html.

7 R. Lanier Anderson, "Friedrich Nietzsche," *The Stanford Encyclopedia of Philosophy, Ed.* Edward N. Zalta, Summer 2017, https://plato.stanford.edu/archives/sum2017/entries/nietzsche/.

8 Alan Watts, "The Tao of Philosophy 4: Seeing Through the Net, 1969," audio transcript, The Library, https://www.organism.earth/library/document/tao-of-philosophy-4.

9 Ben Yagoda, *Will Rogers: A Biography* (New York: Knopf. 1993), 178-79.

10 Abhijit Naskar, *Hometown Human: To Live for Soil and Society* (self-pub., 2021), 101.

11 Harry Farmer, Ryan McKay, and Manos Tsakiris, "Trust in Me: Trustworthy Others Are Seen as More Physically Similar to the Self," Psychological Science 25, no. 1 (January 2014): 290–92, https://doi.org/10.1177/0956797613494852.

12 Kelly Gardner, "How Sesame Street Uses Muppets to Teach Inclusion in the US and Abroad," American University, Washington, DC, April 1, 2021, https://www.american.edu/sis/news/20210401-how-sesame-street-uses-muppets-to-teach-tolerance-in-the-us-and-abroad.cfm.

13 Susan Cain, *Quiet: The Power of Introverts in a World That Can't Stop Talking*, (New York: Broadway Paperbacks, 2013), 4, 15, 170.

14 Daniel Gilbert, review of *Quiet: The Power of Introverts in a World That Can't Stop Talking*, by Susan Cain, Amazon, accessed July 27, 2012, https://www.amazon.com/Quiet-Power-Introverts-World-Talking/dp/0307352153.

15 Wu Youyou et al., "Birds of a Feather Do Flock Together: Behavior-Based Personality-Assessment Method Reveals Personality Similarity Among Couples and Friends," Psychological Science 28, no. 3 (March 2017): 276–84, https://doi.org/10.1177/0956797616678187. See also Martin J. Smith, "Turns Out That Opposites Don't Attract After All," Stanford Graduate School of Business, January 17, 2017, https://www.gsb.stanford.edu/insights/turns-out-opposites-dont-attract-after-all.

16 Elisa Shearer and Amy Mitchell, "News Use Across Social Media Platforms in 2020," Pew Research Center, January 12, 2021, https://www.pewresearch.org/journalism/2021/01/12/news-use-across-social-media-platforms-in-2020/.

17 Amy Roeder, "Social Media Use Can Be Positive for Mental Health and Well-Being," Harvard T. H. Chan School of Public Health, January 6, 2020, https://www.hsph.harvard.edu/news/features/social-media-positive-mental-health/.

18 Michelle Trudeau, "Why People Take Risks to Help Others: Altruism's Roots in the Brain," Weekend Edition, Sunday, NPR, November 23, 2014, https://www.npr.org/2014/11/23/366052779/why-people-take-risks-to-help-others-altruisms-roots-in-the-brain.

Ten

1 Robert Enright, "Eight Keys to Forgiveness," *Greater Good Magazine*, University of California, Berkeley, October 15, 2015, https://greatergood.berkeley.edu/article/item/eight_keys_to_forgiveness.

2 Enright, "Keys to Forgiveness."

3 Viktor E. Frankl, *Man's Search for Meaning*, trans. Ilse Lasch (Boston: Beacon Press, 1959, 2006), 66.

4 Charlotte Lieberman, "Why We Romanticize the Past," Smarter Living, *New York Times*, April 2, 2021, https://www.nytimes.com/2021/04/02/smarter-living/why-we-romanticize-the-past.html.

5 Lieberman, "Why We Romanticize the Past."

6 Lieberman, "Why We Romanticize the Past."

7 Sarah Griffiths, "Can You Trust Your Earliest Childhood Memories?," *Neuroscience*, BBC, May 19, 2019, https://www.bbc.com/future/article/20190516-why-you-cannot-trust-your-earliest-childhood-memories.

8 Griffiths, "Trust Childhood Memories?"

9 Annette Kämmerer, "The Scientific Underpinnings and Impacts of Shame," *Scientific American*, August 9, 2019, https://www.scientificamerican.com/article/the-scientific-underpinnings-and-impacts-of-shame/.

10 Kurt Smith, "Four Reasons to Forgive but Not Forget," PsychCentral, December 10, 2014, https://psychcentral.com/blog/4-reasons-to-forgive-but-not-forget#1.

Eleven

1 Jean-Jacques Hublin et al., "A Long Childhood Is of Advantage," Max-Planck-Gesellschaft, November 15, 2010, https://www.mpg.de/617475/pressRelease20101111.

2 Aldous Huxley, "What a Piece of Work Is a Man," (lecture, Massachusetts Institute of Technology Department of Humanities, fall 1960), https://archivesspace.mit.edu/repositories/2/resources/761/collection_organization. The following titles from this series are available as audio and transcripts: "Ancient Views of Human Nature" (lecture, MIT, October 5, 1960), "The Contemporary Picture" (lecture, MIT, October 13, 1960), "The Individual in Relation to History" (lecture, MIT, October 1960), "Symbols and Immediate Experience" (lecture, MIT, October 26, 1960), and "Why Art?" (lecture, MIT, November 2, 1960).

3 Huxley, "What a Piece of Work."

4 Heidi Godman, "Feeling Young at Heart May Help You Live Longer," Harvard Health Publishing, Harvard Medical School, December 17, 2014, https://www.health.harvard.edu/blog/feeling-young-heart-may-help-live-longer-201412177598. See also Isla Rippon and Andrew Steptoe, "Feeling Old vs Being Old," *JAMA Internal Medicine* 175, no. 2 (2015): 307-09, https://doi:10.1001/jamainternmed.2014.6580.

5 Lindsey Dodgson, "Feeling Younger than Your Age Could Be a Sign That Your Brain Is Healthy, According to New Research," *Business Insider*, July 6, 2018, https://www.businessinsider.com/feeling-younger-than-your-age-could-be-a-sign-your-brain-is-healthy-2018-7.

6 Child Welfare Information Gateway, "Understanding the Effects of Maltreatment on Brain Development," (Washington, DC: US Department of Health and Human Services, Children's Bureau, 2015), https://www.childwelfare.gov/pubpdfs/brain_development.pdf.

7 Jack P. Shonkoff and Deborah A. Phillips (eds.), *From Neurons to Neighborhoods: the Science of Early Childhood Development* (Washington, DC: National Academy Press, 2000). See also *From Neurons to Neighborhoods: Reflections on Four Themes* [10 years later], (Washington, DC: National Academies Press, September 7, 2012), https://www.ncbi.nlm.nih.gov/books/NBK200879/.

8 Savithiri Ratnapalan and Helen Batty, "To Be Good Enough," *Canadian Family Physician* 55, no. 3 (March 2009): 239-41, https://www.cfp.ca/content/cfp/55/3/239.full.pdf.

9 Carlin Flora, "Moderation Is the Key to Life," *Psychology Today*, October 15, 2019, https://www.psychologytoday.com/us/articles/201707/moderation-is-the-key-life.

10 John C. Maxwell, *Failing Forward: Turning Mistakes into Stepping Stones for Success* (Nashville: Thomas Nelson Publishers, 2000, repr., 2007) 1.

11 "Vincent's Life, 1853–1890," Van Gogh Museum, Amsterdam, NL, accessed August 2, 2021, https://www.vangoghmuseum.nl/en/art-and-stories/vincents-life-1853-1890.

12 "Looking for Direction: Biography, 1873–1881," Van Gogh Museum, Amsterdam, NL, accessed August 2, 2021, https://www.vangoghmuseum.nl/en/stories/brotherly-love.

13 Nathaniel Branden, *The Six Pillars of Self-Esteem* (New York: Bantam, repr., 1995) 3.

14 Harvard Professional Development, "Assessing Your Emotional Intelligence: Four Tools We Love," Harvard Division of Continuing Education, November 18, 2016, https://professional.dce.harvard.edu/blog/assessing-your-emotional-intelligence-4-tools-we-love/.

15 Sadhguru (Jaggi Vasudev), "How to Live Joyfully, No Matter What," May 14, 2018, Sadhguru, video, 5:52, https://youtu.be/wvjklSWUj5s.

16 Rebecca Alber, "How Are Happiness and Learning Connected?," *Edutopia*, March 4, 2013, https://www.edutopia.org/blog/happiness-learning-connection-rebecca-alber.

Twelve

1 The Mind Lab, "A Study Investigating the Relaxation Effects of the Music Track 'Weightless' by Marconi Union in Consultation with Lyz Cooper," introduction by David Lewis, Sussex Innovative Center, University of Sussex, UK, accessed August 3, 2021, https://www.britishacademyofsoundtherapy.com/wp-content/uploads/2019/10/Mindlab-Report-Weightless-Radox-Spa.pdf.

2 Christine A. Goodwin et al., "Functional Connectivity within and between Intrinsic Brain Networks Correlates with Trait Mind Wandering," *Neuropsychologia* 103 (August 2017): 140-153, https://doi:10.1016/j.neuropsychologia.2017.07.006.

3 "Jerome L. Singer," Department of Psychology, Yale University, January 1, 2020, https://psychology.yale.edu/news/jerome-l-singer.

4 Scott Barry Kaufman, "RIP Jerome L. Singer, 'The Father of Daydreaming' (1924-2019)," *Scientific American*, December 17, 2019, https://blogs.scientificamerican.com/beautiful-minds/rip-jerome-l-singer-the-father-of-daydreaming-1924-2019/.

5 Jason Gregory, *Effortless Living: Wu-Wei and the Spontaneous State of Natural Harmony*, (Rochester, Vermont: Inner Traditions, 2018), 32.

6 Thich Nhat Hanh, "Thich Nhat Hanh on the Practice of Mindfulness," *Lion's Roar*, repub. December 10, 2019, https://www.lionsroar.com/mindful-living-thich-nhat-hanh-on-the-practice-of-mindfulness-march-2010/.

7 "Harvard Second Generation Study: Grant and Glueck Study," accessed August 4, 2021, https://www.adultdevelopmentstudy.org/grantandglueckstudy.

8 Robert Waldinger, "What Makes a Good Life? Lessons from the Longest Study on Happiness," TEDxBeaconStreet, November 2015, video, 12:34, https://www.ted.com/talks/robert_waldinger_what_makes_a_good_life_lessons_from_the_longest_study_on_happiness.

9 Waldinger, "What Makes a Good Life?"

10 Melanie Curtin, "This Seventy-five-year Harvard Study Found the One Secret to Leading a Fulfilling Life," *Inc.*, February 27, 2017, https://www.inc.com/melanie-curtin/want-a-life-of-fulfillment-a-75-year-harvard-study-says-to-prioritize-this-one-t.html.

11 Liz Mineo, "Good Genes Are Nice, but Joy Is Better," *Harvard Gazette*, April 11, 2017, https://news.harvard.edu/gazette/story/2017/04/over-nearly-80-years-harvard-study-has-been-showing-how-to-live-a-healthy-and-happy-life/.

12 Waldinger, "What Makes a Good Life?"

13 Ian Sample, "Shocking but True: Students Prefer Jolt of Pain to Being Made to Sit and Think," *The Guardian*, July 3, 2014, https://www.theguardian.com/science/2014/jul/03/electric-shock-preferable-to-thinking-says-study.

14 Scott Barry Kaufman and Jerome L. Singer, "The Creativity of Dual Process 'System 1' Thinking," *Scientific American*, January 17, 2012, https://blogs.scientificamerican.com/guest-blog/the-creativity-of-dual-process-system-1-thinking/.

15 Daniel Kahneman, Thinking Fast and Slow, (New York: Farrar, Straus and Giroux, 2011), 19. See also Das Narayan, Nivedita, "Be Your Spontaneous Best," *The Hindu*, March 3, 2019, https://www.thehindu.com/education/be-your-spontaneous-best/article26416752.ece.

16 Kathryn Schulz, "The Rabbit-Hole Rabbit Hole," *The New Yorker*, June 4, 2015, https://www.newyorker.com/culture/cultural-comment/the-rabbit-hole-rabbit-hole.

Thirteen

1 "02: Forest Medicine," *Research*, Nippon Medical School, accessed August 8, 2021, https://www.nms.ac.jp/college/english/research/topics/topics02.html.

2 Mayo Clinic staff, "DASH Diet: Healthy Eating to Lower Your Blood Pressure," accessed August 14, 2021, https://www.mayoclinic.org/healthy-lifestyle/nutrition-and-healthy-eating/in-depth/dash-diet/art-20048456.

3 M. L. Khalil and S. A. Sulaiman, "The Potential Role of Honey and Its Polyphenols in Preventing Heart Disease: A Review," *African Journal of Traditional, Complementary and Alternative Medicine* 7, no. 4 (2010), https://doi.org/10.4314/ajtcam.v7i4.56693.

4 Carolyn L. Todd, "Can Our Bodies Even Tell the Difference between Naturally Occurring and Added Sugars?," *Self*, June 24, 2019, https://www.self.com/story/how-different-are-naturally-occurring-sugars-really-from-added-ones?mbid=synd_yahoo_rss.

5 "Potassium: Fact Sheet for Consumers," National Institutes of Health, accessed September 4, 2021, https://ods.od.nih.gov/factsheets/Potassium-Consumer/. See also "Potassium: Fact Sheet for Professionals," National Institutes of Health, https://ods.od.nih.gov/factsheets/Potassium-HealthProfessional/.

6 Michael Pollan, Food Rules: *An Eater's Manual* (New York: Penguin, 2009), 7. See also Jane E. Brody, "Rules Worth Following, for Everyone's Sake," *New York Times*, February 1, 2010, https://www.nytimes.com/2010/02/02/health/02brod.html and Tim Farris interview, "Michael Pollan: This Is Your Mind on Plants," July 6, 2021, video, 2:02:06, https://youtu.be/76SSms99HAs.

7 Susan J. Torres and Caryl A Nowson, "Relationship between Stress, Eating Behavior, and Obesity," *Nutrition* 23, nos. 11-12 (2007): 887-94, https://doi.org/10.1016/j.nut.2007.08.008. See also Hans Selye, *The Stress of Life* (New York: McGraw-Hill, 1978) and Bruce S. McEwen, "Protection and Damage from Acute and Chronic Stress: Allostasis and Allostatic Overload and Relevance to the Pathophysiology of Psychiatric Disorders," *Annals of the New York Academy of Sciences* 1032, no. 1 (2004): 1–7, https://doi.org/10.1196/annals.1314.001.

8 Erin Blakemore, "What Was the Neolithic Revolution?," *National Geographic*, April 5, 2019, https://www.nationalgeographic.com/culture/article/neolithic-agricultural-revolution.

9 Alex Whiting, "How Stone Age Humans Unlocked the Glucose in Plants," *Horizon: The EU Research and Innovation Magazine*, March 27, 2020, https://ec.europa.eu/research-and-innovation/en/horizon-magazine/how-stone-age-humans-unlocked-glucose-plants.

10 Alan H. Goodman and George J. Armelagos, "Disease and Death at Dr. Dickson's Mounds: The Skeletal Remains of Prehistoric Native Americans Shows That Agricultural Revolutions Can Be Hazardous to Your Health," *Natural History* 94, no. 9 (September 1985), https://www.researchgate.net/publication/305399228.

11 Whiting, "How Stone Age Humans."

12 Yun-Zi Liu, Yun-Xia Wang, and Chun-Lei Jiang, "Inflammation: The Common Pathway of Stress-Related Diseases," *Frontiers in Human Neuroscience* 11 (June 20, 2017): 316, https://doi.org/10.3389/fnhum.2017.00316.

13 Janice K. Kiecolt-Glaser, "Stress, Food, and Inflammation: Psychoneuroimmunology and Nutrition at the Cutting Edge," *Psychosomatic Medicine* 72, no. 4 (May 2010): 365-69, https://doi:10.1097/PSY.0b013e3181dbf489.

14 Martin Juneau, "Why Do the Japanese Have the Highest Life Expectancy in the World?," *Prevention Watch*, March 9, 2021, https://observatoireprevention.org/en/2021/03/09/why-do-the-japanese-have-the-highest-life-expectancy-in-the-world/.

15 Matthew T. Buckley et al., "Selection in Europeans on Fatty Acid Desaturases Associated with Dietary Changes," *Molecular Biology and Evolution* 34, no. 6 (June 2017): 1307–18, https://doi.org/10.1093/molbev/msx103.

16 Christopher Matthews, "Med [Mediterranean] People Shun Med [Mediterranean] Diet," *FAONewsroom*, Food and Agriculture Organization of the United Nations, July 29, 2008, http://www.fao.org/Newsroom/en/news/2008/1000871/index.html.

17 "Alcohol Use and Your Health," Centers for Disease Control and Prevention, May 11, 2021, https://www.cdc.gov/alcohol/fact-sheets/alcohol-use.htm.

18 Hima J. Challa, Muhammad Atif Ameer, and Kalyan R. Uppaluri, "DASH Diet to Stop Hypertension," StatPearls, May 19, 2021, https://www.ncbi.nlm.nih.gov/books/NBK482514/.

19 Arndt Manzel et al., "Role of 'Western Diet' in Inflammatory Autoimmune Diseases," *Current Allergy and Asthma Reports* 14, article no. 404 (January 2014), https://doi:10.1007/s11882-013-0404-6.

20 "Why Dogs Are Good for Us," Andrew Weil blog, accessed August 14, 2021, https://www.drweil.com/blog/bulletins/why-dogs-are-good-for-us/ in Francisco Lopez-Jimenez et al., "Dog Ownership and Cardiovascular Health Results from the Kardiovize 2030 Project," *Mayo Clinic Proceedings, Innovations, Quality and Outcomes* 3, no. 3 (September 2019): 268-75, https://doi.org/10.1016/j.mayocpiqo.2019.07.007.

21 "02: Forest Medicine," *Research*, Nippon Medical School, accessed August 8, 2021, https://www.nms.ac.jp/college/english/research/topics/topics02.html.

22 Matthew P. White et al., "Spending at Least 120 Minutes a Week in Nature Is Associated with Good Health and Wellbeing [sic]," *Scientific Reports* 9, article no. 7730 (2019), https://doi.org/10.1038/s41598-019-44097-3.

Fourteen

1 Gabrielle Lipton, "The Fractal Nature of Almost All Things: Understanding Nature's Fractals, from Galaxies to Ecosystems to the Human Heartbeat," *Global Landscapes Forum*, March 20, 2020, https://news.globallandscapesforum.org/43195/fractals-nature-almost-all-things/.

2 Richard P. Taylor, "Reduction of Physiological Stress Using Fractal Art and Architecture," *Leonardo* 39, no. 3 (2006): 245–51, https://doi.org/10.1162/leon.2006.39.3.245.

3 Terry Marks-Tarlow, ed. *A Fractal Epistemology for a Scientific Psychology* (Newcastle upon Tyne, UK: Cambridge Scholars Publishing, 2019), 274.

4 Marks-Tarlow, *A Fractal Epistemology*, xxi–xxii.

5 Michael Miller, "Emotional Rescue: The Heart-Brain Connection," *Cerebrum: the Dana Forum on Brain Science* 2019, May 1, 2019, https://www.ncbi.nlm.nih.gov/pmc/articles/PMC7075501/.

6 Sarah Yang, "'Trust Hormone' Oxytocin Helps Old Muscle Work Like New, Study Finds," *Berkeley News*, June 10, 2014, https://news.berkeley.edu/2014/06/10/oxytocin-helps-muscle-regeneration/.

7 Loyola University Health System, "What Falling in Love Does to Your Heart and Brain," *ScienceDaily*, February 6, 2014, https://www.sciencedaily.com/releases/2014/02/140206155244.htm.

8 Elizabeth Barrett Browning (1806-61), "How Do I Love Thee?," Sonnet 43, *Poets.org*, https://poets.org/poem/how-do-i-love-thee-sonnet-43.

9 "Elizabeth Barrett Browning," Poetry Foundation, accessed September 12, 2021, https://www.poetryfoundation.org/poets/elizabeth-barrett-browning.

10 Robert C. Roberts, "Dismantling Walls: How Humility and Love Help Us Make It to the Other Side," *The Table*, September 10, 2017. https://cct.biola.edu/dismantling-walls-humility-love-help-us-make-side/.

11 Kaye Cassidy, "Love Your Neighbor: A Common Theme in Major Religions," *Qur'an* 4:36, accessed September 10, 2021, https://www.maryspence.org/stories/love-your-neighbor-a-common-theme-in-major-religions/.

12 Eric Jaffe, "The Psychological Study of Smiling," *Association for Psychological Science*, February 11, 2011, https://www.psychologicalscience.org/observer/the-psychological-study-of-smiling.

13 Ron Gutman [guest blogger for Eric Savitz], "The Untapped Power of Smiling," Forbes, March 22, 2010, https://www.forbes.com/sites/ericsavitz/2011/03/22/the-untapped-power-of-smiling/?sh=3267e957a67b.

14 Ron Gutman [guest blogger for Eric Savitz], "The Untapped Power of Smiling."

15 HeartMath Institute, "Heart-Brain Communication," chapter 1 in *Science of the Heart: Exploring the Role of the Heart in Human Performance*, Accessed September 23, 2021, https://www.heartmath.org/research/science-of-the-heart/heart-brain-communication/.

16 Rollin McCraty et al., *The Coherent Heart: Heart-Brain Interactions, Psychophysiological Coherence and the Emergence of System-Wide Order* (Boulder Creek, CA: Institute of HeartMath, 2006; online December 2009), 3, https://www.researchgate.net/publication/41393262_The_Coherent_Heart_Heart-Brain_Interactions_Psychophysiological_Coherence_and_the_Emergence_of_System-Wide_Order.

17 Mitchell B. Liester, "Personality Changes Following Heart Transplantation: The Role of Cellular Memory," *Medical Hypotheses* 135 (February 2020), https://doi.org/10.1016/j.mehy.2019.109468.

18 Sue McGreevey, "What Makes AA Work?," *The Harvard Gazette*, September 12, 2011, https://news.harvard.edu/gazette/story/2011/09/what-makes-aa-work/.

19 David Cameron, "Having Happy Friends Can Make You Happy," *The Harvard Gazette*, December 5, 2008, https://news.harvard.edu/gazette/story/2008/12/having-happy-friends-can-make-you-happy/.

20 Cameron, "Having Happy Friends."

21 Mariah F. Purol et al., "Loved and Lost or Never Loved at All? Lifelong Marital Histories and Their Links with Subjective Well-Being," *The Journal of Positive Psychology* 16 , no. 5 (June 26, 2020): 651-59, https://doi.org/10.1080/17439760.2020.1791946.

22 Zig Ziglar, "The Born to Win Seminar," Nightingale-Conant Press, 2010, video, https://www.amazon.com/Ziglars-Complete-Born-Collection-Inspirational/dp/B08KTWSK1M?ref_=ast_sto_dp. See also "101 Inspiring Quotes by Zig Ziglar," *Entrepreneurs Way*, Medium, April 19, 2017, https://medium.com/@entrepreneursway0007/101-inspiring-quotes-by-zig-ziglar-448b8ab66865.

Selected Bibliography

As the resources consulted to produce this book are referenced in Notes—and at the risk of excluding authors whose works, opinions, and research I greatly admire—I, nevertheless, am providing here a short list of readings that you may find particularly useful in learning how living mindfully aware is indivisible from choosing thoughts and behaviors that lead to integrated mind-body-spirit well-being, health, and happiness. I present them chapter by chapter.

Introduction

Chopra, Deepak. "Present-Moment Awareness: A Better Way to Stay in Control." *Chopra*. September 15, 2017. https://chopra.com/articles/present-moment-awareness-a-better-way-to-stay-in-control.

Lents, Nathan H. "Why Do Humans Make Art?" *Psychology Today*. September 5, 2017. https://www.psychologytoday.com/us/blog/beastly-behavior/201709/why-do-humans-make-art.

Newberg, Andrew, and Mark Robert Waldman. *Words Can Change Your Brain: 12 Conversation Strategies to Build Trust, Resolve Conflict, and Increase Intimacy*. New York: A Plume Book, the Penguin Group, 2012. Kindle.

Ram Dass. *Be Here Now*. New York: Crown Publishing, 1978.

Siegal, Ronald D. "Positive Psychology: Harnessing the Power of Happiness, Mindfulness, and Inner Strength." *Harvard Medical*

School Special Health Report Book 4. Boston: Harvard Health Publications, May 8, 2014. Kindle.

Tolle, Eckhart. *The Power of Now: A Guide to Spiritual Enlightenment.* Novato, CA: New World Library, 2004. Kindle.

One

Booth, Robert. "Master of Mindfulness, Jon Kabat-Zinn: 'People Are Losing Their Minds. That Is What We Need to Wake Up To.'" *The Guardian.* October 22, 2017. https://www.theguardian.com/lifeandstyle/2017/oct/22/mindfulness-jon-kabat-zinn-depression-trump-grenfell.

Graham, Carol. *Happiness Around the World: The Paradox of Happy Peasants and Miserable Millionaires.* New York: Oxford University Press, 2009.

Lyubomirsky, Sonja. *The Myths of Happiness: What Should Make You Happy but Doesn't, What Shouldn't Make You Happy but Does.* New York: Penguin, 2014. Kindle.

Two

Campbell, Joseph. Interviewed by Bill Moyer. "Follow Your Bliss," *The Power of Myth*, Episode 4. Joseph Campbell Foundation. July 22, 2020. https://youtu.be/s28rwnz18j4.

Chopra, Deepak. "The Importance of Being Aware." *Medium.* September 9, 2019. https://deepakchopra.medium.com/the-importance-of-being-aware-3308e2918020.

Henderson, Joseph Lewis, and Maud Oakes. *The Wisdom of the Serpent: The Myths of Death, Rebirth, and Resurrection.* Princeton: Princeton University Press: 1963, 1990. Kindle.

Keng, Shian-Ling, Moria J. Smoski, and Clive J. Robins. "Effects of Mindfulness on Psychological Health: A Review of Empirical Studies." *Clinical Psychology Review* 31, no. 6 (May 13, 2011): 1041-56. https://doi.org/10.1016/j.cpr.2011.04.006.

Three

Bulley, Adam, Jonathan Redshaw, and Thomas Suddendorf. "The Future-Directed Functions of the Imagination: From Prediction to Metaforesight." In the *Cambridge Handbook of the Imagination*. Edited by Anna Abraham. United Kingdom: Cambridge University Press, 2020. 425.

Corballis, Michael C. *The Wandering Mind: What the Brain Does When You're Not Looking*. Chicago: University of Chicago Press, 2015. 84.

Dennett, Daniel C. *Darwin's Dangerous Idea: Evolution and the Meanings of Life*. New York: Simon and Schuster.

Frank, Adam. "Roll Over Copernicus! Turns Out We Are the Center of the Universe." *Cosmos and Culture*. NPR. March 1, 2011. https://www.npr.org/sections/13.7/2011/03/02/134137113.

Lotzof, Kerry. "Are We Really Made of Stardust?" National History Museum. Accessed May 13, 2021. https://www.nhm.ac.uk/discover/are-we-really-made-of-stardust.html.

Resnick, Brian. "'Reality' Is Constructed By Our Brain. Here's What That Means and Why It Matters." Vox. June 22, 2020. https://www.vox.com/science-and-health/20978285.

Seth, Anil. "Your Brain Hallucinates Your Conscious Reality." TED. July 18, 2017. https://youtu.be/lyu7v7nWzfo.

Watts, Alan. "Essential Lectures 12: 'Conversations with Myself': Mount Tamalpais, 1971." https://www.organism.earth/library/document/essential-lectures-12.

Yulsman, Tom. "Yes, You Are the Center of the Universe (in One Sense . . .)." *Discover.* December 31, 2014. https://www.discovermagazine.com/the-sciences/yes-you-are-the-center-of-the-universe-in-one-sense.

Four

Gilbert, Daniel T. *Stumbling on Happiness.* New York: Vintage Books, 2005.

Rosenberg, Joab. "Only Humans, Not Computers, Can Learn or Predict." *TechCrunch.* May 5, 2016. https://techcrunch.com/2016/05/05/only-humans-not-computers-can-learn-or-predict/.

Glattfelder, James B. "The Consciousness of Reality," in *Information—Consciousness—Reality.* The Frontiers Collection. Springer (April 11, 2019): 515–95. https://doi.org/10.1007/978-3-030-03633-1_14.

Montana, Cate. "The Illusion of Reality: The Scientific Proof That Everything Is Energy and Reality Isn't Real." *Conscious Lifestyle Magazine.* Accessed July 27, 2021. https://www.consciouslifestylemag.com/everything-is-energy-illusion-reality/.

Five

Chopra, Deepak. "A Surprising Answer to 'Who Am I?'" The Chopra Foundation. June 12, 2017. https://choprafoundation.org/articles/a-surprising-answer-to-who-am-i/.

Cook, Gareth. "Does Consciousness Pervade the Universe?" *Scientific American*. January 14, 2020. https://www.scientificamerican.com/ article/does-consciousness-pervade-the-universe/.

Ireland, Tom. "What Does Mindfulness Meditation Do to Your Brain?" June 12, 2014. *Scientific American*. https://blogs.scientificamerican. com/guest-blog/what-does-mindfulness-meditation-do-to-your-brain/.

McKie, Robin. "Why Do Identical Twins End Up Having Such Different Lives?" *The Guardian*. June 1, 2013. https://www. theguardian.com/science/2013/jun/02/twins-identical-genes-different-health-study.

Oyserman, Daphna, Kristen Elmore, and George Smith. "Self, Self-Concept, and Identity." In the *Handbook of Self and Identity*, Second Edition. New York: The Guilford Press, 2013.

Paoletti, Patrizio, and Tal Dotan Ben-Soussan. "Reflections on Inner and Outer Silence and Consciousness without Contents, According to the Sphere Model of Consciousness." *Frontiers in Psychology* 12 (August 2020). Research Institute for Neuroscience, Education and Didactics. https://doi.org/10.3389/fpsyg.2020.01807.

Williams, Caroline. "Different Meditative Types Train Distinct Parts of Your Brain," *New Scientist*, October 4, 2017, https://www. newscientist.com/article/2149489-different-meditation-types-train-distinct-parts-of-your-brain/.

Six

Farber, Neil. "The Truth About the Law of Attraction: It Doesn't Exist," *Psychology Today*. September 18, 2016. https://www.psychologytoday. com/us/blog/the-blame-game/201609/the-truth-about-the-law-attraction.

Lee, Lewina O. et al. "Optimism Is Associated with Exceptional Longevity in Two Epidemiologic Cohorts of Men and Women." *Proceedings of the National Academy of Sciences* 116, no. 37 (August 26, 2019): 18357-62; https://doi.org/10.1073/pnas.1900712116.

Peterson, Christopher, and Lisa M. Bossio. *Health and Optimism*. New York: Free Press, 1991.

Seligman, Martin E. P. *Learned Optimism: How to Change Your Mind and Your Life*. New York: Vintage Books, 2006.

Seligman, Martin. *Authentic Happiness: Using the New Positive Psychology to Realize Your Potential for Lasting Fulfillment*. New York: Free Press, 2002.

Sharot, Tali. *The Optimism Bias: A Tour of the Irrationally Positive Brain*. New York: Vintage Books, 2012.

Seven

Sounders, Beata. "The Vital Importance and Benefits of Motivation." *Positive Psychology*. March 22, 2021. https://positivepsychology.com/benefits-motivation/.

Tolle, Eckhart. "Realizing the 'Deep I.'" Eckhart Tolle. Accessed July 29, 2021. https://eckharttolle.com/realizing-the-deep-i/.

Vilhauer, Jennice. "How Your Thinking Creates Your Reality." *Psychology Today*. September 27, 2020. https://www.psychologytoday.com/us/blog/living-forward/202009/how-your-thinking-creates-your-reality.

Winfrey, Oprah. "Deepak Chopra: Spiritual Solutions." Oprah's SuperSoul Conversations. July 29, 2020. https://www.happyscribe.com/public/oprah-s-supersoul-conversations/deepak-chopra-spiritual-solutions.

Eight

"Mars vs. Venus, the Gender Gap in Health." *Harvard Health Publishing*. August 26, 2019. Harvard Medical School. https://www.health.harvard. edu/newsletter_article/mars-vs-venus-the-gender-gap-in-health.

Esty, Katharine. *Eightysomethings: A Practical Guide to Letting Go, Aging Well, and Finding Unexpected Happiness*. New York: Skyhorse, 2019.

Kando Fi Chor, Juliette. "Second Brain Found in the Heart and Gut Neurons." *Owlcation*. July 25, 2021, https://owlcation.com/stem/ your-second-brain-is-in-your-heart.

Ornish, Dean. "Changing Your Lifestyle Can Change Your Genes." *Newsweek*. June 16, 2008. https://www.newsweek.com/changing-your-lifestyle-can-change-your-genes-91323.

Nine

Cain, Susan. *Quiet: The Power of Introverts in a World That Can't Stop Talking*. New York: Broadway Paperbacks, 2013.

Gardner, Kelly. "How Sesame Street Uses Muppets to Teach Inclusion in the US and Abroad." Washington, DC: American University, April 1, 2021. https://www.american.edu/sis/news/20210401-how-sesame-street-uses-muppets-to-teach-tolerance-in-the-us-and-abroad.cfm.

Gorlick, Adam. "For Kids, Altruism Comes Naturally, Psychologist Says." *Stanford News*. November 5, 2008. https://news.stanford.edu/ news/2008/november5/tanner-110508.html.

Pittaro, Michael. "Social Media and the Bystander Effect." *Psychology Today*. September 19, 2019. https://www.psychologytoday.com/us/ blog/the-crime-and-justice-doctor/201909/social-media-and-the-bystander-effect.

Smith, Martin J. "Turns Out That Opposites Don't Attract After All." Stanford Graduate School of Business. January 17, 2017. https://www.gsb.stanford.edu/insights/turns-out-opposites-dont-attract-after-all.

Trudeau, Michelle. "Why People Take Risks to Help Others: Altruism's Roots in the Brain." *Weekend Edition*. NPR. November 23, 2014. https://www.npr.org/2014/11/23/366052779/why-people-take-risks-to-help-others-altruisms-roots-in-the-brain.

Watts, Alan. "The Tao of Philosophy 4: Seeing Through the Net, 1969." *The Library*. https://www.organism.earth/library/document/tao-of-philosophy-4.

Yagoda, Ben. *Will Rogers: A Biography*. New York: Knopf. 1993.

Ten

Enright, Robert. "Eight Keys to Forgiveness." *Greater Good Magazine*. October 15, 2015. University of California, Berkeley. https://greatergood.berkeley.edu/article/item/eight_keys_to_forgiveness.

Frankl, Viktor E. *Man's Search for Meaning*. Translated by Ilse Lasch. Boston: Beacon Press, 1959, 2006.

Griffiths, Sarah. "Can You Trust Your Earliest Childhood Memories?" *Neuroscience*. BBC. May 19, 2019. https://www.bbc.com/future/article/20190516-why-you-cannot-trust-your-earliest-childhood-memories.

Kämmerer, Annette. "The Scientific Underpinnings and Impacts of Shame." *Scientific American*. August 9, 2019. https://www.scientificamerican.com/article/the-scientific-underpinnings-and-impacts-of-shame/.

Lieberman, Charlotte. "Why We Romanticize the Past." *New York Times*. April 2, 2021. https://www.nytimes.com/2021/04/02/smarter-living/why-we-romanticize-the-past.html.

Smith, Kurt. "Four Reasons to Forgive but Not Forget." PsychCentral. December 10, 2014. https://psychcentral.com/blog/4-reasons-to-forgive-but-not-forget#1.

Eleven

Alber, Rebecca. "How Are Happiness and Learning Connected?" *Edutopia*. March 4, 2013. https://www.edutopia.org/blog/happiness-learning-connection-rebecca-alber.

Branden, Nathaniel. *The Six Pillars of Self-Esteem*. New York: Bantam, reprinted 1995.

Child Welfare Information Gateway. "Understanding the Effects of Maltreatment on Brain Development." Washington, DC: US Department of Health and Human Services, Children's Bureau, 2015. https://www.childwelfare.gov/pubpdfs/brain_development.pdf.

Godman, Heidi. "Feeling Young at Heart May Help You Live Longer." *Harvard Health Publishing*. Harvard Medical School. December 17, 2014. https://www.health.harvard.edu/blog/feeling-young-heart-may-help-live-longer-201412177598.

Hublin, Jean-Jacques et al. "A Long Childhood Is of Advantage." Max-Planck-Gesellschaft. November 15, 2010. https://www.mpg.de/617475/pressRelease20101111.

Maxwell, John C. *Failing Forward: Turning Mistakes into Stepping Stones for Success*. Nashville: Thomas Nelson Publishers, reprinted 2007.

Shonkoff, Jack P., and Deborah A. Phillips, eds. *From Neurons to Neighborhoods: the Science of Early Childhood Development* (Washington, DC: National Academy Press, 2000). See also *From Neurons to Neighborhoods: Reflections on Four Themes* [10 years later]. Washington, DC: National Academies Press, September 7, 2012. https://www.ncbi.nlm.nih.gov/books/NBK200879/.

Twelve

Gregory, Jason. *Effortless Living: Wu-Wei and the Spontaneous State of Natural Harmony*. Rochester, VT: Inner Traditions, 2018.

Hanh, Thich Nhat. "Thich Nhat Hanh on the Practice of Mindfulness." *Lion's Roar*. Republished December 10, 2019. https://www.lionsroar.com/mindful-living-thich-nhat-hanh-on-the-practice-of-mindfulness-march-2010/.

Kahneman, Daniel. *Thinking Fast and Slow*. New York: Farrar, Straus and Giroux, 2011.

Mineo, Liz. "Good Genes Are Nice, but Joy Is Better." *Harvard Gazette*. April 11, 2017. https://news.harvard.edu/gazette/story/2017/04/over-nearly-80-years-harvard-study-has-been-showing-how-to-live-a-healthy-and-happy-life/.

Vaillant, George E. *Triumphs of Experience: The Men of the Harvard Grant Study*. Cambridge, MA: Belknap Press, 2012.

Thirteen

"02: Forest Medicine." *Research*. Tokyo, Japan: Nippon Medical School. Accessed August 8, 2021. https://www.nms.ac.jp/college/english/research/topics/topics02.html.

Liu, Yun-Zi, Yun-Xia Wang, and Chun-Lei Jiang. "Inflammation: The Common Pathway of Stress-Related Diseases." *Frontiers in Human Neuroscience* 11 (June 20, 2017): 316. https://doi.org/10.3389/fnhum.2017.00316.

Manzel, Arndt et al. "Role of 'Western Diet' in Inflammatory Autoimmune Diseases." *Current Allergy and Asthma Reports* 14, article no. 404 (January 2014). https://doi:10.1007/s11882-013-0404-6.

Pollan, Michael. *Food Rules: An Eater's Manual.* New York: Penguin, 2009.

Selye, Hans. *The Stress of Life.* New York: McGraw-Hill, 1978.

White, Matthew P. et al. "Spending at Least 120 Minutes a Week in Nature Is Associated with Good Health and Wellbeing [sic]." *Scientific Reports* 9, article no. 7730 (2019). https://doi.org/10.1038/s41598-019-44097-3.

Fourteen

Cameron, David. "Having Happy Friends Can Make You Happy." *The Harvard Gazette.* December 5, 2008. https://news.harvard.edu/gazette/story/2008/12/having-happy-friends-can-make-you-happy/.

HeartMath Institute. "Heart-Brain Communication." In *Science of the Heart: Exploring the Role of the Heart in Human Performance.* Accessed September 23, 2021. https://www.heartmath.org/research/science-of-the-heart/heart-brain-communication/.

Liester, Mitchell B. "Personality Changes Following Heart Transplantation: The Role of Cellular Memory." *Medical Hypotheses* 135 (February 2020). https://doi.org/10.1016/j.mehy.2019.109468.

Lipton, Gabrielle. "The Fractal Nature of Almost All Things: Understanding Nature's Fractals, from Galaxies to Ecosystems to the Human Heartbeat." *Global Landscapes Forum*. March 20, 2020. https://news.globallandscapesforum.org/43195/fractals-nature-almost-all-things/.

Loyola University Health System. "What Falling in Love Does to Your Heart and Brain." *ScienceDaily*. February 6, 2014. https://www.sciencedaily.com/releases/2014/02/140206155244.htm.

Marks-Tarlow, Terry, ed. *A Fractal Epistemology for a Scientific Psychology*. Newcastle upon Tyne, UK: Cambridge Scholars Publishing, 2019.

McCraty, Rollin et al. *The Coherent Heart: Heart-Brain Interactions, Psychophysiological Coherence and the Emergence of System-Wide Order*. Boulder Creek, CA: Institute of HeartMath, 2006. https://www.researchgate.net/publication/41393262.

McGreevey, Sue. "What Makes AA Work?" *The Harvard Gazette*. September 12, 2011. https://news.harvard.edu/gazette/story/2011/09/what-makes-aa-work/.

Miller, Michael. "Emotional Rescue: The Heart-Brain Connection." *Cerebrum: the Dana Forum on Brain Science*, May 1, 2019. https://www.ncbi.nlm.nih.gov/pmc/articles/PMC7075501/.

Roberts, Robert C. "Dismantling Walls: How Humility and Love Help Us Make It to the Other Side." *The Table*. September 10, 2017. https://cct.biola.edu/dismantling-walls-humility-love-help-us-make-side/.

Taylor, Richard P. "Reduction of Physiological Stress Using Fractal Art and Architecture." *Leonardo* 39, no. 3 (2006): 245–51, https://doi.org/10.1162/leon.2006.39.3.245.

About the Author

Daniel A. Johnson's passion is helping people achieve their dreams. With his *Twelve Insights for Mindful Living: An Awareness Approach to Health and Happiness*, Dan amps up our courage and skills to tackle the seemingly impossible. A sought-after motivational and inspirational speaker and presenter at worksites, conferences, and retreats, Dan shares with business professionals and conference attendees the powerful health and happiness benefits of living mindfully. Executive director of the Wellness Council of Arizona since 1995, Dan has served on the boards and advisory councils of many state and national health and wellness organizations. Early in his career, he served as a personal trainer to athletes as well as cardiac and orthopedic recovery patients. In a life-changing mindful moment, the former co-owner and operator of twenty athletic clubs and fitness centers throughout the Southwest recognized there was more to being fit than a strong body. His insight launched him into intensive study and the practice of mindfulness to attain integrated mind-body-spirit well-being. Today, he helps others awaken their senses to the joys that can be the undercurrent of each waking moment. Dan, his wife, Melinda, and their two dogs reside in Tucson. The couple's daughter, Makenna, an Inclusion Specialist, works with special needs children. For Dan, golf eases life's sand traps, and meditation provides his daily dose of medication.

Made in the USA
Middletown, DE
08 June 2022

66751636R00201